THE PEACE REFORM
IN AMERICAN HISTORY

THE PEACE REFORM
IN AMERICAN HISTORY

Charles DeBenedetti

INDIANA UNIVERSITY PRESS · BLOOMINGTON

Library of Congress Cataloging in Publication Data

DeBenedetti, Charles.
    The peace reform in American history.

    Bibliography: p.
    Includes index.
    1. Peace—History.   I. Title.
JX1961.U6D42   327'.172'09   79-2173
ISBN 0-253-13095-6   3 4 5 6 7 88 87 86 85 84

For Sandy

No one can ever say, finally and with anything like entire objectivity, what the meaning is of the struggle against war portrayed in these pages, even when that struggle shall at last be over. All that the historian can do now is to interpret the continuing struggle in the light of his own day.

Merle Curti, *Peace Or War: The American Struggle,*
    1636–1936

CONTENTS

Preface

There is no reform that Americans have talked of more and done less about than that of world peace. From the time of the Puritan migrations, Americans have thought of themselves as a people uniquely dedicated to the cause of peace. Yet their record of continental and insular expansion has been persistently scarred by acts of war and physical violence. Clearly, stretches of organized violence dominate the great surface of American history. Interestingly, however, there exists beneath that surface a substratum of organized citizen activism which has insistently valued peace as too important to be left to prevailing authority. The purpose of this book is to explore that substratum and to remember that large numbers of Americans have long struggled to do more than talk about living peace. They have worked to sustain it.

Historically, the pursuit of peace has occupied a major part of the American reform tradition, absorbing innumerable individuals and organizations in a commitment to peace as the first principle of social action and reformation. Understandably, the forms of their commitment have been diverse and changing. Many have limited their commitment to specific antiwar activities, standing in opposition to American involvement in various wars for any number of reasons. Others have devoted themselves to the cause of internationalism, arguing that peace would appear with the institutionalization of procedures and organizations established for the prevention and settlement of disputes among nations. Others have subscribed to various pacifist ethics, ranging from utter nonresistance to governing authority to nonviolent resistance to injustice, on the grounds that peace subsists in a *mode* of ongoing human relations that precludes the resort to violence. Others have pursued their peace vision through antimilitarism, certain that the existence of large standing armies posed a threat to individual liberty and constitutional democracy as well as to peace. And still others have worked toward the peace reform as an enterprise integrally connected to their allied interests in the advance of capitalism, feminism, anarchism, or socialism. Plainly, American peace seekers have always been a mixed lot. But then they were not acting out of a need to fit the categories of latter-day historians.

Yet peace reformers have generally operated through American history along two lines of parallel action. First, they have for reasons of principle denounced war (i.e., the highly organized, socially sanctioned violence of one group upon another) as a form of collective behavior that corrupts social order, Christian ethics, and human well-being. Second, they have worked from that principle to establish alternative means of resolving human conflicts and developing forms of group harmony so that peace might persist as a living social dynamic. Refusing to accept war as a necessary part of human existence, peace workers have tried over the course of the American experience either to form ideal communities that would serve as working models for the larger society, or to engage in reform efforts intended to overhaul those political policies, social institutions, or cultural patterns that prevented the triumph of lasting peace. Altogether, they have sought positively to make peace, and not merely to oppose war.

As a reform cause, the American peace tradition has advanced along the sinews of larger national developments. In the colonial period, the concern for peace was derivative, intellectually patterned upon contemporary English attitudes toward war and armies and practically pursued by a strange combination of indrawn Anabaptist sects and irrepressible Quakers. With the outbreak of the American Revolutionary War, peace took on the trappings of a revolutionary reform. It appeared functionally related to the success of that incredible new nation which joined federalism, republicanism, and constitutionalism in a working experiment that promised a welcome escape from the European cycle of war and irresponsible monarchical ambition.

Within its first generation of independence, however, the new American nation found that it could not so easily escape from or reform that cycle. As the Old World suffered the wars of the French Revolution and Napoleonic conquest, Americans fought intermittently with their Spanish, French, and English rivals in North America, until full-scale war erupted between the United States and Britain in 1812. The end of that war in late 1814 opened the first great growth period in America of organized nonsectarian peace seeking. Buoyed by the spreading spirit of evangelical Christianity and a romantic faith in human perfectability, the first major peace societies gathered for the purpose of organizing the nation against the sin of war and on behalf of the blessings of rational peace. Peacemaking gained force as an elemental humanitarian calling. Rising with the North's economic success, the humanitarian peace reform expanded through the indefatigability of single-minded heroes like Elihu Burritt and the gathering strength of organized womanhood. Like the related abolitionist crusade, the antebellum peace reform won the majority of its leaders from male Christian evangelicals and the bulk of its membership from middle-class Northern women. The South stood discreetly apart from its challenge.

After the Mexican-American War, the humanitarian reform slipped into decline and then collapsed completely during the Civil War, when social activists subordinated their peace commitment to the Union's struggle for survival and abolitionism. A new movement reassembled only slowly in the wake of the carnage. Cautiously adjusting to the country's late nineteenth-century rush through industrialization, the postwar peace reform took on the color of a cosmopolitan endeavor, linked abroad to the growing international peace movement and tied at home to a world-minded metropolitan elite of lawyers, businessmen, and politicians. More secular and less sentimental, cosmopolitan peace seekers valued arbitration, Anglo-American cooperation, and mechanistic means of organizing an industrial world of Great Power interdependence. The anti-imperialist outburst against U.S. expansion in the Caribbean and Pacific between 1898 and 1901 interrupted but did not reverse their ambitions.

The peace cause took on the form of an even more practical enterprise in the early twentieth century, as its leadership passed to businessmen-philanthropists like Andrew Carnegie and influential lawyers like Elihu Root. Under their direction, the peace reform in Progressive America became a prestigious and proper calling, devoted to the legal settlement of disputes and the "scientific" study of war and its alternatives. Absorbed in that dual commitment, practical peace advocates formed the American Society of International Law, the Carnegie Endowment for International Peace, and the World Peace Foundation between 1906 and 1911 as specialized agencies for transmitting the experts' knowledge of peace to the masses and encouraging fuller conciliatory gestures among governments. The superficial solidity of the practical peace reform proved unusually attractive. Interdenominational Protestant leaders, who were busy in these same years organizing the Federal Council of Churches of Christ in America, joined the peace parade, as did a scattering of militant federalists like the magazine editor Hamilton Holt, who sought more stringent forms of world order. But neither their prayers nor their exhortations could staunch the bloodletting that began in Europe in 1914 and seemed never to end.

The World War of 1914–1918 stands as the great watershed of the modern American peace reform. While practical peace reformers flailed helplessly against it, the war ground mercilessly on, forcing forward a host of military innovations, social transformations, and intellectual adaptations. Its very totality demanded the mobilization of whole societies for the sake of more efficient means of killing. Its very success in the scientific application of wholesale killing devices—including machine guns, poison gases, and submarines—meant indiscriminate death for combatants and noncombatants alike. And its very endlessness aggravated national hatreds and worked a corrosive social demoralization that peaked with the Russian Revolution in 1917. In their cumulative force, these developments not only shattered the old European order but also pushed to the surface the most disturbing paradox of this century: The very processes of modernization—including industrial interdependence, advancing science and technology, and the bureaucratic organization of mass violence—which made peace a simple necessity of survival had intensified the kind of tribal nationalism and military influence that placed highest value upon state security and protracted struggle. Peace after 1919 seemed more necessary than ever before. Yet it also became more remote.

The modern peace movement arose after 1915 to resolve this paradox. For the next generation, American peace workers struggled to realize their cause through the League of Nations, the World Court, arbitration treaties, disarmament agreements, the Kellogg-Briand Pact, and more equitable economic arrangements. Politically, the new movement swung to the left. Emotionally, it vibrated with an unprecedented sense of immediacy. Internal differences nevertheless persisted. Some internationalists in the League of Nations Non-Partisan Association pushed for U.S. leadership in the collective maintenance of global peace. Others in the Foreign Policy Association favored a more democratic diplomacy and international economic reconstruction as ways of resolving social tensions before they erupted in major conflict. Liberal pacifists in the Women's International League for Peace and Freedom and the Fellowship of Reconciliation promoted transnational nonviolent action in defense of justice, while active resistants in the War Resisters League pledged absolute opposition to complicity in the war system. Despite these intramural differences, however, the peace movement moved forward after 1919 upon the power of a shared awareness of the consuming destructiveness of modern total war. Rationally, the issue seemed simple. Industrial peoples would have peace, or they would perish.

Practically, however, the politics of war and peace proved much more intractable. A clamor of conflicts—including rising anticolonialism in Asia and the Near East, persisting class tensions in the West, Lenin's success in Russia, and the rise of the corporate Right and fascism—produced recurring instability within the Western state system that finally mushroomed in the early 1930s into a global crisis. Mortified by the mounting signs of catastrophe, American peace workers swung to the work of preventing a new European war, and then split in the late thirties over the question of U.S. involvement in that war. In the face of Hitlerism in Europe and Japanese military expansion in Asia, most American peace activists decided after 1940 that war was more necessary for the moment than peace. Indeed, after Pearl Harbor, no war in American history seemed more necessary and less objectionable than that two-front struggle against Nazi Germany and Imperial Japan.

By 1945 the bones of 55 million dead and the atomic obliteration of

Hiroshima and Nagasaki once more appeared to make peace the necessary reform. Yet politically World War II settled little. Nazism was crushed, along with the pan-Asian ambitions of rightist Japan. But peace seemed only more distant. In Washington, America's unmatched industrial might and atomic monopoly failed to prevent U.S. policy makers from feeling growing resentment after 1945 at the Soviet presence in eastern Europe and at Communist activity in the rest of Europe and the colonial world. Obsessed with Stalin's intentions, American leaders rapidly identified peace as a condition of anti-Communist stability, an attitude which they expanded to global proportions with the enunciation in 1947 of the Truman Doctrine. Insistently, official Washington spoke more of security than of peace; and, accordingly, it constructed a national security structure (defined best in the 1947 National Security Act) that was intended to constrain Soviet power, repel leftist revolutionary movements, and maintain domestic conformity behind the government's Cold War commitment to Communist containment through military deterrence.

Rallied to support a frustrating postwar war, most Americans viewed volunteer peace seeking by 1949 as a suspect—if not subversive— endeavor. The organized peace movement understandably suffered as a result. Prompted by fresh cadres of atomic scientists and world federalists, the peace reform enjoyed a brief renascence in the late forties, until the Korean War and a surge of right-wing nationalism shoved the movement hopelessly to the defensive. Fixed in the grip of ultranationalism, American politics offered no serious room for the disarmament, world government, pacifist, and noninterventionist alternatives proffered by peace workers in the 1950s. Officially and popularly, peace subsisted in the assertion of American power. It was too important to be left to concerned citizens.

After 1960, domestic rumblings toward change—starting with the civil rights movement and the drive against atmospheric nuclear testing— brought the peace movement new organizations, new constituencies, and new opportunities. Driven by a combination of feminists, students, and intellectuals, the resurgent peace reform made some promising strides until 1965, when expanding U.S. involvement in the Indochinese War forced peace seekers into antiwar activism and diverted them from their first concerns with the arms race and institutionalized injustice.

Arising from several sources, an antiwar opposition emerged in the middle sixties that included respected congressional critics as well as New Left radicals. But traditional peace workers—ranging from nonviolent resisters to practiced Washington lobbyists—stood at its core. Struggling on several fronts, veteran peace activists helped the antiwar opposition gain public visibility and (after the open bankruptcy of U.S. policy in 1968) political effectiveness. Practiced peace leaders made the opposition into a movement. They organized resistance, promoted dissidence, and promulgated alternatives. They did not in the end stop the bloodletting. But they moderated its reach. And they convincingly identified the war as the logical—and not accidental—result of Washington's commitment to global stability through military deterrence. They exposed the notion that peace could be achieved through war as the ultimate illusion of Cold War America.

More than ever, the U.S.-Indochinese War compelled concerned Americans to reflect upon the purposefulness of their country's presumed commitment to peace and to review the place of the peace tradition in the American experience. And that again defines the purpose of this book. It is intended to survey the place of the peace reform in the context of developing American nationhood by giving new voice to those volunteer middle-class activists who have historically provided moral, intellectual, and organizing force to the nation's successive peace movements. Ideally, we might see through these reformers an alternative vision of America and its promise. It is not necessarily a vision that is either wholly consistent or wholly right. But it is the one that best encompasses the persisting hope that people might collectively realize at least order and at most harmony on a global scale.

Perhaps that vision always was and will remain a mere hope. Yet that is no reason to ignore the pursuit of that hope over time in America by resolute men and women. For they alone were the people who worked creatively and intelligently to resolve the largest power conflicts of their times. And they alone have bequeathed to us some of the few available methods and principles that might yet save us in the closing years of this century from those impulses toward death and self-destruction that still dominate global politics.

Except for the concluding chapter, this book represents an attempt at a broad synthesis of existing scholarly writing. My largest intellectual debt therefore is due to those many scholars who have worked over the past generation to reconstruct aspects of the American peace tradition. Their individual contributions are cited in the chapter notes and the bibliographical essay. More immediately, a number of friend-critics did their best to improve this book. Michael Lutzker, David Patterson, and Lawrence Wittner each reviewed those chapters dealing with topics best known to (and through) them, while Peter Brock, Charles Chatfield, Merle Curti, and Warren Kuehl read the manuscript in its entirety. Stubbornly, however, I did my part. Those errors of fact and interpretation that remain are thanks to me.

Other people helped in other ways. The faculty and administration of the University of Toledo provided both moral encouragement and institutional support. Alice Weaver, JoAnne Hartough, and the interlibrary loan staff of the Carlson Library persevered in supplying me with books and articles. Carol Oleson, Jihad Kassis, Carl Katafiasz, and David Chelminski each assisted at different times in the research. My friends gave me some much-appreciated attention; and my family reminded me of those things more important than bookwork. For their contributions to this study, I thank David, who invited me into his games and reveries; Laura, who shared with me her concerns and accomplishments; and, most of all, Sandy, who made everything special.

THE PEACE REFORM
IN AMERICAN HISTORY

Chapter One
The Sectarian Reform

Europeans did not conquer North America without violence. Yet some deliberately sought in their colonial ventures to establish peace practices that gave new dimension to the Western peace tradition. In one of the more underrated achievements of the period 1620–1763, religious sectarians dedicated to the reconstitution of primitive Christianity and distinguished by their estrangement from governing authority founded in British North America a social commitment to the primacy of organized peace. Weary of Old World violence, resolute members of Protestant Europe's most radical reform sects moved to North America not simply out of an aspiration for peace. They aimed to live it as literal imitators of the True Christ.*

Radical religious sects proliferated across Europe between 1525 and 1660 in response to the overriding problem of the age: the collapse of traditional authority. Weakened by the Protestant Reformation and the rising nation-state, the customary sources of religious and secular authority disintegrated in spasms of violent dislocation that pushed forward seekers of a new truth. Most found it in Jesus Christ. Determined to emulate His original way, scatterings of simple Christians gathered in various communities that rejected involvement in secular affairs in favor of preparation for the Second Coming. Inevitably, the sectarians' determination to live

---

*Unlike a church, a sect is "a religious group which is gathered or called out of some natural organic group or state church on positively anticonformist grounds, sometimes by a charismatic leader, but as often by some principle of greater strictness, more singleminded dedication, or more intense abnegation of the world and its attractions." It is distinguished by its voluntarism, exclusivity, a perfectionist bent toward pure beliefs and practices, and an eschatological sense of Christ's imminent Second Coming to earth. Sydney E. Ahlstrom, *A Religious History of the American People* (New Haven: Yale University Press, 1972), p. 230.

3

solely by Christ's authority brought them into conflict with the power of established churches and the developing nation-states. Yet the radicals thrived in the face of contention, and they succeeded in bearing their convictions intact when they migrated to the New World. By 1763 nearly 60,000 inward-looking Anabaptist communitarians and extroverted Quakers had established in British North America a dissenting peace tradition that resulted from their unbending Christian devotion. In a society rich with dissenters, colonial peace reformers defined a sectarian peace vision that remained the bedrock of organized peace action in North America until the end of the nineteenth century.

In the New World, the largest social reality encompassed the protracted conflict among reds, whites, and blacks for identity and survival. Each entered upon this struggle with attitudes toward war and peace that were both unique and complex. For example, West African peoples historically accepted a "customary law" that regulated intergroup relations and controlled warfare. Some, like the Ashanti, used diplomacy in realizing their aims without war, while others, like the Ibo, negotiated differences with rivals through priests or representatives from neutral towns. A few West African people even selected champions to serve as duelists in the resolution of group disputes.[1] Those peace traditions weakened dramatically, however, in the midst of the sixteenth-century wars that spread in the wake of the expanding slave trade; and most disappeared altogether among the victims of transatlantic enslavement. Africans carried much of their traditional cultures to the New World. But they were compelled to adapt a great portion of this heritage—including various peace traditions—to the implacable new reality of slavery.

Native Americans varied in their attitudes toward peace and war from the pacific Hopi of the Southwest to the violent Sioux of the northern Plains. Typically, Indians perceived peace within a religious context that embraced their relationship with natural and supernatural forces. The Creeks' corn ceremony, for instance, began with a "peace day" on which all debts were to be settled and quarrels ended, while Plains Indians undertook extended "peace journeys" for purposes of trade and conciliation. More strikingly, the calumet, or peace pipe, was a symbol of peaceable intent for natives from the Atlantic to the Rockies. After seeing it in operation, one white observer was moved to report that "the Sceptres of our Kings are not so much respected" as an instrument for promoting and sealing intergroup harmony.[2]

Customarily, Indians viewed war as an episodic exercise that offered a minimum of violence and a maximum of opportunity for the individual warrior to humiliate an enemy without inflicting physical harm. Killing among even the bitterest rivals was discouraged; and, if a warrior did die, the victim's family was entitled to compensation from the attacking group. Waged mostly for revenge and prestige, Indian battles never involved large standing armies or protracted sieges. War parties seldom numbered more than a few score men who preferred brief hit-and-run skirmishes over set-piece battles.

Ironically, the very modesty of Indian warfare reinforced fears on the part of invading Europeans of the natives' barbaric ways. The sudden swoop into the enemy's camp, which the Indians valued as a sign of craft and daring, appeared to Europeans as proof of aboriginal stealth. Likewise, the Indian avoidance of open battle convinced colonists of the natives' heathen preference for those forbidding forests that swarmed with uncontrolled furies. Even the natives' best mechanisms for containing conflict—most notably the League of the Iroquois—spread awe and fear among encroaching Europeans. Although capable of mounting war parties from the Hudson River Valley to the Illinois country, the Iroquois Confederation worked most successfully to control tribal rivalries and organize woodland Indians in profiting from the Anglo-Dutch-French competition for furs. Combining political imagination, effective war parties, and a federative spirit, the Iroquois managed to hold the balance of power in the North American interior from the start of the seventeenth century until the eve of the American Revolution.

Incredibly, the first extension of European peace values to North America began with the great Puritan migrations of the 1630s, and continued through the worst civil disorder in English history and the bloody Thirty Years' War in Europe. The achievement was doubly unusual because Puritans were known as loyal members of a "military civilization."[3] For fifty years these English Calvinists had been caught up in a bitter struggle to purify the Church of England of remaining Roman influences. Then, in the late 1620s, a variety of forces combined to drive nearly 20,000 Puritan dissidents over the next decade to Massachusetts Bay colony, where they

resolved to build a model biblical commonwealth. Striving relentlessly for sanctity, New England Puritans worked unyieldingly
to establish a Christo-centric social order whose tenets derived
from Scripture. Yet they proved strangely ambivalent when con-
fronting matters of war and peace.

Puritans in North America generally met the war/peace question
by oscillating between two of Christianity's most durable traditions: the just war and the crusade. Conscious of teachings dating
back to St. Augustine, New England clergymen felt most satisfied
with the just war position. Encouraged by contemporary English
divines like William Ames, they maintained that war was morally
acceptable when it was defensive in nature, prosecuted toward the
end of justice, authorized by legitimate authority, protective of
noncombatants, and waged with reasonable proportionality between the degree of violence and the justness of the end to be at-
tained. In theory, the Puritan reiteration of the just war idea was
intended to work a limiting effect upon a necessary evil. In practice, however, it helped lend sanction to the Puritans' attacks upon
their red neighbors. More subtly, Puritan support of the just war
doctrine strengthened in the seventeenth century the growing
claim of the centralizing state to a monopoly of the public warmaking power. It helped convert the universal war/peace maxims
of the Roman church to the state-building needs of secular
authority.[4]

Periodically, however, Puritans moved beyond the just war position and endorsed war as a positive good when conducted as a
crusade in defense of the True Faith. In part, the Puritan vision of
war as crusade derived from their feeling that they were the New
Israelites, a chosen people designated like their Old Testament
forebears as an "armed band of the Lord."[5] Even more, it resulted
from their practice of viewing right behavior in military terms. Seeing life as a battle against sin and Satan, Puritans exalted the
soldierly virtues of courage, discipline, and sacrifice as vital to individual saintliness and necessary social order. Puritans were, most
literally, obedient Christian soldiers. They were warrior-saints who
were expected to organize and do battle with a tenacity essential to
those in Christ's service. Sometimes the soldierly impulse among
Puritans left them spiritually drained and socially fractious. But it
usually served them well. More than most, they were prepared for
the shocks of revolution, regicide, and civil war that struck England between 1644 and 1660 with unexpected ferocity.

At home, New England Puritans worked diligently to sustain a commonwealth of harmony and peaceability. Although sure of man's inherent sinfulness, they went out of their way to emphasize the importance of consensus and concord within the province. When looking to the outside, however, Puritan leaders lived in expectation of major violence. Surrounded by the hostile French and unpredictable natives, they waited in self-conscious emulation of Old Testament Israelites for their God to try them with war. "War is the greatest of all outward Judgements," one Puritan elder declared.[6] It was God's test of their faith and His punishment for their flagging religious zeal.

Puritans met their test well. Over the seventeenth century, they confronted their Indian neighbors with growing animosity and periodic violence (most notably the Pequot War of 1635 and King Philip's War of 1675–1676) which eventually resulted in the elimination of local native resistance. In the process, Puritans not only experienced and survived divine judgment but also passed through that uniquely New World experience which Richard Slotkin has aptly termed "regeneration through violence." With other colonists, Puritans found in the New World an opportunity to regenerate their souls, their church, and their fortunes. Rapidly, however, they also realized that the surest way toward individual and social regeneration was by means of violence. Violence broke open the way toward new opportunity; and the belief in regeneration through violence became a formative feature of American life and thought.[7] It proved a disturbing signal for those who saw in the New World new hope for lasting peace.

While Puritans conquered in America, England staggered through a revolution and civil war that produced a limited monarchy, a rich body of radical republican thought, and unprecedented religious ferment. Nearly two hundred sects sprang up in mid-seventeenth-century England in enthusiastic attempts to create a literal Christian order that would function through a Rule of the Saints in anticipation of Christ's impending return. The followers of one group called themselves the First Publishers of Truth. Made up mostly of veteran religious seekers and former military officers, these enthusiasts concluded late in the 1640s that, since Christ revealed Himself in an Inner Light within every person, Christians must help everyone to uncover and live by the indwelling spirit. Led by an itinerant cobbler, George Fox (1624–1691), and other lay ministers, these self-described "changed men" crisscrossed England in the 1650s, urging listeners to recognize the Christ within them and deriding the "false pride" of existing political and religious authorities.[8] Their enemies had a name—Quakers—for these seekers who trembled at the thought of the inner spirit. They called themselves "Friends in the Truth," or simply "Friends."*

Exerting unusual appeal among the gentry and middle-class wholesalers, Quaker enthusiasts originally accepted the necessity of force as a means of achieving the Rule of the Saints. By the early 1660s, however, they shifted under a wave of persecution initiated by the restored Stuart monarchy into an ambiguous pacifist posture. Wavering between their respect for legitimate authority and the radical implications of the egalitarian Inner Light, Quakers came only gradually to reject war (initially, in fact, they permitted defensive preparations and support of warring governments) on the grounds that it was "contrary to the light of the lord Jesus Christ."[9] Like their allied "testimonies" against oath taking and for simplicity, the Quakers' pacifism grew less from any Sermon on the Mount literalism than from respect for "the ever-present and ever-teaching Spirit of Christ."[10] It was one track in a larger way illuminated by the Inner Light.

In practice, pacifism worked to bridge the inward and outward emphases of the Quaker way. Quietly bearing the Inner Light, Quakers sought a personal peace that was "purely inward, subjective, unilateral, if you like—a search for peace of mind."[11] Yet they were equally determined to serve as messengers of Christ's truth. As a result, itinerant Quaker ministers both lived pacifism for the sake of inner peace and proclaimed it publicly as the working way to Christ's earthly kingdom. Plainly, pacifism was no protective covering for a Quaker retreat from this world. It was rather one more tactic in the Friends' strategy of overtaking the world for Christ through the projection of the saving Inner Light.

Almost from the start of the sect, Quakers fanned out across the Atlantic from Barbados to Massachusetts Bay. Everywhere, they opposed, for reasons of conscience, militia drills, oath taking, jury service, and war and religious taxes. Frequently their commitments cost them their property. Sometimes they paid with their lives. In Puritan Massachusetts, where the experiential nature of the Inner

---

*The collective term, Religious Society of Friends, was not adopted until almost 1800. Richard Vann, *The Social Development of English Quakerism* (Cambridge: Harvard University Press, 1969), p. 129.

Light contradicted the scriptural bases from which local government drew its authority, colonial magistrates banished, tortured, and then executed a handful of Quakers late in the 1650s. Elsewhere the treatment of Friends varied according to their relationship with the governing authorities. In Rhode Island, Quaker colonists took a free and active part in running the province. In Virginia, they were initially persecuted and then grudgingly tolerated.

Seeking greater autonomy in the New World, several well-placed English Quakers succeeded in the 1670s in securing from the Crown a proprietary colony in the Jerseys. The enterprise became embroiled in a host of controversies, however, and seemed quite unsuitable as a safe Quaker refuge. Subsequent attempts among Friends to gain a second colonial foothold failed until 1681, when a well-born Quaker convert named William Penn (1644–1718) settled a family debt with King Charles II by accepting the proprietorship of a huge tract in the lower Delaware Valley. He called it "Pennsylvania." With other enthusiasts, Penn intended to establish there a "holy experiment" in the working Quaker way. He also hoped to turn a profit.

Penn was the first authentic peace hero in Anglo-American history. The hard-living son of a prominent naval officer, Penn first became attracted to Quakerism during his studies at Oxford. Converting to the new way in the mid-1660s, he drafted (often from prison) some powerful tracts in defense of religious toleration, and joined radical Whigs like Algernon Sidney in struggles for constitutional self-government and fuller civil liberties. Alternating between rationalism and spiritualism, Penn developed an intense religiosity which anchored a body of beliefs that were socially conservative, politically radical, and commercially adventuresome.

Confident in his convictions, the young convert supported London Friends in sponsoring the Quakers' West Jersey colony in the 1670s and accepted the Pennsylvania proprietorship in the expectation of profit. But Pennsylvania was far more than a business venture for Penn. It was the one place where persecuted Quakers could escape Restoration England and establish a model Christian community that operated on a voluntary social consensus and without physical coercion. It was the one place to work out the New Testament in the New World, with the help of radical republican theories that Penn absorbed from his contemporaries. Striving toward the world's boldest attempt at planned social harmony, he and his associates aimed to fashion a polity rooted in the vision that peace depended upon justice, "which is a fruit of government, as government of laws is from society, and society from consent."[12] No other radical Whig pamphleteer captured so cogently what came to be an overpowering American concern with peace, order, and popular self-determination.

In support of these assumptions, Penn drafted in 1682 a constitutional Frame of Government that provided unusually broad representative government and extensive religious toleration. In the same way, he took great pains to accommodate the natives' needs. Citing their common dependence upon the Great Spirit, Penn recognized the Indians' coequal right to the land and the importance of negotiating differences in good conscience. Through patience and not weapons, Quakers and Indians carved out a record of peaceable relations that remains unmatched in the meeting of migratory peoples. Nearly 12,000 English Friends flowed across historically Indian land in the last years of the seventeenth century. Yet conflict remained minimal and violence rare.

The Pennsylvania experiment was furthermore unique in the way that it welcomed other radical sects. At Penn's urging, the first group of pietistic German Mennonites, under the leadership of Francis Daniel Pastorius, migrated to the present-day Germantown section of Philadelphia in 1683. Other radical pacifist separatists followed a generation later. In 1710–1711, communities of Swiss Mennonites settled further inland, followed by members of the German Church of the Brethren (or Dunkers) in 1719, Schwenkfelders from Lower Silesia in the mid-1730s, and Moravians in the early 1740s.* Nearly all were farmers attracted to the richness of the Pennsylvania soil. Most were furthermore heirs to sixteenth-century Anabaptism and were encouraged by the Quakers' respect for their separatist preference for introverted rural communities that refused in any way to participate in the state's politics or wars.

Although they arrived later in North America, Anabaptist pacifist sects antedated Quakerism by more than a century. Springing up first in Zurich and then in south Germany in the 1520s,

---

*Several Amish arrived in 1727. Headed by Jakob Ammann, this conservative faction had broken away from the parent Swiss Mennonites between 1693 and 1697 because of differences in religious practices and personality. John A. Hostetler, *Amish Society* (Baltimore: The Johns Hopkins University Press, 1963), pp. 27–34.

Anabaptism originally represented those groups of radical Christians who believed that the way to a saving primitive Christianity was through voluntary adult baptism within a gathered community, and not through simple membership in an inclusive state church. Congenitally contentious, Anabaptist leaders quarreled as vigorously among themselves as they did with the hostile church and state authorities whose very legitimacy they challenged. Even worse, the early Anabaptist eschatological vision contained a revolutionary potential that became real in 1535, when apocalyptic-minded seekers descended upon the north German town of Münster, proclaimed a terror-filled Rule of Saints, and then collapsed before a Catholic counteroffensive.

After the Münster disaster, Anabaptism broke into several parts. Some of its members gradually re-formed under the inspiration of the former Dutch priest Menno Simons (1492–1559). Traveling through the rural Netherlands and northern Germany, Menno used his impressive organizational powers to gather a sect that stressed an other-worldly quietism. Unconcerned with secular authority, Mennonites adopted pacifism as part of their rejection of the powers of this world. Even more, they lived pacifism as a sign of their willingness to suffer in this world for Christ's sake. Mennonites gladly identified themselves as "defenseless Christians." "Our weapons are not swords and spears," Menno explained, "but patience, silence, and hope, and the word of God."[13] They would suffer for Christ, but not kill for Him.

From a similar impulse, other radical pietists moved to Pennsylvania, committed to a nonresistant pacifism that subsisted in communal separatism. Like the Mennonites, the Dunkers and Amish accepted state governing authority—or the Sword—as necessary to the control of human corruption. Yet they refused to participate in state affairs on the grounds that worldly power begot sinfulness. Aware that they could neither ignore secular power nor overcome it, Anabaptist sectarians withdrew into introverted rural communities and adopted a "Bible-centered, church-centered, vocational nonresistance."[14] They were simple nonresistants, determined only to abide by Christ's injunction that His imitators resist not evil.

In Pennsylvania, the indrawn German peace sects did little to help Penn in coping with the province's mounting problems: factional infighting, tensions with imperial authority, and a rising tide of land-hungry non-Quakers. Beginning in the 1680s, colonizing Friends became ensnarled in angry quarrels over the distribution of land and the powers of the proprietorship, moving Penn at one point to plead, "For the love of God, me, and the poor country, be not so governmentish, so noisy and open in your dissatisfactions."[15] But the contentiousness continued. Indeed, it reached a new level in 1693, when the colonial Assembly's refusal to supply men and monies for the Anglo-French war provoked a bitter conflict with imperial authorities that was only compounded by Penn's waning influence in London.

Identified as too sympathetic to the Crown, Penn drew a two-year jail term after the Glorious Revolution of 1688–1689, and briefly lost his governmental powers in Pennsylvania. While in prison, he wrote his famous "Essay Towards the Present and Future Peace of Europe" (1693–1694), a landmark exposition of the need for a collective order that would provide peace through an "imperial parliament" of European sovereigns. Penn's "Essay" originated in his religious faith in the universality of the Inner Light. But it moved forward through his rational attacks on war's wastefulness. In addition, his argument contained a subtle protest against Quakerism's growing tribalism and its mounting emphasis on personal peace. Working peace, Penn maintained, must be organized and institutionalized in social forms. It could not live long in the individual human heart, since "the Safety of the Society" rested upon "the Safety of the Particulars that constitute it."[16]

Yet Penn was unable to impress his social vision of peace upon the "holy experiment." Although he made a second visit to Pennsylvania over 1699–1701, provincial politics remained quarrelsome; and relations with the proprietorship grew more strained. Perplexed and frustrated, Penn suffered a stroke in 1712 and lingered six years before death. The proprietory interest in the meantime passed to his non-Quaker heirs, who showed more interest in profit making than in making a Christian society.

Intriguingly, however, circumstances forced the slow pacification of Pennsylvania politics. Starting early in the 1700s, an influx of Scotch-Irish settlers who cared little for the Inner Light but much for the Indians' lands swept into the colony. Pressing into the interior, the new colonists demanded the forcible removal of the natives; and they showed sharp hostility toward the Philadelphia Quaker merchants, whose commercial success made them a power in imperial as well as provincial politics.[17] Anxious to protect their experiment from disastrous new stress, Friends from throughout the colony joined in a vigorous attempt to heal continuing factionalism and establish firmer group discipline.

Politically, their success was striking. "The ability of the Quakers to avoid serious contention," says Alan Tully of the years 1726–1755, "was the single most important reason why Friends were able to dominate Pennsylvania politics to such a degree and why, in turn, politics were so stable."[18] Religiously, however, Quakers paid a price for their renewed group discipline. Most meetings withdrew into a kind of pious tribalism that undercut the Society's traditional interest in evangelization. Affirming the quietist ideal of a people apart, Quakers intensified philanthropic activities among themselves. But they otherwise withdrew—except for antislavery activism—from fuller attempts to spread the spiritual and humanitarian implications of the Inner Light.[19]

Yet the Quaker retreat from social activism positively strengthened their pacifist commitment. Beginning in the 1740s, Quaker politicians faced strong new demands from the family proprietors, imperial authorities, and non-Quaker colonists for more aggressive action in the back country against the French and Indians. At first they tried typically to deflect the pressure. Employing policies first adopted in the 1690s, Friends in the provincial Assembly declined to vote tax monies specifically for imperial wars. But they did agree to contribute funds in general "for the king's use" and authorized voluntary enlistment in the militia.[20] Their equivocation was understandable in the face of a classic dilemma. Fighting the danger of "greater complicity" in the King's wars, Quaker politicians sought desperately to reconcile their sectarian refusal to bear arms with their worldly desire to maintain a legitimate government in the physical defense of its citizens.[21]

This attempt to reconcile religious conviction and political reality worked until 1755, when the outbreak of the French and Indian War precipitated an irresolvable crisis. Pressured by imperial authorities and an antipacifist Assembly faction headed by Benjamin Franklin, a group of Quaker assemblymen led by Isaac Norris II ignored militant pacifist protests and supported a special war tax as compatible with their commitment to peace. Their action finally cracked the Quakers' political unity and policy-making effectiveness. Goaded by dissidents like John Churchman and John

Woolman, a faction of reform Friends attacked the war levy and demanded the withdrawal of all conscientious Quakers from the Assembly. Some responded. In June 1756 six Quakers quit the Assembly in a dramatic display of their determination to protect their Christian peace commitment against the claims of the state. They had no illusions as to the effectiveness of their protest against the war tax, but they felt sure of its necessity. As one Friend explained while war preparations mounted, "I found it best for me to refuse paying demands on my estate which went to pay the expenses of war; and although my part might appear at best a drop in the ocean, yet the ocean, I considered, was made up of many drops."[22]

Reinforcing the new pacifist militancy, the Philadelphia Yearly Meeting, the strongest coordinating body among Friends in the colonies, cautioned its members against holding any public office within the warring state. The Meeting also urged Friends to respect their peace testimony at the risk of state confiscation of their property and proposed supervision of any "disorderly walkers" who might be tempted to assist the war effort. Acting forcefully in retreat, the Quakers toughened their pacifism and protested attempts to distinguish between moral behavior in the political and religious spheres. "There is no distinction in Christianity between civil and religious matters," the reformer Anthony Benezet declared in 1757.[23] The two were one.

Working from this conviction, Quaker reformers did not view their withdrawal from public authority in Pennsylvania as a loss for Penn's "holy experiment." On the contrary, they had succeeded in showing for seventy-five years that pacifism could work for public order.[24] Now they intended to employ it for the sake of larger social justice. Standing apart for the first time from provincial politics, Pennsylvania Quakers formed the Friendly Association* in 1756 as a neutral mediating agency between warring reds and whites. It was the first step in what became a Quaker tradition of acting as reconcilers between expanding Europeans and various North American natives.

Embarrassingly, however, the Friends' peacemaking practices became overshadowed in the early 1760s by the wealth that Philadelphia Quaker merchants were accumulating in the lucrative wartime trade. The anomaly of prospering from social evil troubled

---

*More formally, the group was titled "The Friendly Association for Regaining and Preserving Peace with the Indians by Pacific Means."

many Quakers, but none more than John Woolman (1720–1772). A simple tailor from Mount Holly, New Jersey, Woolman began preaching against the dangers of Quaker wealth and worldliness in the 1740s, when he experienced an intense personal crisis after assisting in the sale of an enslaved woman. Denouncing materialism and reemphasizing the virtue of simplicity, he thereafter pursued an itinerant ministry through the Middle and Southern colonies, out of a determination to assist "the pure flowing of divine love" through human affairs.[25] "The only effective dissolvent of the love of power," ran his message to the worldly, "was the power of love."[26]

Urging Friends to socialize their faith, Woolman argued for support of the poor, defense of Indian rights, and an end to slavery. Pressed by him and other Quaker reformers, Friends became by the 1760s the first group of white Americans to turn from slaveholding toward outright abolitionism. The New Jersey tailor also helped in the work of the Friendly Association, and refused along with his friend Benezet to pay war taxes in support of the French and Indian War. He was an uncompromising—and vocal—Christian war-resister. Direct and unaffected, Woolman furthermore set down a religious *Journal* that stands as a moving testimony to the ways in which one person can alter human relations in a manner that was at once simple, decent, and loving. He was an altogether rare creature, devoted to "living in the real substance of religion, where practice doth harmonize with principle."[27] Gentle if unyielding, he was the first native-born peace hero in Europeanized America.

Yet Woolman's very uniqueness as an aggressive seeker of peace through justice was indicative of the larger containment of the sectarian peace reform in eighteenth-century America. Colonial peace activism claimed in Penn and Woolman some remarkable leaders. But the core of the reform centered in what came to be called the Historic Peace Churches—those Pennsylvania-based Anabaptist remnants and the 50,000 Quakers who were scattered by 1763 in nearly eighty meetinghouses from Massachusetts Bay to the West Indies. Apart from a few spiritual adventurers like Woolman, most were relentlessly plain people. Simple and unassuming, they undertook to live peace; and, as they did, they demonstrated powerfully how ordinary people can bring about an extraordinary advance when they mold their behavior around a few basic truths. Richard Hofstadter once observed that "There are times—however rare—when striking historical achievements are made by men of an excessive simplicity."[28] The rise of the sectarian peace reform marked one such achievement. Radical religious dissidents had migrated to North America to achieve Christ's peace without violence. They remained to stand in its witness; they built in the process a tradition.

Chapter Two
The Revolutionary Reform

Between 1763 and 1815, the thirteen British colonies in North America worked an uncommon number of revolutionary achievements as they completed an uncharted course toward national independence. In rapid succession, American patriots raised up resistance to their English sovereign, waged and won an anticolonial revolutionary war, created a constitutional republic with imperial pretensions, and then secured these achievements in a bitter struggle against European hostility and domestic discontents. Peace plainly was at a premium in these formative years of American nationhood. Yet American leaders nonetheless strove ideologically and institutionally to graft the peace reform to their revolutionary purpose. No other government permitted so many men of conscience to avoid military service. No other country erected so many constraints against a peacetime standing army. No other people defined their collective identity so firmly with the work of redeeming the world for peace.

The first powerful expressions of America's revolutionary peace destiny appeared in the 1770s, when radical patriots finally decided upon the need for complete independence. Identifying British overlordship with recurring conflict, radical leaders urged other colonists to turn with them from the monarchical European system of war and conquest to the peaceable service of model republicanism and working commerce. With Britain as "our master," Tom Paine wrote in 1776, "we became enemies to the greatest part of Europe, and they to us; and the consequence was war inevitable. By being our own masters, independent of any foreign one, we have Europe for our friends, and the prospect of an endless peace among ourselves." If the country were united and self-governing, he further predicted, America could cross the continent and thus eliminate

17

"the future use of arms from one quarter of the world."[1] Let there be no misunderstanding, Paine insisted:

> Our plan is peace for ever. We are tired of contention with Britain, and can see no real end to it but in a final separation. We act consistently, because for the sake of introducing an endless and uninterrupted peace, do we bear the evils and the burdens of the present day.[2]

From the start, the revolutionaries' promise of global peace through American national independence was based on a synthesis between universality and uniqueness that shaped not only America's developing nationalism but also popular perceptions of peace. America was basically "the product," as Sidney Ahlstrom has written, "of two traditions: one, particularist, providential, supernaturalistic, Puritan and Judaic; the other, universalist, rational, naturalistic and cosmopolitan."[3] In Revolutionary America, these two visions operated most visibly through the outworkings of evangelical Protestantism and Enlightenment rationalism. The two were opposed in many ways. Experiential and individualistic, evangelical Protestantism viewed God as transcendent, man as corrupt but redeemable, and history as the fulfillment of scriptural prophecy. Conversely, Enlightenment rationalists saw man as perfectible, history as the expansion of progress through reason, and natural laws as the governing forces of the universe. The two traditions additionally perceived peace in different ways. While evangelicals looked for it in the spreading Kingdom of God, rationalists treated peace as part of the progress through reason that grew with interlocking commerce along "natural" lines among free republics.[4]

In the heat of revolutionary politics, however, the two traditions fused to form the bases of modern American nationalism and the people's peace vision. Both traditions identified Americans as a chosen people, a people apart. Both saw for America a higher mission, whether in service of God or of universal natural rights. Both viewed the American mission as the means toward larger human fulfillment, whether in the Christian millennium or in a rationalistic utopia. And both believed that, in pursuit of this mission, America acted essentially outside of history, whether suprahistorically on God's behalf or ahistorically apart from the Old World. On all counts, America signified for evangelicals and rationalists the opening of a triumphant new epoch. America's birth heralded an era "when universal love and liberty, peace & righteousness, shall prevail"; proclaimed one preacher, "when angry contentions shall be no more, and wars shall cease, even unto the ends of the earth." "The birthday of the world is at hand," agreed the deist Paine. "We have it in our power to begin the world over again."[5] With America, the universal and the unique were one.

In practice, evangelical Protestantism and Enlightenment rationalism combined in the 1760s to produce that "apocalyptic Whiggism" which gave driving force to the Revolution.[6] Rooted in a century of left-wing political opposition and activated by pulpit jeremiads, "apocalyptic Whiggism" expanded after 1763 on the common beliefs that man was corrupt, power corrosive, and liberty tenuous. It spread even more in the wake of the colonists' growing fears of Britain's use of the peacetime standing army. Heir to a tradition of antimilitarism, Anglo-Americans generally disliked war because it increased the public debt, taxes, and executive power. But they especially feared it for the ways in which it strengthened the standing army. Dominated by an elite officer corps and manned by ruffians, the traditional standing army stood apart from the larger society and stuck together through severe discipline and strict obedience to command. It was in colonial eyes an institution that was dangerous on every count: its makeup menaced public morals; its irresponsibility threatened civilian authority; and its power made it irresistible to tyrants.[7]

The troubles of mid-seventeenth-century England bred antimilitarism into colonial bones; and the observed behavior of contemporary European professional armies and English imperial garrisons added strength to the sentiment.[8] Yet colonists did not act upon their suspicions until 1763, when Britain began for the first time to station thousands of regular troops in the colonies. Then the old apprehensions turned after several crises into antimilitarist action. As British troops became the crudest symbol of imperial power, the colonials chafed at their presence. Several clashed openly with royal regulars in the Hudson Valley in 1766 and in Boston in 1770. Many more viewed the troops as a standing contradiction to claimed provincial liberties. In 1776 Thomas Jefferson articulated a longstanding belief when he asserted that the establishment of a standing army and the King's attempt "to render the Military independent of a superior to the Civil Power" were high among those royal "injuries and usurpations, all having in direct object the establishment of an absolute Tyranny over these States."[9] The misuse of the military power presented a singular justification for revolution.

Paradoxically, the antimilitarism that shaped early American nationalism nearly undercut the country's main means of nation making—the Continental Army. The colonial fear of a large standing army—plus the power of localism—consistently weakened attempts to support a national fighting force. The Continental Congress was notoriously tightfisted in funding the army, and enlistments were erratic and brief. State bounties failed to attract recruits into national service; and, when some states passed conscription laws in attempts to man General George Washington's army, they provoked major outbreaks of antidraft violence.[10] Antimilitarist defenders of the local militia distrusted advocates of a centralized national military establishment, while leaders of the Continental Army felt contempt for the military unreliability of the militia. Understandably, their differences intensified as the war grew more costly, and persisted even after victory.[11] Indeed, the struggle over the means of building an effective national defense for a society committed to antimilitarism continued for another generation.

Sectarian pacifists in the Historic Peace Churches endured other kinds of conflict during the Revolutionary War. Although Philadelphia Quaker merchants played a leading role in colonial protests in the early 1760s, the radicalization of provincial politics prompted most Friends to retreat by 1770 into wholehearted neutralism. "[W]e do not believe in revolutions," a handful explained in 1776, "and we do not believe in war. . . . We are out of the whole business and will give aid and comfort to neither party."[12] Tied to the Atlantic trading community and the English Society of Friends, American Quakers generally stood by their pacifist testimony during the war despite some internal fractures. A small group of Free Quakers quit the Philadelphia Yearly Meeting in the mid-1770s to support the revolutionary effort. A faction of Quaker Loyalists likewise carried their doctrine of nonresistance into open support of the Crown. And Friends with sympathies toward neither side quarreled among themselves over the payment of war taxes and the use of the rebels' Continental currency.

Most Quakers respected the sect's traditional injunctions against the bearing of arms or the payment of soldier-substitutes. But their behavior from conscience came at a price. Inflamed local patriots executed two unresisting Friends in Pennsylvania. In an attempt to force them to bear arms, Continental Army soldiers tied muskets to the backs of fourteen Quaker conscientious objectors* at the Valley Forge encampment before General Washington ordered their release. One North Carolina Quaker received forty lashes for his refusal to shoulder a musket, while countless draft-age Friends were arrested and jailed throughout the rebel colonies for their objection to military service.

More generally, Quakers suffered for their peace witness by losing property. Often, foraging troops summarily seized their livestock or harvest. Sometimes local rebel authorities levied distraints (or legal claims) upon Quaker holdings as a means of making them pay for their neutralism. In addition, Friends clashed repeatedly with warmaking governments over the use of loyalty test oaths, the rebels' Continental currency, and the payment of tax monies which might support the war effort.

Ineluctably, the continuing tension between peacemaking Quakers and warmaking authorities moved Friends to withdraw further from public politics and into a deeper tribalism. Interestingly, however, the growing Quaker emphasis on group discipline and self-purification not only strengthened the Friends' sense of sectarian exclusivity but also accelerated their traditional humanitarian impulses. In 1770 the Philadelphia Yearly Meeting opened the first school for freed blacks in North America. Six years later, the Meeting prohibited the ownership among its members of enslaved people. At the same time, the outbreak of war inspired Friends into relief work. Within months of the Battle of Bunker Hill, Quakers were providing aid to noncombatants in eastern Massachusetts; and they proceeded as the violence expanded to organize help for uprooted people from New Jersey to Georgia.[13]

The Friends' enlarging benevolence became most manifest in the work of Anthony Benezet (1713–1784). In 1776 this longtime Quaker reformer, who had been born of French Huguenots and raised in England, drafted one of the earliest pacifist treatises in American

---

*Actually, the term "conscientious objection" did not come into use until World War I. Before then, religious objectors to war were called "non-resistants" or "non-combatants." Edward N. Wright, *Conscientious Objectors in the Civil War* (New York: A.S. Barnes edition, 1961), pp. 1–2.

history. Conveying his *Thoughts on the Nature of War*, Benezet condemned war as "the premeditated and determined destruction of human beings, of creatures *originally formed after the image of God*." Arguing from faith and history, he held that people peaceably prospered in production and trade until innate greed provoked warfare that persisted until exhaustion required new peace. There was only one way to break this pattern, Benezet believed. Christian peoples must act as responsibly as Christian individuals, and reconcile their governments to the "divine government, the fundamental law of which is LOVE."[14] At best, Benezet hoped that his *Thoughts* would demonstrate the utter dispensability of war. At least, he felt that it would "lessen, if not remove, any prejudice which our Friends' refusal to join in any military operation may have occasioned" among other colonists.[15]

Impatient with preachments, Benezet also worked to alleviate war-caused suffering. He gradually moved in the face of the human hurting to two radical conclusions: (1) war was too evil to originate in the will of an all-loving God; and (2) it was too destructive to remain the sole concern of traditional peace sects. Moving beyond Quaker meetinghouses, he distributed leaflets and urged audiences everywhere to act directly against war. He preached and practiced tax refusal, badgered British and American military officers to reflect upon their work, and demanded that Christians act—and not simply pray—in unison against the war menace. Quite realistically, he never underestimated the magnitude of the cause or the barriers before it. It was "a fundamental Truth," he believed, "that Christ overcame by patient suffering, leaving us an example . . . that we should follow his steps; but this mode of conquest is so contrary, & so irksome to proud nature, which so impatiently bears the thought of submission; very few indeed are willing to be as pilgrims & strangers in their passage thro' life."[16]

Benezet's challenge made little impression, however, upon biblically bound Anabaptist pacifists. Holding to their other-worldly witness, Mennonites, Dunkers, and other scattered peace sectarians declared their devout neutralism during the war and adapted to local conditions. Unlike the Quakers, most purchased exemptions from military service and willingly served in war-related work. Like the Quakers, they suffered fines for their refusal to enroll in the militia, and endured the confiscation of property for their opposition to revolutionary loyalty oaths. For the most part, rural sectarians continued to live out their lives in a religious witness, holding to the practice of peace on the grounds that they were "accountable to none but God." "It is our fixed principle," they maintained, "rather than take up Arms to defend our King, our Country, or our Selves, to suffer all that is dear to us to be rent from us, even Life itself, and this we think not out of Contempt to Authority, but that herein we act agreeable to what we think is the mind and Will of our Lord Jesus."[17]

Living in the "two Kingdoms" of God and man, both Quakers and rural peace sectarians petitioned and argued in support of their principled objection to war. But they declined in all other ways to defend their peace witness. And civil authorities had neither the desire nor the means to subordinate their witness to the will of the state. The result by war's end was tacitly sanctioned confusion. The new country possessed no coherent policy toward war objectors. Pacifist claims rather drifted in "a legal limbo, part privilege and part right." The country was covered, as Richard Renner has observed, by a "statutory mosaic of alternative service schemes, fines, conditional exemptions of varying rigor, provisions for distraint, and simple disregard of the whole issue."[18] Nor were there any attempts to institute a national solution. Evidently, the civil status of conscientious objectors was not important until time of war.*

Although the end of the Revolutionary War in 1783 eased the problems of sectarian pacifists, it did not resolve popular antimilitarist fears or demands for a reliable military establishment. With British authority eliminated, American patriots rather broke into open quarrel over how they might build a constitutional republic that would be strong enough to defend the country but flexible enough to tolerate the extensive exercise of individual liberties. The momentous task of securing the Revolution by institutionalizing republicanism was complicated further by the

---

*The list of American peace sects was lengthened in 1774, when an English perfectionist community called Shakers migrated to upstate New York. Headed by Mother Anne Lee, the Shakers (more formally, the United Society of Believers) aimed to "follow peace with all men" out of a sense of Christian literalism. Living simply and celibately, Shakers refused to bear arms, but were willing to pay war taxes (at least until 1815) and provide war relief. Their numbers grew to about 1,000 in 1815 as they experimented with different communal arrangements in order to re-create literally Christ's own Jerusalem in America. Edward D. Andrews, *The People Called Shakers: A Search for the Perfect Society* (New York: Oxford University Press, 1953), p. 212.

Americans' clear ambition for continental conquest and European trade. "Wars then must sometimes be our lot," Jefferson wrote of the country's commercial desires, "and all the wise can do, will be to avoid that half of them which would be produced by our own follies, and our own acts of injustice; and to make sure for the other half the best preparations we can."[19]

Persisting domestic tensions and periodic mob actions such as Shays's Rebellion in 1786 aggravated the republican dilemma of how to avoid militarism while establishing a respectable military. Anxious to sustain public order for the sake of freedom, American nationalists like Washington and General Henry Knox tried in the early 1780s to create a national military force that would maintain both state security and republicanism. But to revolutionaries who had struggled on the local or state level, plans for a national military establishment raised the first threat of a counterrevolutionary military coup d'etat. Their fears were understandable. As one historian has concluded, "at no other time in American history—save perhaps the Reconstruction years and the era of the Cold War—had militarism so seriously threatened the United States" as in the first years of the republic.[20]

Postwar fear of military rule first crystallized in 1783 following the founding of the Society of the Cincinnati. Organized by top Continental Army officers and conservative politicians, the Cincinnati formed the groundwork of social and political solidarity for the postwar officer corps. Antimilitarist critics immediately attacked the Society as an upper-class nest of power seekers; and, even as it died of inanition, the Cincinnati left memories of the military's ambition for advantage in an open society. At the same time, nationalist plans for a peacetime military establishment proved worrisome. In April 1783 General Washington submitted to the Congress his "Sentiments on a Peace Establishment," in which he called for the establishment of a small regular army of citizen-soldiers garrisoned in frontier forts and coastal fortifications. Three years later, Secretary of War Henry Knox proposed the formation of an "energetic national militia" and the standardization of equipment and training.[21] But neither proposal moved legislators, who looked to the local and state militia as the nation's best line of defense. Local revolutionaries worried too much about military autocracy and too little about European invasion to overcome their fears of any established force that appeared as a standing army.

They believed that the oceans secured America well enough in peace.

The conflict over a national military establishment expanded during the fight over the ratification of the 1787 Constitution, as each side insisted that its approach would best prevent the rise of peacetime standing armies. Defending the new Constitution, the authors of *The Federalist* argued that a strong national government commanding a small regular army would enhance the security of the republic without endangering popular liberties. Recent changes in finance, industry, and national rivalries had produced "an entire revolution in the system of war," Federalists explained, "and have rendered disciplined armies, distinct from the body of citizens, the inseparable companions of frequent hostility." In the face of these changes, standing armies would "inevitably result" in America from the ongoing decline of the Articles of Confederation government, whereas their existence under the Constitution was "at most, problematical and uncertain."[22]

Antifederalists meanwhile feared the militaristic implications of the proposed new government. Many suspected that the president would serve as a "military king." Some fretted over the future of the militia. Others worried that a national military establishment would cause the multiplication of executive officers, moving placemen to "swarm over the land, devouring the hard earnings of the industrious—like the locusts of old, impoverishing and desolating all before them." A few emphasized the need to respect the scruples of conscientious objectors. And all feared the rise of a peacetime standing army, "that grand engine of oppression," which the new Constitution promised to streamline rather than reduce.[23]

With the adoption of the Constitution, plans to promote a nationwide peace reform took on brief new life in the early 1790s. Perhaps the most arresting proposal was Benjamin Rush's idea for a national peace office. A Philadelphia physician and onetime Continental Army Surgeon-General, Rush was a fascinating figure who blended evangelical Christianity with a scientific intelligence that placed him in the company of Benjamin Franklin and Thomas Jefferson. He was also a humanitarian who took peace seriously. Writing in 1793, Rush urged the formation of a national peace office under the direction of a man who was "a genuine republican and a sincere Christian, for the principles of republicanism and Christianity are no less friendly to universal and perpetual peace, than they are to universal liberty." The proposed office would establish throughout the country free schools which promulgated pacific Christian principles. It would also distribute an American edition of the Bible to every family; work to eliminate all capital punishment laws; and seek the elimination of militia parades, military titles, and uniforms. It should maintain a museum that featured a collection of swords that had been beaten into plowshares, and sponsor in an adjacent assembly hall the daily appearance of a choir of young women who would sing "in praise of the blessings of peace."[24] In all ways, Rush's proposal aimed to substitute a culture of peace for the glamor and heroism of war. It seemed a laughable if laudable idea. Yet it pointedly framed a problem that would perplex peace reformers well into the twentieth century: how was peace to be sought as long as war seemed so attractive?

In the 1790s, however, Rush's point became obscured in the spreading glorification of the Revolutionary War. Absorbed in a spirit of "martial republicanism," American nationalists hailed the war as a splendid example of how an oppressed people used limited violence to secure peace and justice through a united effort. Patriots honored military leaders, memorialized battles, and devised national histories that lauded the Revolutionary struggle as the greatest advance in recent human progress. The War of Independence became the weld of national identity—and the most virtuous exercise of violence. "[I]f ever there was a holy war," Jefferson allowed, "it was that which saved our liberties and gave us independence." It would be "sanctioned," he predicted, "by the approbation of posterity through all future ages."[25]

Positive peace proposals also failed to advance in the 1790s because of major red-white violence in the Old Northwest. Inevitably, the worsening Indian wars reopened the question of national preparedness and revived the conflict between the nationalist proponents of a centralized military establishment and the antimilitarist defenders of the militia system. Caught between frontier violence and French Revolutionary tensions in Europe, nationalists like Washington and Knox reiterated their demands for a small regular army and strengthened coastal defenses. And for once Congress responded with assent. In its first defense bill, the Uniform Militia Act of 1792, the government created a new category of "federal volunteers" that was more than a militia but less than an army. Hesitantly, American leaders proceeded over the next several years to create "a small national establishment backed by a standardized, federalized militia" that was the equivalent of the modern reserve.[26] But they deferred consistently to anti-militarist apprehensions. What became the American army was too small to function as a classic, European-style standing force. Yet it was much better organized than the traditional militia. It was an army of a new mode, tailored to the unique demands of an antimilitarist but aggressive republican people.

While quarrels over military organization subsided after 1792, arguments over the use of the armed forces rose sharply over the decade. Dividing into Federalist and Republican factions, political partisans battled violently over the executive's use of the army against domestic dissidents during various popular tax rebellions and in the face of an undeclared Franco-American naval war. And then there occurred a most remarkable event—the election of 1800. Without military intervention, power passed in America through electoral means to the principal opposition group, with the concurrence of the defeated incumbents. Thomas Jefferson's peaceful accession to presidential power in 1801 not only showed that the mechanics of the Constitution's electoral provisions worked despite dreaded factionalism but also proved that power could change hands in the world's only imperial republic without a military coup. Antimilitarist opposition to a peacetime standing army and to military influence in civilian politics would remain powerful elements in subsequent American history. But the fear of military intrusion that dominated so much of early American politics diminished sharply after 1800. "At a time when the French were turning to Napoleon the Americans turned to Jefferson," Henry Steele Commager has observed, "and the Jeffersonian era outlasted the Napoleonic."[27]

It was also an era highly mindful of right religion. Bubbling among the political tensions of the 1790s was a religious fermentation that signaled the second Great Awakening of pietistic revivalism. Originating in New England in an atmosphere of supposed spiritual decline, the Awakening naturally stressed the importance of individual regeneration and personal salvation. Yet it contained a social reform impulse that produced organized crusades against vice and intemperance and in behalf of peace, sabbatarianism, and foreign missions. Operationally, the drive shaft that connected the needs for personal salvation and social conversion lay in the spirit of millennialism that had long permeated Protestant America. Living in anticipation of Christ's impending return, evangelical Protestants worked to prepare themselves and American society for divine judgment on the assumption that they were "the last peculiar people which he [God] means to form, and the last great empire which he means to erect, before the kingdoms of this world are absorbed in the kingdoms of Christ."[28] They sensibly intended to make clear the way of the Lord.

But the millennialist expectations of Protestant reformers took on new direction after 1807 with the worsening of Anglo-American relations. Aggravated by agricultural depression within America and by Napoleon's success in Europe, differences between Washington and London expanded over such matters as British aid to northwestern Indian tribes and American trade with France. Inevitably, the darkening diplomatic climate produced anxious policy debate at home. Northeastern merchants warned that a naval war with Britain would destroy American commercial prosperity. Federalist politicians complained that the Republicans' anti-British policies entailed a subservience to imperial France that threatened the very independence and fragility of the American republic. New England clergymen condemned Washington's de facto alignment with the Napoleonic antichrist. In spite of the apocalyptic flavor of their protests, domestic critics worked little effect upon Republican policy makers. Yet they did lay the basis for the formation of a full-scale antiwar movement that arose in June 1812, when the United States declared war on Britain and prepared to invade Canada.

Domestic opposition to the War of 1812 was as vehement and widespread as any in American history. Signs everywhere indicated that the conflict actually was "the most unpopular war that this country has ever waged."[29] The administration's official declaration of war passed a divided Congress by 19–13 in the Senate and 79–49 in the House. The War Department could never man the army to more than half its authorized strength. The Congress provided for 50,000 recruits, but less than 10,000 men proved willing to join for the one-year term of service. Typically, Kentucky, which churned with prowar enthusiasm, contributed fewer than 400 volunteers to the national war effort. In fact, the New England states supplied nearly twice as many regiments to national service as did the southern states. Yet Federalist New England was the hotbed of domestic opposition.

Antiwar activism took many forms as it moved to a peak in 1814. When Congress declared war, Massachusetts Governor Caleb Strong called for a public fast of atonement for America's attack upon "the nation from which we are descended, and which to many generations has been the bulwark of the religion we profess."[30] Northeastern financiers consistently refused to subscribe to national war loans, while the officers of the Harvard Corporation awarded five honorary degrees to leading antiwar critics in 1814. Nor were the lower classes silent. Nantucket islanders calmly declared their neutrality in the conflict. And, in early 1813, a mob in Newburyport, Massachusetts, attempted to free a group of British prisoners of war in one of a dozen acts of collective protest that struck Massachusetts, Rhode Island, and Connecticut.

Perhaps the best-known instance of popular defiance took place late in 1814, when twenty-six Federalists met at Hartford to protest the war, demand an overhaul of national defense policy, and urge several policy and constitutional changes upon the Madison administration. Even more flagrant antiwar action occurred clandestinely. In November 1814 Governor Strong dispatched secret peace feelers to British General Sir John Sherbrooke in Halifax, Nova Scotia, in an attempt to discern British intentions in case Strong attempted to break with the administration and withdraw Massachusetts from the Union. Luckily for the country, peace returned before Strong could pursue his plans.

Sectarian pacifists meanwhile clung to their peace witness in the face of varying wartime pressure. Pennsylvania officials rarely imprisoned conscientious objectors, although they laid heavy fines and property distraints upon them. Peace sectarians in the antiwar Northeast won unprecedented respect and status, while Quakers in the South suffered imprisonment and property distraints. Pressed by the war, Quakers furthermore developed a keener sense of personal responsibility for society's violence. In New Jersey, a free black Quaker farmer who subsisted from the produce that he sold to workers at an iron foundry stopped sales when he learned that the shop was casting cannon for war service. Isolated and ordinary, the Friend's decision was on one level a simple act of personal heroism. On another plane, however, it reflected the deepening integration of personal witness and social commitment that was shaping the Society of Friends into the most dynamic agency of social reform in nineteenth-century America.[31]

At the same time, mainstream American churches waged "a veritable civil war" over the righteousness of America's struggle against Britain. Baptists and Presbyterians supported the Madison administration. Congregationalists condemned the war as an attack on Protestant England in behalf of Napoleonic satanism, while millennialists on all sides argued whether the crisis signaled divine punishment or a positive challenge for spiritual renewal. Aggravating internal division over the war, the churches' controversy made American peace negotiators at Ghent "more circumspect about breaking discussions and more willing to achieve peace."[32]

But nothing sped the making of peace like the exigencies of war. In December 1814, a few months after Napoleon's exile to Elba and the British defeat on Lake Champlain, American and British envoys concluded a settlement that returned Anglo-American relations to the *status quo antebellum*. Politically, the United States salvaged little more from the war than fuller security along the Great Lakes. Psychologically, however, the country felt a charge of national pride that expanded after Andrew Jackson's victory at New Orleans in January 1815.

Hailing the fight as a second War of Independence, Americans took immense satisfaction in the feeling that they had maintained their national honor in the face of repressive British maritime practices. A more full-bodied spirit of nationalism—activated more by the war's end than its conduct—swept the country toward a stronger sense of Union and away from the bitter memories of antiwar dissension. "You might say," Samuel Eliot Morison has observed only half-jokingly, "that it was our most popular war when it was over and our most unpopular while it lasted."[33]

The turn of events was curious but not inexplicable. The postwar nationalist surge quickly suppressed the country's deep wartime division because both were expressions—if different in time and place—of the same "sanctified nationalist ideology" that ultimately captivated both prowar enthusiasts and antiwar dissidents.[34] Convinced of their uniqueness, Americans after 1815 more than ever looked upon themselves as God's chosen people, a people apart. Yet they felt equally sure that they possessed a universal responsibility for global redemption. Steeped in evangelical Protestantism and Enlightenment rationalism, nationalists who had been moved by the "apocalyptic Whiggism" of the 1760s felt singularly predestined after 1815 to lead the world toward a "republican millennium" of peace and plenty.[35] And they resolved to advance as one.

America in 1815 was an impressive achievement. In a half-century of struggle, revolutionary Americans established through anticolonial warfare, resistance to foreign threats, and resolution of domestic tensions an independent constitutional republic imbued with imperial aspirations and expansive peace ideals. National leaders had wrested self-dominion from foreign overlordship, proclaimed a free trade economy in an age of closed empires, and devised a novel federal system for the distribution of governmental power. In addition, they advanced far in the work of reconciling the individual's need to live by conscience and the state's insistence that it order peace through power; and they checked the spread of that militaristic spirit which was historically the bane of republics. Ingeniously, American nationalists established a government that was designed to order but not control. Ambitiously, they organized a highly diverse people around a common vision: America existed to spread the revolutionary peace ideals of free trade, antimilitarism, and self-governing republicanism to a waiting world.

Chapter Three
The Humanitarian Reform

At the turn of the nineteenth century, scattered bands of war-weary Christians invented the modern nonsectarian peace movement by means of a new reform instrument—the private volunteer society. Gathering spontaneously in various cities, reformers prayed, planned, and eventually organized a humanitarian peace reform distinguished by its concern for men as Christian creatures. Solidly patriotic and Protestant, humanitarian peace reformers identified war as a moral evil that God and progress intended to destroy through the free will of enlightened men. And they resolved to be first among those men. They determined to spread among Christian peoples "a new reverence for man" by helping "men to see in themselves and one another the children of God. . . ."[1]

Humanitarian peace workers were typical romantic reformers: individualistic yet organized, rationalistic yet sentimental, personally conservative yet socially radical, humanly optimistic yet scripturally literalist. Priding themselves on their paradoxes, they founded a few dozen state and local societies before 1828, when the American Peace Society (APS) arose as the national consolidation of their efforts. Within a decade, the APS mushroomed into national prominence and then broke into contending factions. Dogged by internal division, organized peace seeking gradually lost momentum after 1840 in the face of the growing slavery controversy. Then it collapsed altogether with the outbreak of the Civil War.

Interestingly, humanitarian peace reformers encountered from the very start those problems that would grip latter-day peace activists. What should be the first object of peace seeking: conversion of the individual human heart, or comprehensive social reformation? What defined the enemy: international war, collective violence, or all forms of coercion? What was the role of a peace movement: to join like-minded reformers in a broad coalition, or to prepare a purified party of believers for radical peace action? Similarly, as antislavery advocates and proponents of national self-determination, humanitarian reformers experienced firsthand two of the most painful dilemmas in American reform history. How could peace-minded people end slavery without the violent overthrow of the constitutionally sanctioned system of property and power in America? How could they help in the triumph of liberal nationalism in Europe (especially Germany and Italy) without upsetting catastrophically the imperial state system? The first dilemma was resolved in the most vicious bloodletting in the nineteenth-century West—the American Civil War. The second was at the bottom of the political chaos of the twentieth century.

In early December 1815 nearly forty influential New York City merchants and clergymen formed the New York Peace Society (NYPS) as the world's first nonsectarian organization for the purpose of emphasizing the incompatibility of war and the Gospel. Its founders aimed "not to form a popular society, but to depend, under God, upon individual personal effort, by conversation and circulating essays" to expand peace principles through the churches.[2] Two weeks later a like-minded group of Boston-area philanthropists established the Massachusetts Peace Society (MPS) in order to join interested sympathizers in demonstrating the pacific intent of the Gospel and in helping to organize similar groups elsewhere. Strangely, the two new societies each arose in ignorance of the other. Yet together they effected a singular achievement: they gave birth to the first American peace movement.*

The first American peace movement originated in an environment dominated by two factors: a generation-old longing for peace, and a belief that the recent war with Britain was an act of divine judgment that signaled the nation's need to turn back to God. Clearly, William Gribben has written, the most pressing matter for Protestant America after 1815 was "national reform, the rooting out one by one of every vice that might provoke divine vengeance."[3] Moved by this concern, northeastern Protestants in particular at-

*In these same weeks, the Rhode Island Peace Society organized, and the Warren County Peace Society formed in northeastern Ohio. One month later the London Peace Society was founded, and in 1821 the Société des Amis de la Morale Chrétienne et de la Paix organized in Paris.

tempted in the first third of the nineteenth century to erect a "benevolence empire" that would conquer society for right Christian
conduct. Redoubling efforts that had begun with the second Great
Awakening, Protestant leaders struggled to tie the popular need for
personal salvation and missionary purpose to the work of "orderly
benevolence"; and they found in voluntary associations a tool most
appropriate to their purposes.[4] After 1800 Protestants in the northeastern states assembled a host of societies—including the American Board of Commissioners for Foreign Missions and the American Bible Society—for the purpose of promoting home and foreign
missions, temperance, and the availability of tracts and Bibles.
They organized within a generation nearly a dozen major reform
efforts intended to facilitate America's progress toward a Christian
commonwealth. One was the peace movement.

Socially, leaders of the first American peace movement were
well-educated members of an urban northeastern middle class who
sought to convert their private religious energies into visible social
improvement. Personally conservative, most were Congregationalist and Unitarian gentlemen accustomed to social deference and
committed to moral improvement through gradual enlightenment.
Many were Quaker-influenced but not Friends.[5] And all were sympathetic with contemporary British reformers, although they remained firm in their American patriotism. Mixing Christian millennialism with faith in inexorable human progress, humanitarian
peace reformers believed that they were living at the dawn of a new
age, when Protestant America would lead the world to victory over
sin and heathenism. Their particular role in this new era was to
overthrow the false idol of war.

In large measure, the character of the first American peace
movement was typified in the lives and work of two early leaders,
David Low Dodge (1774–1852) and Noah Worcester (1758–1836). A
staunch Federalist, Dodge was a prosperous Connecticut merchant
who recalled throughout his life how the death of two step-
brothers in the Revolutionary War had "almost deranged" his
mother.[6] After a religious conversion experience in 1798, Dodge
helped in the formation of several benevolent enterprises, including the New York Bible Society and the New York Tract Society,
before his life was transformed by two events. In 1805 he nearly
shot an innkeeper who had inadvertently stumbled into his room
late at night. Three years later, he survived an attack of spotted
fever. After his recovery, Dodge concluded that he had

no more doubt, from the spirit and example of Christ and the precepts of the Gospel, that all kinds of carnal warfare were unlawful for the followers of Christ, than I had of my own existence. At this solemn moment the Word of God appeared a reality; a sure foundation on which to rest my eternal hopes. From this period, my war spirit appeared to be crucified and slain; and I felt regret that I had not borne some more public testimony against it.[7]

He quickly recovered lost ground. Between 1809 and 1815 he published two classic peace pamphlets and organized several sympathizers to work against all war. After an abortive attempt to form a peace society in 1812, Dodge and his associates established the NYPS in 1815. Naturally he became the group's first president.

Like Dodge, Worcester was a man of strong religious conviction who had been deeply affected by the Revolutionary War. Born in rural New Hampshire, Worcester was a fife-major in the Continental Army and a veteran of Bunker Hill. Entering the ministry, he settled in the Boston area, where he was moved by the power of Federalist antiwar sentiment during the War of 1812. In 1814 Worcester wrote *A Solemn Review of the Custom of War*, a seminal tract that urged Christians, for the first time, to organize against war in volunteer peace societies and to establish an international system for the peaceable settlement of disputes. With Dodge's tracts, Worcester's proposals established the intellectual groundwork for the world's first organized peace activism. Skillfully, their writings blended reason and evangelical Christianity into an attractive mixture of rational analysis and spiritual uplift. Their words armed humanitarian peace reformers with the weapons that they would use for the next generation in pursuit of their holy cause.

Together, Dodge and Worcester believed that war was a barbarous anachronism that destroyed good order, subverted human liberty, and inhibited Christ's global victory. Both maintained that war ensnared people in vice, intemperance, and Sabbath-breaking. Both also held that God intended to end war through men. God "works by human agency and human means," Worcester explained. God had ended dueling and the slave trade within the British Empire by altering the climate of public opinion. In the same way, "God can put an end to war" by blessing "the benevolent exertions of enlightened men."[8]

Yet Dodge and Worcester differed in their preferred strategies for achieving peace. Worcester chose to move from religious arguments to secular conclusions. He attacked war most vigorously as a standing contradiction of Christ's way. Yet his prescription for peace—an organized peace movement of "important civil characters"—was strikingly world-minded and conservative. Sidestepping the issue of defensive war,* Worcester urged Christians to unite and renounce "the heathenish and savage custom" of war, support good rulers, and cultivate "a mild and pacific temper among every class of citizens." He never quite abandoned, however, his millennialist expectations. Through peace, Worcester hoped to give "a new character to Christian nations" and thereby save the world.[9] The techniques were simple: promote enlightenment about the war evil and its alternatives. The stakes were immense: God's victory on earth.

Dodge meanwhile argued from secular premises to a radical Christian peace position. Condemning war as an oppressor of the poor and a threat to republicanism, he urged Christians to destroy its evil by moving into a "lamblike" obedience to Jesus's literal way. Speaking in millennial tones, Dodge denounced even defensive war as being contrary to the Gospel; and he urged organizing peace seekers to practice total forbearance on the grounds that "The spirit of martyrdom is the true spirit of Christianity." Christians must remember that their kingdom was not of this world, Dodge held. Rather Satan "is the god of this world . . . [and] the mainspring of all warlike powers, and when he is bound wars will cease. . . ." Christians must therefore work to bind Satan and war "until God, in his providence, raises up some to bear open testimony against it; and as it becomes a subject of controversy, one after another gains light, and truth is at length disclosed and established."[10] Yet Christians must never expect the outworking of peace in this world. Real peace would come only with transcendence of the world.

Although their differences would grow sharper later, the varying emphases of Worcester and Dodge appeared slight in 1815. Instead, the NYPS and the MPS worked to distribute peace literature, assist unpaid agents in the field, and encourage the formation of local and state societies. With their help, nearly fifty societies appeared in the immediate postwar period in a reform triangle that stretched

---

*"And as soon as offensive wars shall cease," he promised, "defensive wars will of course be unknown." Noah Worcester, *A Solemn Review of the Custom of War*, in Peter Brock, ed., *The First American Peace Movement* (New York: Garland Publishing Co., Inc., 1972), p. 4.

from Maine to Philadelphia to Ohio. Dominated by businessmen, educators, and clergymen, the new groups contained, like other benevolent societies, a streak of New England humanitarian uplift. Like the other reformers, they also quarreled over their very purpose.

Intramural division over the nature of peace activism crystallized around the question of defensive war. While the NYPS attacked defensive war as contrary to Christ's teaching, the MPS ignored the issue for fear of stunting the movement's popular appeal. Both sides recognized the significance of the issue. To Dodge, tolerance of defensive war would shift the emphasis of the peace movement "from the divine prohibition of war, to the mere question of its expediency and utility."[11] To Worcester and MPS leader William Ellery Channing, repudiation of defensive war would crush their attempts to rally popular sentiment against war and behind the establishment of an international system for the settlement of disputes.

Painfully, division over the issue of defensive war grew larger in the 1820s while the working peace movement grew weaker. Poorly organized and underfunded, the country's new peace societies drifted toward irrelevance. Local and state groups shriveled in size and effectiveness. Opportunities to advance went untried. Beginning in the mid-1820s, for instance, antimilitarist sentiment flared throughout the Northeast because of worker opposition to compulsory militia drills. But no mechanism existed to convert this resentment into positive peace action.

Organized peace seeking rather slipped in strength until a retired New England sea captain named William Ladd (1778–1841) gave it new life after 1825. Helped by family wealth and a Harvard education, Ladd was a genial philanthropist who underwent a religious conversion in 1816 that turned him within a few years to the peace cause. A popular speaker and tireless campaigner, he brought to the crusade a combination of common sense and uncommon moral power. Ladd felt sure that the age of barbarism had passed, and that "at no time since the apostolic age has pure and undefiled religion so generally prevailed, as at the present; nor has peace among Christian nations been so general." He cited the decline of the slave trade and the growing opposition to slavery and to the militia as signs of progressive human enlightenment; and he insisted that everyone must assist in God's work of abolishing the war evil. Ir-

repressibly optimistic, Ladd urged peace seekers to work first for
the conversion of public opinion, "for the continuance of war rests
entirely on that." He allowed that the triumph of God's millennial
peace might require some time. "But that it will be accomplished,
we are certain; and that it will be done by means of peace societies,
in connection with the extension of the Christian religion, is
probable."[12]

Anxious to promote peace for the sake of a triumphant Christianity, Ladd decided that the country's shrinking peace movement
needed to become national in scope and more efficient in operation. He therefore journeyed among volunteer peace workers from
Maine to Ohio, preaching the virtues of a central organization.
Encouraged by their response, Ladd joined other peace leaders in
May 1828 and presided at Dodge's New York City home over the
formation of the American Peace Society (APS). It was the first
secular peace organization with national aspirations in American
history. Operationally, the APS affiliated itself with state and local
societies (including the NYPS and the MPS) and welcomed the membership of anyone willing to enlighten men's minds against the
custom of war. Temperamentally, it combined a firm Christian
commitment with a rational faith in the resolvability of all international disputes. The Society promoted negotiation, arbitration,
and the eventual settlement of all disputes by "a *Congress of
Christian Nations*, whose decrees shall be enforced by public opinion that rules the world; not by public opinion as it now is, but by
public opinion when it shall be enlightened by the rays of the gospel of peace."[13] The abrasive question of the justifiability of defensive war was set aside, and with good reason. Peace leaders realized
that they required organization above purification. They decided to
devote their energies to sustaining an ongoing peace movement,
believing that the whole war evil would succumb in good time.

In its first years, the APS worked as a traditional agency of organized benevolence. It distributed tracts, sponsored speakers, and
encouraged local sympathizers who helped advance its "silent and
gradual influence on the minds of men."[14] Ladd served as the Society's main traveling agent (mostly at his own expense) until 1835,
when the Congregationalist minister George C. Beckwith (1800–
1870) joined him for a salary of $2 per day plus expenses. With their
encouragement, the APS attempted to spur public interest in the
peace cause by offering a $1,000 award for the best essay on the idea

of a congress of nations. The Society also went to great lengths to win church support. Leaders of the APS urged various denominational organizations and individual ministers to pray for peace and press for a congress of nations. Prompted by church petitions, the Massachusetts senate endorsed the need for international arbitration and a congress of nations. Similar petitions were presented in the legislatures of other states and in the Congress, but increasingly they were dismissed as abolitionist propaganda.

The tendency to equate the peace and abolitionist crusades rose sharply after 1830 because the two movements were, in fact, working in progressively closer collaboration. Actually, they had never been far apart. Both shared common roots in Quaker sensibilities and the New England conscience. And both drew deeper inspiration from the "vibrant romantic radicalism" that sprang in the 1820s from the religious revivalism of Charles Grandison Finney and other itinerant preachers.[15] Stressing the divine bases of law and of the individual's responsibility for sin, revivalists spread through the North and West an optimistic message that combined perfectionism, millennialism, universalism, and illuminism.* Their words generated extraordinary popular appeal. Sparking with enthusiasm, revivalism supercharged the reform culture of Protestant America, impelling it toward immediate action. With social sin more palpable, reformers became less patient; and compromise became less tolerable.

At the same time, the peace crusade drew closer to abolitionism as slavery came to dominate American politics. In 1829 a free Boston black named David Walker issued a powerful *Appeal* against the benevolent reform of gradual emancipation and African colonization. Two years later, Nat Turner led a group of at least twenty slaves in a sweep across Virginia's Southampton County that left nearly sixty whites dead and the entire South in panic. In 1832 the South Carolina legislature nullified a federal tariff law that it deemed injurious to the state's slave economy. Mixed with ugly threats of secession, the legislature's action brought about a constitutional confrontation with the Jackson administration before an

---

*The first held that perfect sanctification or complete holiness was achievable; the second was concerned with last things; the third held that Christ died to save all men; and the last maintained that recent revelations had imparted to men new truths. Sydney E. Ahlstrom, *A Religious History of the American People* (New Haven: Yale University Press, 1972), p. 476.

uneasy settlement was reached. In May, while the Nullification
Crisis simmered, a wealthy South Carolina planter named Thomas
Grimké attacked his state's position and called for a peaceful settlement in a spirit of Christian pacifism. Nor did he stop there.
Anticipating a predictable response, Grimké went on to criticize
American Revolutionary leaders for using violence in the cause of
independence. It was the boldest pacifist pronouncement within
memory. Frontally, Grimké attacked the one national icon that
pacifist leaders had long recognized as the "great barrier" to their
cause.[16]

Grimké's "most sensational statement of the pacifist case" not
only sparked the first serious debate within the peace movement
over the relationship between organized peace activism and pacifism[17] but also provoked a furious counterattack in the South.
While northern reformers praised him, Grimké's opposition to
nullification and his plea for civil concord earned him enormous
enmity in the slave states. The gentle South Carolinian only
strengthened southern suspicions that there was an inner connection between abolitionism and volunteer peace seeking. In fact, the
southern reaction to his call marked the end, for all practical purposes, of any attempt to advance the humanitarian peace reform
beyond the North and West. By association, the peace crusade was
narrowed, along with the rest of romantic Protestant reformism,
into a sectional cause.

Southern suspicions of the existence of a link between organized
peace seeking and abolitionism became confirmed in the early
1830s as the two reforms advanced with a common sense of immediacy and behind a corps of like-minded leaders. Abolitionism
grew strong after 1830, following the failure of the benevolent
gradualist approach, and abetted by white political crises, black
militancy, and the millennialist sense of personal responsibility for
social sin that spilled out of religious revivalism. Committed to
victory through moral suasion, abolitionist sentiment spread
through small-town New England and the rural Northwest with
unusual force. It claimed a contagious spirit of religious perfectionism, receptive (and mostly female) audiences, and some powerful voices. Arthur Tappan and Theodore Weld bore it through western New York and the Ohio Valley. William Lloyd Garrison
(1805–1879) projected it across New England.

As much as anyone, Garrison led the way for American abolitionism. More than anyone, he personified radical pacifism. The unschooled son of a Newburyport, Massachusetts, sailor who had abandoned his family early in the boy's youth, Garrison made up for a lack of formal education through intellectual power and an unusual ability to attract gifted allies. Several talented people—including Henry C. Wright, Samuel May, Amasa Walker, and Angelina and Sarah Grimké—joined him in his undeviating commitment to the socialization of Christ's redeeming way. A Baptist with Quaker sympathies, Garrison entered the abolitionist movement forcefully in January 1831, when he distributed the first issue of *The Liberator*. Insisting upon the universalization of freedom, he called upon Christian America to free its slaves for the sake of Christ and the salvation of the country. Identifying abolitionists as "Christian warriors," he proclaimed that "ours is the cause of God" and destined to inevitable triumph. But Garrison was not prepared to use violence on slaveholders. He repudiated calls for slave insurrection and urged slaves to remain obedient "and patiently wait for a peaceful deliverance through the omnipotence of truth."[18]

Garrison's social radicalism resulted from his opposition to wrongs wreaked upon creatures made in God's image. His pacifism emerged from his determination to emulate Christ's nonresistant purity. Merging the two convictions, Garrison concluded in 1835 that true social reformation could only occur as individuals renounced violence and took up Christ's way to prepare for the millennial establishment of God's kingdom. Preaching perfectionism, he insisted that real Christian reformers must surrender control of their lives in order to save themselves and the world. The nonresistant pacifist must therefore return good for evil and "*forgive* every injury and insult, without attempting by physical force or penal enactments, to punish the transgressor." A nonresistant must abjure the violence of man in order to live with God.[19] He must never quit fighting for right, but he must lay aside means that were wrong.

Organizationally, Garrison and his followers maintained a distinction between nonresistance and abolitionism. Practically, however, the distinction meant little in the face of prevailing mob violence. Beginning in 1834, American society rattled through one of the most violent periods in peacetime history. Organized bands attacked abolitionists 167 times in outbursts of mob action that culminated in November 1837, when the editor Elijah Lovejoy was killed attempting to defend his printing press in Alton, Illinois. The ferocity of the antiabolitionist attack forced Garrisonians into a more critical consideration of their position. Concluding that reliance on individual moral suasion was no longer adequate, they decided in the mid-thirties that America's salvation required total conversion from human government to the government of God. They chose to live as nonresistant Christian anarchists—responsible only to God—in order to save sinful men.[20]

The growing Garrisonian emphasis on living nonresistance through Christian anarchism gained momentum because of the very spirit of the times. Inspired by a faith in man's potential perfection, advocates of the most extreme or "ultra" objective moved forward in the 1830s in every reform endeavor. The antislavery crusade shifted from promoting gradual emancipation and colonization to advocating outright abolition. The temperance cause turned from moderation to legal prohibition. And the peace reform advanced from benevolent opposition to international war to a nonresistant attack upon all forms of human coercion. Clearly, as John Demos has observed, "Non-resistance was in some ways the most 'ultra' of all the nineteenth-century 'ultraisms.'"[21] Crossbred from perfectionism and millennialism, it demanded absolute emulation of Christ's loving way. It also called for full opposition to human governments that prevented the individual from reconciling his behavior in conscience with God's will.

Tactically, the American Peace Society offered the natural ground for the movement's shift toward "ultraism." Although it opposed all war, the Society collaborated with several local peace organizations whose members were split over the necessity of defensive war. Ladd tried to evade the issue, but it would not subside. In 1836 the ardent Garrisonian Henry C. Wright traveled throughout New York and New England as APS field secretary. With his tacit encouragement, nonresistant sentiment mushroomed with a power that forced the issue of defensive war before the Society's annual convention in May 1837. Pressured by Ladd, the majority delegates voted to amend the constitution to declare that "all war is contrary to the spirit of the Gospel," and that the Society existed "to illustrate the inconsistency of war with Christianity, to show its baleful influence on all the great interests of mankind, and to devise means for insuring universal and permanent peace."[22]

Only partly appeased, nonresistants attacked the Society for not rejecting all forms of force and for remaining open to nonpacifists. What kind of peace society, laughed Garrison, welcomed the support of "belligerous commanders-in-chief, generals, colonels, majors, corporals, and all!" Sensitive to the nonresistants' criticisms as well as to mutterings from more conservative members, Ladd and George Beckwith (who became APS secretary in 1837) arranged at the organization's spring 1838 convention for the passage of two resolutions designed to clarify the 1837 constitutional revision. But their action only further antagonized the nonresistants, who feared a retreat from the Society's new opposition to all war. The air needed to be cleared. At Garrison's urging, his friend Samuel May agreed to join Ladd and Wright in laying plans for a general convention in September 1838 that would "have the subject of Peace searched to the bottom. . . ." "We propose," May promised, "not to evade any question that may be found incidental to the decision of this one, namely; how is the evil that is in the world to be overcome? By violence, or sacrifice?"[23]

Meeting in Boston, the September convention drew almost two hundred delegates, nearly all from New England. In an early test of factional strength, the delegates granted voting rights to the women in attendance, prompting Beckwith and his conservative followers to withdraw in protest. With their departure, the radical pacifist majority formed an independent New England Non-Resistance Society (NENRS), a tiny organization whose name considerably exaggerated the modest influence that it exerted in eastern Massachusetts. The new group won few adherents. But it did boast in its defining Declaration of Sentiments (drafted by Garrison, who served as corresponding secretary) a remarkable statement that stridently showed how perfectionism, millennialism, and Christian anarchism had carried nonresistance by the late thirties into revolutionary pacifism.

Holding that its members were bound by a kingdom "not of this world," the Declaration resolved "to carry forward the work of peaceful, universal reformation" through "THE FOOLISHNESS OF PREACHING" and the "spiritual regeneration" of corrupt human institutions. Society members pledged to oppose all military undertakings (including preparations, monuments, office, and dress), and to live peace with a universal sense of human equality. Denying that they were anarchists, Garrison and his followers declared that they would obey all human ordinances that supported Gospel teachings, and renounce all those that did not. They were gathering "to speak and act boldly in the cause of GOD" in order to hasten the reign of Christ, and suffer in the meantime the persecution of His enemies. "If we suffer with him," Garrison promised, "we know that we shall reign with him. . . . Our confidence is in the LORD ALMIGHTY, not in man."[24] Nonresistants were only lowly imitators of the Son of Man.

Garrison and his allies hailed the NENRS for transforming love into "a vastly greater moral force" than Christian reformers had ever wielded. "Passive non-resistance is one thing"; Maria Weston Chapman explained in reference to the Historic Peace Churches, "active non-resistance another. We mean to *apply* our principles."[25] Privately, however, Garrison feared that the nonresistant revolution would be long in coming. Between lethargic public opinion and "the nature of things," nonresistance "must be the slowest and most difficult of all reforms." It was comparatively easy to support temperance or abolition, because those reforms focused upon health and the oppressed. "But to be a Peace man, in the true acceptation of that term, is to be forever powerless (physically) against injury, insult, and assault—to trust solely to the living God for protection—to be incapable of returning blow for blow, either personally or by proxy."[26] It was a testimony that few could take, and fewer still could uphold.

Initially, it appeared that New England Transcendentalists, who began to exert impressive intellectual influence in the 1830s, would provide precious support to nonresistance. But few showed interest in the peace reform. Only Bronson Alcott supported nonresistant ideals; and none of the Transcendentalists belonged to the APS. Curiously, their lack of interest resulted from the Transcendentalists' confidence in the inevitable triumph of peace, their ambivalence toward war, and their veneration for the self-reliant individual. Peace, as Ralph Waldo Emerson declared in 1838, was surely rising through "the eternal germination of the better." Its universal victory was a certainty. "The question for us is only *How soon?*"[27] Yet Emerson conceded that war possessed real appeal insofar as it provided a theater for those qualities of action, vigor, and "absolute self-dependence" that defined heroism. With war retaining this primitive appeal, peace would not progress through "*routine and mere forms*" like volunteer societies, or through appeals to "that bloated vanity called public opinion." Instead, it must grow through the "private opinion" and "increased insight" of "the cultivated soul" who showed the highest heroism by refusing to take another man's life.[28]

Meanwhile, the formation of the NENRS provoked a short-lived but bitter argument within reform circles over the "no-government" implications of nonresistant anarchism. "There is such a thing," Ladd said drily, "as going beyond the Millennium."[29] Moderate abolitionists like Theodore Weld complained that the nonresistant attack upon government smacked of anarchy, while Garrison tried to explain that revolutionary nonresistance stood not for anarchy but for Christian anarchism—the government of God. Sharp and angry, the "no-government" controversy was complicated by the interest that some reformers showed in model communitarian experiments (such as John Humphrey Noyes's Perfectionist gathering and Adin Ballou's Hopedale Community), which sought to create alternative models of peaceable social behavior.

Neither the NENRS nor the communal experiments, however, long affected the workings of the organized peace reform. Isolated in its purity, the NENRS shriveled shortly after 1840 into a Boston-area fellowship, while the larger appeal of revolutionary nonresistance faded as its proponents drifted in different directions. In addition, nonresistance grew weaker in the early 1840s as abolitionists argued over the role of women in the movement and over the construction of a winning political strategy. Attacking calls for third-party political action, Garrison turned to emphasize the theme of "No Union With Slaveholders" at the expense of radical pacifism. Insistently, he held that nonresistance was "destined to pour new life-blood into the veins of Abolition."[30] But he declined to push the two reforms in working combination.

Leaders of the APS meanwhile nagged opinion makers and propagandized for a congress of nations. President Ladd also made special efforts to recruit women to the peace cause. Observing that many men dismissed peace ideals as to effeminate, Ladd argued that there was "something peculiarly appropriate" about feminine peace action. "Men make war," he thought, "—let women make peace." Reminding them that war was a moral evil, the APS president urged women to pray, rear children pacifically, form female peace societies, and, most of all, hold the Christian church to its peace duty. He wanted America's Christian women to bring about a most radical reform, as Alice Kessler Harris has written, but only through "the most conservative of methods."[31]

Numerically, women constituted a sizable minority—at times the majority—of the APS's audience. But the Society's male leadership showed less interest in their presence and potential than in the idea of a congress of nations. Starting in the 1830s, the Society solicited several plans to implement such a project. In 1840 Ladd gathered the best proposals for publication behind an introductory "Essay on a Congress of Nations" that he personally composed. The statement became an instant peace classic.

Insisting that nations be held accountable to the same moral laws that bound individuals, Ladd suggested the creation of a two-tiered system of international justice: (1) a congress of ambassadors from "the most civilized, enlightened, and Christian nations" who would define international law and plan for peace; and (2) an international court "of the most able civilians in the world" who would arbitrate or judge cases brought before them by the mutual consent of the disputants. In this manner, he held, statesmen could not only separate diplomatic peace practices from juridical action; they could also superintend the development of true international government. Slowly, the congress would take on the work of a legislature; the court would serve as the judiciary; and executive authority would be left to public opinion, "the queen of the world." Extolling the power of public opinion, Ladd asserted that the hope of the peace reform "relies chiefly on the United States, Great Britain, and France, pretty much in proportion to the voice which the people have in the government." The APS enthusiastically concurred. Legalistic, moralistic, and nationalistic, Ladd's plan perfectly captured the Society's governing sentiments. In fact, it defined the scope of APS activities for the next three generations.[32]

Beyond Ladd's "Essay," the most significant peace advance of the 1840s involved the strengthening of international ties. In 1843 the world's first international citizen peace congress took place in London. In general terms, the meeting marked one milestone in the larger international reform congress movement that began with an antislavery meeting in 1840 and culminated in the 1870s, when over 200 meetings took place throughout Europe around such issues as temperance, peace, prison reform, and improved communications.[33] More immediately, however, the 1843 peace congress

reflected the rising level of cooperation among Anglo-American reformers and demonstrated the value of the APS. With Beckwith and
Amasa Walker representing the Society, more than three hundred
delegates gathered to share information, coordinate efforts, and
build international public support. The convention supported
Ladd's "American Plan" (as Europeans had termed the "Essay") and
backed the idea of transnational peace associations among the
world's working classes. It also endorsed the principle of international free trade, and urged the inclusion in all international
agreements of clauses requiring the arbitrated settlement of
disputes.

The idea of stipulated arbitration first gained force in 1842, when
the New York jurist William Jay succeeded upon Ladd's death to
the presidency of the APS. Son of a former Supreme Court justice,
Jay championed the idea of obliging nations to include arbitration
clauses in all future agreements. He felt sure that the proposal possessed both practicality and promise. Citing precedent, Jay argued
that at least 23 different international controversies (including a
recent Anglo-American quarrel over Maine's boundary) had been
submitted successfully to arbitration in the generation before 1840.
Looking to the future, he predicted that those nations which bound
themselves *in advance* to arbitrate their differences would greatly
increase international security and diminish the danger of war. At
Jay's behest, the APS promoted, with a fair degree of success, the
idea of stipulated arbitration along with that of a congress of nations. British peace leaders especially liked the proposal and supported it strongly at the peace congresses that followed the 1843
London convention.[34]

Early in 1848 American peace seekers cooperated with their
European counterparts in convening a second international congress in Paris, until street fighting that spilled out of the '48 Revolution drove them to Brussels. Meeting there in September, 300
delegates passed resolutions supporting a universal code of law and
international disarmament. One year later they gathered again in
Paris in the most impressive international demonstration of organized citizen peace strength before 1890. Over 1,500 peace workers
applauded a stirring address by the author Victor Hugo and resolved their collective support of improved communications,
postal reform, and a common system of weights and measures.
Subsequent congresses in Frankfort in 1850 and London in 1851

matched neither the size nor the enthusiasm of the Paris meeting. Yet they cumulatively indicated that the cause was moving forward and not back. Altogether, as Merle Curti has observed, the international peace congress movement "probably represented the greatest single accomplishment of the early movement."[35]

In America APS leaders praised the congresses as signs of true international cooperation against war. At the same time, the Society campaigned actively to ease recurring Anglo-American tensions over the questions of Texas and Oregon. Circulating petitions and urging arbitration, the APS began to operate openly as a modern volunteer peace society: it informed, organized, and concentrated citizen pressure in behalf of the peaceful resolution of complex quarrels. Unfortunately, however, the Society could not resolve its own problems. Instead, it suffered new controversy after 1842 and a new schism in 1846.

While the characters were different from those in the "ultra" nonresistant quarrel of the 1830s, the issue remained the same: a minority opposed the Society's willingness to enroll nonpacifists and its emphasis on the abolition of war at the expense of working toward related reforms. Personally more pacifistic, veteran peace reformers like Samuel Coues, Joshua Blanchard, and Amasa Walker urged a more explicit commitment to the sanctity of all human life and argued against the Society's narrow concern with the institution of international war. Suppressing their discontent, these moderates chafed in uneasy alignment with the more conservative Society faction headed by Beckwith. Then in 1843 they found a leader in Elihu Burritt (1810–1879).

Burritt was a blacksmith by trade, a scholar by temperament, and a peace activist by compulsion. Born to poverty in New Britain, Connecticut, he grew up in a world steeped in evangelical Christianity and the values of Yankee self-improvement. After working as a blacksmith and a Yankee peddler, Burritt began a lecturing career in the late 1830s that met his literary ambitions as well as his peculiar gift for languages (he eventually mastered over forty). Billing himself as the "Learned Blacksmith," he became a popular lyceum speaker and was addicted to a succession of social reforms. Finally, he found peace. War was the "sin-breeding sin of sins," Burritt concluded in 1843. Protestant Americans must "despair of any permanent world-wide, transforming reform, until Christianity is divorced from its unnatural, ungodly wedlock with the spirit, the fiendish spirit of War."[36]

Burritt's conversion followed from his guiding faith in the spiritual unity of all living things and his conviction that peace was the divinely ordained condition of man and nature. Joining the APS in 1843, the "Learned Blacksmith" quickly came into conflict with Beckwith's conservative followers and allied with the moderate pacifists. With his encouragement, the moderates pressed the Society between 1844 and 1846 to take an explicit stand against all violence and in defense of "the sanctity of human life in all circumstances." The issue "is not whether Christianity, under any circumstances, tolerates international war," Burritt explained, "but whether the *Society* can be most efficient with or without asserting the radical principle."[37]

The differences came to a head at the Society's annual meeting in May 1846. After discussions that were "something like a riot," Beckwith's conservative majority approved resolutions requiring the Society to remain apart from "extraneous" reforms like abolition and open to all Christian peace seekers, "whatever their views respecting defensive wars." Serious peace workers aimed to overcome *"only* THE GREAT DUEL OF NATIONS," Beckwith tried to explain.[38] But Burritt and his allies dissented vigorously and quit their official positions within the Society (although not the organization itself). With their withdrawal, the organized peace movement lay broken in three parts. Revolutionary nonresistants like Garrison rejected all physical force and opposed any kind of coercion. Moderate pacifists like Burritt upheld "the strict inviolability of human life," but accepted the coercive function of orderly government. And conservatives like Beckwith opposed the custom of international war as being contrary to Christianity, though sometimes necessary for defensive purposes.[39]

Tactically, Beckwith and his associates worked after 1846 to move the rump APS into converting public opinion and devising alternative means of settling international disputes. "We dream not of accomplishing all this at once," he wrote of his peace vision, "or ever without the gospel; but we do hope, by God's blessing on a right application of its pacific principles, to drive the custom eventually from Christendom, and then to spread permanent peace, hand in hand with our religion over the whole earth." Beckwith conceded the social utility of war. Identifying it as "a judicial process, a tribunal of justice between nations," he treated war as the customary means by which nations defended their rights, redressed wrongs, and inflicted punishment.[40] It was a respected institution;

and, like any institution, it required substitutes, such as a congress of nations, before it would subside.

The APS gained an unexpected boost in 1845, when the brilliant Boston lawyer Charles Sumner (1811–1874) made an impassioned plea during the city's July 4th celebration for the United States to renounce the false lure of military glory and seek "The True Grandeur of Nations" in peace and righteousness. Acting visibly for the first time in support of his concern for peace (he had been a member of the APS executive committee since 1841), Sumner condemned war as an outlaw judicial institution and denounced the "heathen patriotism" that sustained it. Calling for a higher and truer patriotism, he declared that Christianity and progress had carried the law of love above the law of force and that, when men recognized this reality and acted upon it, they would abolish war, disarm, and establish permanent peace. It was simply a matter of will. *"Believe that you can do it,"* he proclaimed in a perfect expression of the humanitarian reform spirit, *"and you can do it."*[41]

Sumner's July 4th address set off a groundswell of enthusiasm among peace reformers and made him the most prominent national peace leader of the 1840s. But the enthusiasm for peace was scarcely enough to contain President James Polk's continental ambitions. After reaching a settlement with Britain over the Oregon territory, the president turned in early 1846 to deal with Mexico over their conflicting claims in Texas and over U.S. aspirations for California. Fighting quickly displaced diplomacy. In May open warfare broke out between the two nations and abetted the spread within America of an expansionist spirit of Manifest Destiny. Almost as fast, clusters of antiwar opposition sprang up in different parts of the country.

Though noisy and visible, opponents of the Mexican-American War were too diverse and too divided over the slave question to collaborate in a working coalition. Division within the Whig Party typified the difficulties of antiwar activism. While rhetorically antiwar, the Party was split between antislavery northern Whigs, who denounced the war as naked aggression by the southern Slave Power, and prosouthern elements, who disliked the war because it raised the explosive question of slave expansion into the territories conquered from Mexico. Worried and confused, Whig leaders agreed upon the need to criticize Polk's leadership. But internal tensions and memories of the fate of the antiwar Federalists in 1812 (plus the success of Whig generals like Zachary Taylor) restrained them from attacking the war too vehemently or cutting off congressional funding. The Democratic Party likewise contained contending pockets of antiwar dissent. Antislavery followers of former President Martin Van Buren protested Polk's plans, while the proslavery supporters of South Carolina Senator John Calhoun feared that the war would enhance executive authority and diminish southern influence in national politics.

Outside of partisan politics, antiwar protest was sharpest in New England. Unitarian and Congregationalist churches issued strong attacks upon Polk's policies, and the APS also voiced its opposition. Federal enlistments were smallest in the northeastern states, and intellectual notables like Emerson condemned the antilibertarian menace of warmaking governments. In July 1846 Emerson's friend Henry David Thoreau was jailed in Concord for refusing to pay taxes toward the support of a war that he viewed as a sinful extension of the Slave Power. Thoreau's protest—which he recorded three years later under the title "Resistance to Civil Government"—was less an antiwar action than an affirmation of the individual's right to resist government-sanctioned wrong. But it contributed in 1846 to a larger climate of disaffection.

Interestingly, several prominent opponents of the war equivocated over the crucial question of expansion. The Unitarian minister and antiwar advocate Theodore Parker, for instance, dismissed the Mexicans as "a wretched people" who would soon fall before America's inevitable conquest of the continent. But he insisted that the American conquest proceed righteously, by "the steady advance of a superior race . . . by commerce, trade, arts . . . by anything rather than bullets."[42] Garrisonian abolitionists did not agree. They opposed any expansion of the American slave empire. "I desire to see human life at all times held sacred"; Garrison wrote in the middle of the war, "but, in a struggle like this,—so horribly unjust and offensive on our part, so purely one of self-defense against lawless invaders on the part of the Mexicans,—I feel, as a matter of justice, to desire the overwhelming defeat of the American troops, and the success of the injured Mexicans."[43] His words were one early indication of the nonresistants' capacity to tolerate violence, a capacity that would expand tremendously after 1854.

Rising from several sources, antiwar sentiment grew to its fullest strength in late 1847, when it converted mounting public impatience with the war into a political climate that frustrated Polk in his attempt to conquer all of Mexico and forced him to accept a more limited conquest. The war ended in early 1848, but the effects of the opposition lingered. At its best, antiwar dissidence helped to contain the violence and prevent further bloodletting. At its worst, it aggravated domestic political passions and sectional distrust. Antiwar activists persuaded many northerners that the expanding southern Slave Power was poisoning the national mission because of its urge to conquer and not liberate. Warring for slavery's expansion constituted a "national infidelity," declared the Reverend Parker. It entailed nothing less than "a denial of Christianity and of God."[44]

While dissidents attacked Polk's war, the irrepressible Burritt launched a positive series of resourceful actions in the late 1840s. Hard-working despite poor health, the "Learned Blacksmith" criticized APS leaders for exaggerating the need to convert key opinion makers and showed his preference for carrying the peace reform to the masses. Anxious to excise "the spirit of war from the hearts of the people," he developed in the late forties some of the most imaginative transnational enterprises in modern peace activism. In 1846 he opened the "Friendly Address" movement, an exercise in "people-diplomacy" by which different cities were paired (such as the Bostons of England and Massachusetts) and citizens by the thousands exchanged greetings and expressions of goodwill.[45]

In the same year, he formed during a visit to England the League of Universal Brotherhood (LUB). Rooted in Burritt's faith in human unity and his admiration for the temperance pledge, the LUB was open to anyone who made an absolutist vow to pursue "all legitimate and moral means" toward the abolition of war and "whatever else tends to make enemies of nations, or prevents their fusion into one peaceful brotherhood," or denies "the image of God and a human brother in every man of whatever clime, colour, or condition of humanity." Sweepingly comprehensive, the LUB was basic to Burritt's plans for "the evangelization of the world."[46] With the help of Quakers and other English reformers, he promoted the Brotherhood in towns throughout Britain, and cooperated with moderate pacifists like Amasa Walker and Joshua Blanchard in establishing an American branch in May 1846. Within six months the LUB claimed the support of over 30,000 Englishmen and 25,000 Americans. Most members came from the English working class or the rural American northeast and midwest. But the impressiveness of the League's grassroots appeal was offset by its lack of leadership and direction. The American branch weakened rapidly in the early

1850s, while its English counterpart survived until 1858 only because of Burritt's dogged determination. The LUB lasted barely a dozen years; yet it was the largest and most uncompromising nonsectarian pacifist organization yet known among Western peace seekers.

An inveterate popularizer, Burritt also worked to convert modern communications and transportation techniques to serve the cause of peacemaking. In 1849 he drafted the first "Olive Leaves," brief peace statements that he sent for the next several years to newspapers for release throughout America and Europe. He likewise campaigned for the adoption of a one penny ocean postage as an inexpensive means of maintaining transoceanic goodwill, and worked for government-assisted migration of impoverished European workers to America. His concern for working people seemed bottomless. Early in his career, Burritt confessed that he coveted "no higher human reward for any attainment I may make in literature or science, than the satisfaction of having stood in the lot of the laboring man." Out of this conviction, he proposed in 1850 the creation of an international workingman's parliament as a means for achieving peace and laid plans for "an organized strike of the workingmen of Christendom against war" in case the nations failed to establish a congress of nations and effect disarmament.[47]

But Burritt had no solution for Europe's immediate discontents. In 1848 a bandoleer of revolutions exploded across the continent in the name of liberal nationalism and against the old imperial order. Within months, however, every revolt failed; and with them fell the best hopes of Western liberals for a peace built on free trade, enlightened national self-determination, and democratic public opinion. Yet American reformers remained undeterred by the European failure and confident of ultimate victory. Hailing peace as "the universal expression of the Spirit of the Age," Charles Sumner urged America in 1849 to go forth as "the Evangelist of Peace," holding out to the world "a Magna Charta of International Law, by which the crime of War shall be forever abolished." The laws of God, progress, and nature were moving the nations in such a way, the Massachusetts Whig senator promised, that, "without renouncing any essential qualities of individuality or independence," they would soon

> arrange themselves in harmony; as magnetized iron rings . . .
> under the influence of the potent, unseen attraction, while
> preserving each to its own peculiar form, all cohere in a united

chain of independent circles. From the birth of this new order shall spring not only international repose, but domestic quiet also; and Peace shall become the permanent ruler of the Christian States.[48]

Staughton Lynd has called Sumner's 1849 oration "the most comprehensive indictment of war by any American in the nineteenth century."[49] Certainly, it conveyed most passionately that reasoned optimism which carried the humanitarian peace reform so far in the face of mid-nineteenth-century reality.

Inevitably, however, reality intruded at the expense of organized peace seeking. In 1853 Britain joined France in a war in the Crimea against Russia, and the British peace movement destroyed itself while rallying to the government cause. In a larger way the American peace movement sank in irrelevance after 1854 as national politics overflowed with bitter sectional animosities. In May 1856 Sumner suffered a severe physical beating on the Senate floor for his criticism of southern slaveholders. A few months later, bloody clashes erupted in Kansas between free soil and proslavery factions. Members of the 36th—or "armed"—Congress flaunted handguns in the House and Senate chambers. And, most shockingly, John Brown led 21 men in October 1859 in an attack upon the federal arsenal at Harper's Ferry, Virginia, in a futile attempt to spark a massive slave insurrection and effect emancipation through the sword.

The national reverberations set off by Brown's raid finally drove most peace reformers into a fateful passivity. Since 1850, top peace seekers had either retreated from their peace principles or drifted into political purposelessness. The League of Universal Brotherhood fell into a fatal tailspin, while Burritt opened an abortive campaign for gradual emancipation. The American Peace Society similarly slipped in strength. With 300 life members (half living in Massachusetts, and one-third clergymen), the Society spent the fifties evading the slavery question and attacking the institution of international war. Its preachments worked little effect. Its attractions diminished sharply. In 1860, for the first time since its formation, the APS was unable to hold its annual business meeting for lack of a quorum. Dejectedly, one officer speculated that "the entire permanent cure of war may prove the work of all future time, a reform to end only with the end of the world itself."[50]

Most radical pacifists shifted meanwhile to tolerate violence when it worked toward emancipation. Professing to be "amazed" at the change in her own beliefs, Angelina Grimké Weld decided in July 1854 that reformers had "to choose between two evils, and all that we can do is to take the *least*, and baptize liberty in blood, if it must be so." One year later, the ardent nonresistant, Charles Stearns, who had once accepted imprisonment over militia service, chose to take up arms in violence-ridden Kansas after he concluded that "These Missourians are not men." "When I live with men made in God's image, I will never shoot them"; Stearns explained, "but these pro-slavery Missourians are demons from the bottomless pit and may be shot with impunity."[51]

In 1859 the Rev. Samuel May, a veteran Garrisonian who had once organized nonviolent crowds to free captured runaways, publicly acknowledged the need for violence in the fight for emancipation. Shortly after, the fiery Henry Wright decided that the sin of slavery "is to be taken away, not by Christ, but by John Brown." Garrison reluctantly agreed. Portraying Brown as a misguided but genuine hero, the abolitionist leader urged radical pacifists to stand aside and let God visit His judgment upon unrepentant America. Garrison insisted that he remained an "ultra" peace man. Yet he openly praised God for the fact that there were armed men coming forward in the North who were

> so far advanced that they will take those weapons out of the scale of despotism, and throw them into the scale of freedom. It is an indication of progress, and a positive moral growth; it is one way to get up to the sublime platform of non-resistance; and it is God's method of dealing retribution upon the head of the tyrant.[52]

Most peace reformers tolerated or welcomed antislavery violence after 1850, for two reasons. Emotionally, some decided that the dilemma of promoting peace in a slave republic was unbearable in the face of the growing opportunity to contain and reverse slavery. Ideologically, too, some could reconcile violence with their peace beliefs. Strangely enough, Garrisonian nonresistants, who believed first in the sovereignty of God and the individual's right to private judgment, developed several ideological loopholes which allowed them to accept violence when it worked toward God's liberating purposes. Firm millennialists, nonresistants in the 1850s no longer looked for self-purifying individual perfection. But they were willing to stand in witness as God wreaked His purifying judgment upon a sinful people and advanced peace through national trial.[53]

During the secession winter of 1860–1861, peace reformers either professed pro-Unionism or a wish that the South might secede peacefully. Some attempted to mediate sectional differences. Many more prayed. But none supported the idea of a war for the Union until April, when the Lincoln administration first deployed federal forces at Fort Sumter and rallied conservative reformers to the cause. In May 1861 delegates to the APS's annual meeting declared the conflict to be an internal rebellion and announced their support of the Union. With Beckwith's encouragement, the Society offered its services to the president and turned to strengthen Anglo-American relations. A small minority, headed by Joshua Blanchard and Amasa Walker, opposed both the war and the majority Society position, but with scant success. "It has indeed been a *sifting* time here," Burritt wrote to some English friends. "Men who we thought stood strong & firm upon the rock, have been washed away."[54]

Garrison and his supporters meanwhile shifted from initial equivocation into complete support of the Union cause. Overcoming their early confusion, nonresistants found meaning in the war when Lincoln released the Emancipation Proclamation and established abolition as an essential northern objective. Joyously, Angelina Grimké Weld declared that the Union Army was "the angel of deliverance" that was rescuing the nation from wrong and "refounding it upon the rock of justice."[55] One great humanitarian reform was being vindicated, though at the expense of another.

Antiwar opponents did appear in both the North and the South, but their work had little significance for the lasting peace reform. Conservative "peace" Democrats in Ohio and New York consistently attacked the Lincoln administration for its abolitionist policies and exploited popular disaffection with the first national conscription laws in American history. Unionists in pockets of the Confederacy likewise condemned the rebellion as a war for the planter class fought at the expense of slaveless small farmers. Perhaps the most subtle antiwar activism took place in Ohio, where Clement Vallandigham organized a network of dissidents in protest and sometimes espionage. Certainly the most extravagant expression of opposition erupted in New York City in July 1863, when a mob enraged by changes in federal draft laws went on a three-day rampage against blacks and wealthier whites before caving in to exhaustion and federal troops.

The main defense of an enduring peace witness in America's most devastating war fell to those members of the traditional peace sects, plus the newer Seventh-Day Adventists, who opposed the violence for reasons of conscience. Most Quakers, whether in the North or South, sympathized with the Union's crusade against slavery, but they refused military service and the payment of war taxes. Most draft-liable Quaker men furthermore refused to pay commutation money in lieu of service or to pay fees to secure substitutes. In addition, some absolutists demanded unconditional exemption from all war service claims on the constitutional grounds of freedom of conscience. Government officials retreated only part way, however, before the Friends' fullest demands. Union authorities issued property distraints against Friends who refused war taxes, while Quakers in the South lived in "a continual state of crisis" because of the Confederacy's persisting manpower demands.[56] Quaker draft resisters suffered physical abuse in various army encampments on both sides of the battlelines, and several southern Friends escaped to the North to avoid forced draft conscription.

The wartime experiences of the few thousand Mennonites, Brethren, and other rural-based pacifist remnants paralleled those of the Quakers. Like the Friends, the traditional German peace sectarians formally opposed military service and support of the warmaking state. But they quarreled among themselves over the propriety of war taxes, commutation monies, and political activism. Mennonites and Brethren usually proved willing to pay a commutation fee in lieu of service, but they declined to hire substitutes. In return, they were either ignored or subjected to penalties that varied according to local conditions and the whims or requirements of warmaking authority.

Perversely, the authorities' attitudes toward the traditional German peace sects were complicated by the recent appearance of "millenarian nonresistants" like the Christadelphians and Seventh-Day Adventists.[57] Strict sabbatarians and living members of Christ's world, these new-style pacifists refused to participate in man's wars in order that they might be better prepared to do violence for the Lord on the day of His return. In many ways, these millennial-minded pacifists were a throwback to the zealous German Anabaptists of the 1630s. But in the 1860s they only added more texture and complexity to an American pacifism whose variety already taxed the imagination of governing officials. Their conditional acceptance of violence only made it more difficult to define the scope of genuine conscientious objection.

In practice, warmaking authorities treated conscientious objectors in ways that varied from occasional brutal punishments to overall leniency.[58] Objectors in the North generally went their way without hardship, while their counterparts in the South felt greater stress because of the Confederacy's manpower needs and because of local suspicion of their longstanding antislavery sentiments. Politically, influential Friends, who enjoyed unusually easy access to Union leaders, helped to relieve pressure on conscientious objectors. In February 1864, in response to Quaker demands, the Lincoln administration went out of its way to define hospital work as a legitimate alternative to army service for pacifist sectarians. It was the first alternative service legislation in American history, and it added strength to the Quaker determination to stand against war and for humanitarian relief.

Altogether, over 1,500 conscientious objectors endured hardship and sometimes death during the Civil War in defense of their highest beliefs. But countless others found in the war a new form of belief. "For the first time," Michael Howard has written, "millions of men discovered that war was terrible but that it was necessary and might be splendid, and found in the concept of their Nation a cause for which they really were prepared to die." Their discovery made for a new and better nation. But it ended the prewar humanitarian belief that moral power was increasing every day "in geometrical ratio," and it killed the first American peace movement.[59]

Chapter Four
The Cosmopolitan Reform

Between 1865 and 1901 the peace reform passed along with the rest of American society from the politics of Reconstruction into the age of industrialism and empire. Exerting at first only limited appeal, a new breed of peace seekers progressively responded to the tensions and opportunities of America's rise to world power by joining European activists in pressing for an international system of peacekeeping *machinery*. And they created in the process a more cosmopolitan peace reform. Unlike their antebellum predecessors, postwar peace workers cared more about the Anglo-Saxon race than mankind, and more about world order than Christ's work. Unabashed social Darwinists, cosmopolitan reformers viewed peace less as a means of social salvation than as a self-conscious effort in Great Power (and especially Anglo-American) cooperation. They consequently promoted specific proposals, directly pressured responsible policy makers, and called for an "international conscience" that identified "true patriotism" with international law and order.[1] Their approach brimmed with hope. But it also contained contradictions that became palpable in 1898, when the McKinley administration intervened in the Spanish-Cuban War and launched a war for overseas empire. Some peace leaders supported Washington's drive toward war and empire as compatible with their peace vision. Others helped form a major anti-imperialist movement to reverse the Republican decision to conquer for peace.

In the days after Appomattox, the peace movement slowly regathered upon its traditional bases among sectarian pacifists, radical pacifists, and New England reformers. The problems besetting the American Peace Society typified the pains of postwar readjustment felt by most peace workers. Headed by George Beckwith and like-minded associates, the Society held hard to its contention that the Civil War was simply an internal rebellion, and persisted in its attempts to interest preachers and other opinion shapers in the idea of a congress of nations and an international court. Society leaders established a midwestern department in 1865 and helped in the formation of the Universal Peace Union and the Peace Association of Friends in North America. But they really initiated no serious peace work before 1868, "because of the doubt whether the popular feeling was such as to permit a presentation of peace claims."[2]

Anxious for respectability, the APS furthermore ignored the postwar domestic strife between business and labor, and failed to articulate a coherent response to Washington's violent pacification of the Plains Indians. Trapped between its peace longings and its conservative sensibilities, the Society slipped in membership, funds, and relevance. In the early 1870s so many of its original members died off that the Society became "practically a new organization."[3] Then the Panic of 1873 set off an economic depression which plunged the organization into a financial crisis that required a decade to resolve.

Prewar radical pacifists meanwhile showed even less strength. William Lloyd Garrison passed the postwar years in quiet triumph, enjoying official acclaim for his lifelong fight for abolition. But neither Garrison nor his new popularity gave force to the cause of radical pacifism. Seeking a new organizational base, a group of one-time Garrisonians—including Joshua Blanchard and Ezra Heywood—moved to help the young Quaker Alfred Love (1830–1913) in forming the tiny Universal Peace Union in 1866. But their effort was inadequate to the need of reinvigorating the radical pacifist appeal. Based on the principles of Garrisonian resistance, the UPU stood as an uncompromisingly "radical peace society" that aimed to overcome the sin of war through a combination of mechanical means (e.g., disarmament and arbitration) and the living of the Christian ethic of love and nonviolence. Members of the UPU left nothing to moderation. They sought to build a force-free America through "the leadership of an intellectual-spiritual elite" which exhorted men to act upon their highest instincts.[4]

Alfred Love in most ways seemed to embody those instincts. A successful Philadelphia woolens merchant, Love emphatically refused both lucrative government contracts and military service during the Civil War. More positively, he learned from the war to extend his pacifism into all phases of life; or, as Robert Dougherty has put it, "he emerged as an active pacifist rather than someone who simply believed in pacifism."5 Under his direction, the UPU supported several related reforms, including temperance, black civil rights, improved Indian relations, industrial arbitration, and the women's rights crusade.

The Union's tactics were equally eclectic. Leaders of the UPU petitioned, preached, and employed innovative techniques—such as the public beating of Civil War swords into plowshares—in attempts to rally public support. They established branch operations in four northeastern states and made contact with European peace activists. They sponsored a public reception for former President U.S. Grant in 1879; and they enlisted nearly 200 prominent public figures—including Grant and William Howard Taft—as titular vice-presidents. Yet they failed to expand beyond a base of support among a 400-member remnant of progressive Quakers, Shakers, and Rogerenes, and they never raised an annual budget above $1,000. Tellingly, UPU members did not suffer the popular abuse that had showered antebellum Garrisonians until 1898, when a wartime Philadelphia mob hanged Love in effigy. Otherwise, the UPU was permitted to live in peace and die in peace, as it did in 1913 upon Love's passing.

While the UPU never escaped Love's shadow, it depended heavily for support among women. Women made up at least one-third of the Union's membership, while the lawyer and feminist Belva A. Lockwood (1830–1917) served as the organization's most effective lobbyist. Strangely, however, feminists otherwise failed to sustain organized peace activisim among women in the early postwar years. Women assembled a wide range of independent reform organizations in the last third of the nineteenth century. But their peace efforts were weak and shallow.

The most promising postwar feminist peace effort took place in September 1870, when the Franco-Prussian War moved the eminent Boston reformer Julia Ward Howe (1819–1910) to issue "An Appeal To Womanhood Throughout the World." Characteristically couching her call in biblical terminology, Howe urged Christian women everywhere to issue "a sacred and commanding word" against war and in favor of an international women's peace congress. Organizational meetings were held in New York and Boston over the next several months; and, in early 1872, Howe visited London in an attempt to convene a women's peace congress and initiate "a Wo-

man's Apostolate of Peace." She failed, however, to gain the active
support of either sex. The male officers of an international peace
meeting gathered in Paris refused to permit her to speak before the
general membership, while feminists showed a decided preference
for the temperance and suffrage campaigns. "I could not help seeing that many steps were to be taken before one could hope to
effect any efficient combination among women" in the peace
creed, Howe recalled. "The time for this was at hand, but had not
yet arrived."[6]

Difficulties also dogged members of the Historic Peace
Churches. Sectarian pacifism received a brief infusion of strength
in the 1870s, when communities of Russian-German Hutterites
migrated en masse to the Great Plains in flight from Old World
conscription and in confidence that the U.S. government would respect their conscientious opposition to war. But the Hutterite
influx could not offset the overall softening of the sectarian witness. The Brethren, Mennonites, and other religious nonresisters
persisted in their inward-looking ways in the postwar period, while
the Quaker peace vision grew blurred. In 1867 a group of midwestern Quakers formed the Peace Association of Friends in North
America in an attempt to strengthen and even spread the sect's
peace testimony; and Friends everywhere took an active interest in
healing the Indian-white hatreds that had been aggravated by Washington's wars of conquest in the West.

But the Quakers' distinctive peace commitment otherwise diminished in postwar America. Partly, their commitment diminished because the very absence of wartime governmental pressure loosened the communal bonds of the Society and eased
sectarian demands upon the younger members. At the same time,
the commitment contracted because the Quakers' very success in
their missionary activity in the West won to the group new members who valued the experiential Inner Light but ignored the testimony of actively nonresistant love. Distracted and divided,
Friends failed to concentrate their full strength behind organized
pacifism in the last part of the nineteenth century. Yet they still
contributed, in people like Benjamin Trueblood and Hannah Bailey,
a disproportionately large number of leaders to the advancing peace
reform.

Hearteningly, the generally "static character" of the postwar
peace movement was offset after 1865 by the first impulses toward

a more cosmopolitan peace-mindedness.[7] Inspired by prominent political thinkers like Francis Lieber (1800–1872) and David Dudley Field (1805–1894), there appeared in the 1860s a small but potent body of lawyers and businessmen who sought to collaborate with like-minded European peace seekers in pressing governments directly to humanize war, establish judicial and arbitral means of settling disputes, and regularize the functional infrastructure (e.g., the international postal service, communications, and consular services) of the emerging system of industrial interdependence. Centered in northeastern cities, these cosmopolitan peace advocates were war-hardened reformers who had little use for panaceas or preachments. But they did believe that the Civil War had left for the country two large lessons: (1) that America was part of an Atlantic community; and (2) that government could serve as a useful instrument for social improvement.[8] Moving forward without illusions, they resolved to show new concern for world politics. In addition, they determined to concentrate on the development of legal processes which would control social progress at home and would assist America in its rise to international power, while avoiding European political entanglements.

The first important expression of the cosmopolitan peace reform appeared in 1863, when the Columbia University Professor Francis Lieber submitted to the U.S. War Department his *Instructions for the Government of Armies in the Field, General Orders No. 100.* Cautionary in tone, Lieber's *Instructions* offered "the first clear statement of the laws of war," and emphasized the need for the control and containment of war's violence.[9] Even total wars were not to be waged without respect for rules. Significantly, Lieber's work paralleled European advances that peaked in 1863, when government representatives agreed in Geneva to create a neutral organization of "internationally connected national associations" which would care for wounded soldiers beneath the protection of a new flag that featured a red cross on a white field. One year later, a congress of governmental plenipotentiaries met again in Geneva and adopted the "Convention for the Amelioration of the Condition of the Wounded in Armies in the Field" as a formal agreement which lent the shield of neutrality to wounded soldiers, ambulances, and military hospitals.[10] Seemingly, European and American reformers were coming to agree that if war could not be abolished, it should at least be made more civilized.

Lieber meanwhile expanded upon his peace interest in 1865, when he publicly urged the U.S. government to submit its wartime differences with Great Britain to international arbitration. His proposal was well-taken. Anglo-American relations turned sour in the postwar years because of disputes over American access to the North Atlantic fisheries, Irish-American forays into Canada, and—especially—the *Alabama* claims question. Highly complex and emotionally charged, the *Alabama* claims sprung from Washington's demand for indemnity for Union losses suffered as a result of Britain's wartime failure to prevent the release from English shipyards of Confederate warships. It constituted the most explosive question in postwar Atlantic diplomacy. Treading gingerly through a minefield of controversy, British and American policy makers succeeded in early 1871 in establishing a Joint High Commission which concluded the Treaty of Washington. Ranging across a variety of issues, the 1871 Treaty of Washington provided for the submission of the *Alabama* claims to a five-member international arbitration tribunal which met in Geneva, Switzerland, and handed down its judgment to the contending but accepting parties in September 1872. American peace seekers were cheered by the triumph of reason over rancor. The arbitration settlement seemed "thrilling evidence that mankind had at last turned the corner to better days."[11]

The Treaty of Washington and the Geneva claims settlement accelerated interest among cosmopolitan peace seekers in the codification of international law and the regularization of arbitration procedures. In 1866 the prominent law reformer David Dudley Field called for an international committee of jurists to develop a revised and updated code of law for the consideration of major governments. Encouraged by an affirmative European response, Field coordinated an international effort that produced a landmark *Draft Outline of an International Code* in 1872. In the same year, Elihu Burritt and James Miles of the American Peace Society called for the creation of a permanent arbitration system that rested upon a government-approved code of international law. Intrigued with Field's work, the APS leaders joined him and other notables in pressing successfully for the convocation in Brussels in 1873 of an international code and arbitration congress that resolved itself into the Association for the Reform and Codification of the Law of Nations. Establishing branches in Europe and America, the Association served as the main stimulant behind the international law reform cause until 1895, when it was reorganized into the International Law Association. Also in 1873, a more exclusive group of legal experts (with Lieber as the only U.S. representative) established in Ghent the Institute of International Law, as a scientific center for training and study. Altogether, these advances reflected sharply the new international-mindedness of European and American peace seekers. They were bench marks in that "extraordinarily rapid growth" of internationalism which produced 130 new international nongovernmental organizations—and the very term "international organization"—in the last quarter of the nineteenth century.[12]

During the 1880s cosmopolitan impulses quickened with a force that gave driving power to resurgent peace activism. In 1882 the educator Robert McMurdy and the former governor of Kansas, Frederick Stanton, formed the National Arbitration League in an attempt to popularize arbitral ideals. One year later the national Women's Christian Temperance Union president Frances Willard experienced "a distinct illumination" in favor of the peace cause, following a visit to San Francisco's Chinatown, and enlisted her organization in peace work with the help of the tireless Quaker activist Hannah Bailey.[13] In 1886 the APS established a Pennsylvania auxiliary which soon emerged, under the leadership of the Philadelphia Baptist minister Russell Conwell, as the autonomous Christian Arbitration and Peace Society.

Three years later, representatives from the WCTU, APS, and UPU attended in Paris the first Universal Peace Congress held since 1851. While it advanced no specific program, the Paris congress marked the first in a new series of European meetings that demonstrated the expanding power of the international peace reform. Also in 1889, the English peace leader Randal Cremer and a handful of European sympathizers formed the Interparliamentary Union as a clearinghouse for Western legislators committed to the maintenance of the international bourgeois order through a world court. Four years later the International Peace Bureau arose in Berne as another center for cooperating peace activists.[14]

The revitalization of American peacemaking in the 1880s resulted from several factors. In large part, it followed in the wake of the impressive European peacemaking advances. Partly, too, it derived from an enlarging awareness on the part of leading American business and reform figures of the country's growing involvement in a world shrinking daily through improved technology and communications. In addition, American peace seeking surged forward with the help of official encouragement and informal promptings. Government policy makers like Secretary of State James Blaine stressed the need for international peacekeeping mechanisms, while influential Protestant clerics like the Reverend Josiah Strong reminded Americans of their global Christian responsibility. Altogether, as Warren Kuehl has remarked, a host of material, political, and moral factors were converging upon world-minded Americans late in the nineteenth century to produce "a growing sense of cosmopolitanism" and support for the new machinery of the world peace movement.[15]

The distinctively cosmopolitan nature of the resurgent peace reform resided in its practical-mindedness, racial Anglo-Saxonism, and reasoned Christian optimism. Encouraged by businessmen like the steel baron Andrew Carnegie (1835–1919), cosmopolitan peace reformers worked to promote specific proposals—such as an Anglo-American arbitration agreement—rather than attack the wickedness of war. War was not "to be settled by singing," declared the APS leader Benjamin Trueblood. Peacemaking must rather "command the attention and respect of the practical people in the world."[16] Even more, cosmopolitan reformers were distinguished by their commitment to the triumph of peace through the domestic and global extension of Anglo-American racial supremacy. They determined to strengthen ties between those British and American peoples who had "a common destiny as the exponents of the highest freedom and the highest civilization."[17] Finally, this new breed of American peace seekers felt sure that they were riding the wave of the future. "The real tendency of the world involves the full coming of democracy and the completion of the organization of industry," declared the ebullient Josiah Strong.

> We are entered upon the final stage of industrial development, which is the organization of a world-industry. This world-tendency involves also the complete development of a world-life, a world-conscience. And all these involve ultimate international arbitration.[18]

Secure in these assumptions, a reinvigorated peace movement advanced after 1890. Early in the nineties, the Brahmin reformer

Robert Treat Paine (1835–1910) and the Quaker educator Benjamin Trueblood (1847–1916) assumed the leadership of the quiescent APS and recharged it with new influence. In 1895 two genial Quakers, Albert and Alfred Smiley, opened their Lake Mohonk, New York, resort for what proved to be the first of 22 annual summer conferences of notable national leaders favorable to the cause of international arbitration. One year later, over 300 delegates gathered in Washington for a National Arbitration Conference (which, significantly enough, excluded female participants) that pressed for a special Anglo-American arbitration agreement. Suddenly, a surge of peace activism was driving the cosmopolitan reform forward in three directions. Geographically, it was gaining a broader base of cooperation. Organizationally, it was achieving continuity. Politically, it was becoming fixed upon a special Anglo-American relationship.

Late-nineteenth-century peace seekers promoted the general ideals of international arbitration and a world court, and attacked "the sorcery of militarism" and the European arms race.[19] But they first sought an Anglo-American arbitration treaty. In 1887 the leading British peace activist Randal Cremer approached Andrew Carnegie with a proposal for an Anglo-American treaty agreement to submit to arbitration all future disputes between the two powers. Carnegie, an irrepressible optimist who believed that the law of human progress worked through Anglo-American racial superiority, took sharp interest in the project; and he used his good offices to facilitate a visit by Cremer and other British legislators to various American cities. Some political figures, like the Ohio Republican Senator John Sherman, expressed support for the idea. But the proposal worked little immediate effect on an American political system that was dominated by an extremely close party balance. Republicans saw little gain in chancing cooperation with America's oldest rival. And Democrats, anchored to a large Irish constituency, saw much to be lost. Yet the idea gripped peace seekers throughout the nineties. Nearly everyone agreed, as David Patterson has observed, that "such a treaty was the first, most logical step toward a peaceful world order."[20]

The power of the Anglo-American arbitration idea derived from Anglo-Saxonist sentiments that grew along with the domestic difficulties of the 1890s. After 1890, industrial America's long-developing lines of tension—including rapid urbanization, labor unrest, agrarian discontent, and nativist resentment with growing immigration—caught fire in a crisis that reached epic proportions with the onset after 1893 of the worst economic depression in the nation's history. Stirred by the crisis, propertied Americans reacted in part by developing a new nationalism that would help to excuse the suffering and defend the existing industrial capitalist system. For the first time, state legislatures mandated the use of patriotic textbooks and daily flag flying at schools. New patriotic societies took form; and reverence for the flag became an organized ritual.[21] Yet the new-fashioned nationalism enhanced rather than excluded an affinity for things British. Groups of concerned Christians, including Social Gospel reformers and Salvation Army volunteers, strengthened their trans-Atlantic connections and sympathies. American imperialists like Theodore Roosevelt talked of overcoming the domestic crisis by creating an overseas empire after the British example, while anticolonialists like Carnegie applauded England's free-trade principles and hailed Britain as the model of a society that had endured crises while preserving order and individual liberty. Strikingly, Anglo-Saxonism helped inform a nationalistic ideological consensus for both defenders and reformers of the prevailing American order.[22]

It also shaped the ethos of the cosmopolitan peace reform. Evolutionists and optimists, cosmopolitan reformers assumed the existence of an identity between Anglo-American peoples based on a common heritage, language, and respect for social principles that preserved liberty within order. They in no way viewed that identity as subversive of an independent American nationality. On the contrary, Anglo-Saxonism appeared among peace seekers to be the first vehicle toward a liberal international system of voluntary peace, which would flourish as it joined Europe's diverse nationalities beneath the same moral law. What they detested was anti-English prejudice. Resentment of Britain was "our national insanity and our national sin"; said Edwin D. Mead, "and this is the place where the American devoted to internationalism and the cause of peace and reason among men has to begin his work, as schoolmaster and doctor and moralist."[23] Battling to win public opinion, cosmopolitan peace workers blended the rhetoric of evangelical Christianity with the scientific idiom of racial Anglo-Saxonism toward the goal of redeeming the world for peace. In the process, they imprinted upon the American internationalist tradition an Anglo-American cast that lasted well into the twentieth century.

Bolstered by racial Anglo-Saxonism, the appeal of an Anglo-American arbitration agreement grew throughout the 1890s. Trueblood fixed the idea as the top priority of the APS. The National Arbitration Conference argued hard for the proposal, while the Lake Mohonk conferences annually reiterated its value. The idea gained further force because of international political developments. In 1895 a long-simmering border feud between Venezuela and the British crown colony of Guiana boiled into a full-scale diplomatic crisis. The United States interceded diplomatically on the Venezuelan side; and, after weeks of tension, the two powers agreed to submit the controversy to an ad hoc arbitral tribunal at The Hague. Politically, the settlement of the Venezuelan boundary dispute not only increased America's imperial preeminence in the Hemisphere but also reinforced the Anglo-Saxonist insistence that the racial affinities between Britain and America (and consequently their very destinies) required that the two powers agree to submit all of their future disputes to arbitration.

Moved by this belief, Secretary of State Richard Olney agreed early in 1897 with British ambassador Sir Julian Pauncefote on a treaty arrangement that would oblige the two countries to submit all financial and territorial differences over a five-year trial period to a complicated system of arbitrated settlement. Immediately, the agreement captured the support of peace leaders in England and America. Rightly viewing the agreement as the greatest step toward the peaceful resolution of disputes since the *Alabama* claims settlement, American peace activists pressed for Senate ratification of the treaty. But their effort fell far short. The Senate remained far too suspicious of England, too apprehensive over immediate international problems, and too dubious about mechanical peace agreements to support Olney's proposal. The proposed arbitration treaty died on the Hill in the spring of 1897.[24]

The fascination felt by cosmopolitan reformers for the entwined ideals of arbitration and Anglo-Saxonism gradually drew the mainstream peace movement away from any involvement with nonresistant—and socially concerned—pacifism. The Universal Peace Union remained in the nineties the most visible center of nonsectarian pacifist activism in the country. Seeking to restructure American society on literal Christian lines, Alfred Love and UPU leaders tried to popularize their position by sponsoring after 1893 an annual series of summer meetings in Mystic, Connecticut. The festive Mystic meetings attracted thousands of visitors to joyous communal celebrations that featured games, peace displays, and the climactic release of hundreds of confused doves of peace. But, by any measure, visitors appreciated Love's showmanship more than his message. Throughout the nineties, the membership of the UPU remained small and its influence minimal.

Perhaps the most significant development in radical pacifism after 1887 involved the spread to the United States of the teachings of the Russian literary giant Leo Tolstoy (1828–1910). A nobleman by birth, Tolstoy professed a faith in literal Christian anarchism, upholding the inviolable sanctity of human life and denouncing force—and not merely violence—as contrary to human dignity. Aiming to replace the human law of violence with the Christian law of love, he attacked the state and property holding as the main sources of everyday evil; and he urged individuals to resist nonviolently the state's illegitimate power and pursue freely the life of love and cooperation. In America, Tolstoy's ideas proved most influential as they radiated through prominent individuals. Reform-minded figures like the Chicago settlement house worker Jane Addams, Democratic Party leader William Jennings Bryan, and the lawyer Clarence Darrow were each affected in different ways by the Russian's emphatic Christian anarchism, while eminent Boston reformers and intellectuals established an active Tolstoy Club in 1889.[25] All tried energetically to convert Tolstoy's words into works.

Reflecting the openness of late nineteenth-century peace activism, Tolstoyans, sectarian pacifists, and arbitrationists collaborated politely through most of the 1890s. But their relations grew strained in April 1898, when the U.S. government declared war on Spain and launched coordinated attacks upon Spanish holdings in Cuba, Puerto Rico, and the Philippines. Washington's decision for war followed the failure of a three-year attempt by Spain to crush the Cuban independence movement; and it occurred in anticipation of a partition of China by the great European powers. The international implications of the decision were complex and profound, but American military forces found the conflict wonderfully simple. Within four months, U.S. military pressure succeeded in overcoming Spanish resistance in Cuba, Puerto Rico, and the Philippines, and in facilitating the annexation of Hawaii. Four months later, Spanish and American negotiators agreed in Paris to a peace treaty that provided for U.S. occupation of Cuba and the cession to America of Puerto Rico and the Philippines.

Brief, cheap, and successful, the war with Spain proved unusually popular in the United States. Enthusiastic volunteers applied for military service in such numbers that the Army accepted 100,000 more men than it could equip, while the Mormon Church supported McKinley's crusade at the cost of its half-century tradition of selective pacifism.[26] Citizen peacemakers were meanwhile unusually passive. The tiny UPU recorded its vigorous protest. But APS leaders subordinated their "intense disappointment" with the war to their larger certainty that the international peace movement would "break forth somewhere in a new tidal wave after the war closes, just as it has done after each of the war periods of the century." "What we fear," wrote Trueblood,

> is that its center of gravity, which has, ever since the movement began a century ago, always been in our country, may move from us never more to return. When a nation once forfeits a high prerogative which God has given it, it rarely if ever regains it.[27]

Plainly, the peace movement did not rally many against the war. Yet it did abet the spread of a surprisingly powerful anti-imperialist movement.

The anti-imperialist movement of 1898 rested upon a generation of opposition to U.S. expansion overseas. Starting early in the 1870s, liberal Republicans like Charles Sumner and Carl Schurz launched strong attacks upon Washington's ambition for conquest in the Caribbean. Early in the 1890s anti-expansionist sentiment again flared, when Schurz and the editorialist E. L. Godkin assailed demands for greater naval building, larger military budgets, and the seizure of selected territory like Samoa and Hawaii. Ridiculing references to America's "manifest destiny," anti-expansionists defended the country's traditional commitments to political unilateralism, military independence, and exemplary moral conduct. Insistently, they maintained that overseas conquest would do nothing but subvert America's unique experiment in constitutional republicanism.

Drawing upon this tradition, the anti-imperialist movement emerged in the spring of 1898 as growing numbers of Americans became disturbed with reports that the administration was planning to annex the Philippines to a new American empire. Organizationally, the movement took life on June 15, 1898, when a large crowd of Boston reformers met at Faneuil Hall to organize the Anti-Imperialist League as a means of preventing the war to pacify

Cuba from being "perverted into a war of conquest" in the Pacific.[28] Headed by 67-year-old Gamaliel Bradford, a direct descendant of the Bay Colony's first governor, the Anti-Imperialist League attracted the support of prominent feminists (women reportedly made up half of the Faneuil Hall gathering) as well as the whole range of Boston reformers. But mostly it mirrored the international sentiments of New England Mugwumps.

Conservators of the pre-Civil War reform temper, Mugwumps pursued after Reconstruction a variety of causes—including civil service reform, women's suffrage, and temperance—out of a dedication to civic purity and a faith in moral suasion. They wanted to keep an industrializing America pure. Irascible and independent, Mugwumps were generally older than other political activists. And they were determined to secure the future upon the most positive achievements of the past. Proudly nationalistic, Mugwumps wanted to sustain an America that was prosperous but not plutocratic, internationally respected but not imperialistic. They wanted to salvage constitutional republicanism in the Age of Empire.

Shaped by Bradford and the former Radical Republican leader George Boutwell, the Anti-Imperialist League became the centerpiece of a remarkably heterogeneous movement that included publicists like Schurz and Godkin, industrialists like Carnegie and George Foster Peabody, clergymen like A. A. Berle and Henry Van Dyke, feminists like Josephine Lowell and Jane Addams, pacifists like Ernest Crosby and Edward Atkinson, urban reformers like Hazen Pingree and Samuel "Golden Rule" Jones, educators like David Starr Jordan and William Graham Sumner, black activists like Booker T. Washington, white supremacists like Ben Tillman, labor leaders like Samuel Gompers, and legal authorities like Thomas Cooley. Independently, they organized sympathizers, spoke in public meetings, and wrote and distributed pamphlets, books, and articles. Collectively, they raised a host of persuasive arguments against McKinley's decision to seize the Philippines as a forward base for America's Asian power.[29]

Some anti-imperialists insisted that a republic was constitutionally incapable of absorbing an empire, warned of the international complications attendant upon America's involvement in imperial politics, and fretted about the Monroe Doctrine. Many held that imperialism was economically unsound and subversive of the free-trade bases of competitive capitalism, and a number opposed expansion for distracting from the need for domestic reform. A few disliked the conquest of highly competitive cheap labor, while others worried that the annexation overseas of colored people would weaken white supremacy at home. Most believed that imperialism was simply wrong. Animated by many different concerns, anti-imperialists coalesced mainly in that they agreed upon two points. They realized that McKinley's Philippines policy signaled a major break from America's past containment in the Western Hemisphere. And they feared that such a break would fatally corrupt American constitutional principles, competitive capitalism, and democratic freedoms. Imperialism would cost America its purity.

Initially, the Anti-Imperialist League organized in order to dissuade the McKinley administration through moral pressure from seizing the Philippines. When that tack failed, the League collaborated with several affiliated organizations, which sprang up spontaneously across the country, in an attempt to prevent Senate ratification of the Paris Peace Treaty. Winning the support of dissident Republicans like George Hoar, anti-imperialists generated fierce pressure on Capitol Hill before the Treaty was ratified by one vote on February 6, 1899. To the disgust of many, the Senate approval took place with the support of Democratic Party leader and sometime anti-imperialist William Jennings Bryan. Even worse, fighting broke out two days later in the Philippines between American troops and Filipino patriots led by Emilio Aguinaldo.

The eruption of the Filipino-American War transformed the Anti-Imperialist League into a national movement with a mass constituency. Working with other anti-imperialist elements, League membership expanded to over 30,000 in a growth spurt that made it the largest antiwar organization per capita in American history. Mugwumps, older Republicans, and a range of Bryanite and conservative Democrats stood behind the movement in a suprapartisan bond that was extraordinary in those highly partisan times, while labor, farm, and black leaders extended the cause beyond class and racial lines. Finding receptive audiences, anti-imperialists distributed literature and placed speakers around the country as they pursued two simple goals: an immediate suspension of hostilities in the Philippines, and a congressional pledge of Philippine independence. Sensibly, they declined to address the differences that divided them over such significant issues as the length of the American withdrawal and the future disposition of the islands.

In action, anti-imperialists crossed the country organizing, agitating, and trying to build a popular backlash against the drive toward empire. Sometimes the government presented them with an issue. In May 1899, for instance, Postmaster General Charles Emory Smith ordered the removal of Edward Atkinson's anti-imperialist tracts from the mail bound for the Philippines in what Fred Harvey Harrington has called "the most sensational episode" in the anti-imperialist struggle.[30] The administration action provoked an immediate outcry over government censorship and the abuse of First-Amendment freedoms. For several weeks the controversy simmered, while popular demand for Atkinson's pamphlets climbed. Then federal officials decided to organize a measured retreat rather than risk a larger confrontation that might further strengthen the anti-imperialist appeal.

With Washington operating most cautiously, anti-imperialist leaders were obliged to orchestrate strains of antiwar sentiment that emanated from several different sources. In the South and West, for instance, anti-imperialist activists played on local desires to bring the troops home by pleading that the youthful volunteers "did not enlist to fight niggers."[31] In Chicago, on the other hand, black leaders satirized the imperialists' philanthropic claims by forming the Black Man's Burden Association as a reminder of racial oppression at home and a warning against its extension to the Philippines.[32] Trying to harmonize these various sentiments, over 100 delegates from anti-imperialist leagues in 30 states met in Chicago in October 1899 and formed the American Anti-Imperialist League under the chairmanship of George Boutwell. Chicago became the head of the movement. But Boston remained the brains. And the whole country vibrated with its energy.

Over the winter of 1899–1900, the anti-imperialist movement slipped from a campaign of mass mobilization into the confusion of electoral politics. Unable to stop the war through popular agitation, anti-imperialist leaders toyed briefly with the idea of mounting a third-party effort for the 1900 presidential election. Then, in August, most decided to support the Democratic candidacy of William Jennings Bryan. Sincere if shallow, Bryan was a sometime Christian pacifist and a full-time political strategist. After service as a colonel with the Nebraska volunteers during the Spanish-

American War, the Democratic leader protested McKinley's Pacific policies but then decided grudgingly to support the Senate ratification of the Paris Treaty.

In late winter 1899, however, the forty-year-old "Boy Orator of the Platte" turned more fully toward anti-imperialism; and he became one of the movement's most powerful spokesmen. Hearkening to scriptural injunctions and the Declaration of Independence, Bryan attacked imperialism as one more indication of eastern plutocratic subservience to foreign ways, and he shrewdly tied his rural populist following in the West to the side of eastern Mugwumps and independents. By doing so, Bryan revived the antiplutocratic theme that he had played in 1896 and solidified his hold on the Democratic Party. Anxiously, Filipino patriots hoped for his success. Guerrilla elements geared their attacks to strengthen Bryan's anti-imperialist appeal, while Aguinaldo reportedly promised to halt the fighting if the Democrat were elected.[33]

But a large minority of conservative anti-imperialists rejected Bryan's appeal. Convinced that Bryan was a demagogue, Carnegie and Hoar returned to the Republican fold and supported McKinley, while conservative Democrats like Grover Cleveland simply sat out the race. At the same time, U.S. military forces gradually but visibly ground down the insurrection. The result was a McKinley victory that was even more decisive than the election of 1896, and a devastating blow to the anti-imperialist movement. The cost in the Philippines was even greater. Between the outbreak of war in February 1899 and its official end in June 1902 (serious scattered resistance continued at least until 1904), anywhere from 250,000 to 600,000 men, women, and children died in battle or because of war-related disease. Official U.S. losses were put at over 7,000 casualties and $600 million.

Shattered by Bryan's humiliation, the anti-imperialist movement retreated into its hardcore bases in the urban Northeast. Various leaders either died or retreated into mainstream politics. But those who remained became even more critical of Washington's anti-guerrilla war and the domestic sources of U.S. imperialism. Edward Atkinson attributed imperialism to the growing "trustification" of the American economy by irresponsible monopolies anxious for foreign markets. George Boutwell blamed white American racism for providing the drive force to the U.S. suppression of the Filipinoes. The elitist Godkin complained that mass democratic participation in the Spanish and Filipino conflicts showed how modern war was turning into a savage mob blood rite.

Frustrated by its venture into electoral politics, the shrinking anti-imperialist movement drifted after 1900 into attempts to challenge the constitutionality of American imperialism and to expose American atrocities in the Philippines. The first tack failed in the spring of 1901, when the Supreme Court ruled in the *Insular Cases* that the Constitution indeed applied to colonial holdings subject to congressional legislation. But the revelation of atrocities produced some temporarily encouraging results. Spurred by the anti-imperialist charges, the Senate Committee on the Philippines and Secretary of War Elihu Root jointly investigated widespread allegations of U.S. war crimes in the islands.

Their findings confirmed what anti-imperialists had long maintained. Fighting an irregular war against a colored people, U.S. armed forces had habitually tortured rebel suspects, shot prisoners or unlucky civilians, and burned and looted conquered areas. Yet there was little negative reaction within the country to the official confirmation of U.S. atrocities. Several commentators dismissed the victims as "only niggers."[34] Most editorialists excused U.S. military conduct as consistent with the irregular nature of the war, while leaders of organized Protestantism showed more concern with the Army's plans for licensed brothels in Manila than with war crimes.[35] Perversely, the very power of national pride that anti-imperialists had hoped would shame Americans, once aware of the atrocities, into opposing the war moved most people into accepting the crimes as the accidental but acceptable cost of a liberating war.

The anti-imperialist movement finally deflated during 1902. In February, Aguinaldo was captured, and the Filipino resistance suffered an irreversible loss. Five months later, President Theodore Roosevelt, who had succeeded to the White House on McKinley's death at the hands of an assassin in September 1901, declared the war formally ended. Stubbornly, however, the Anti-Imperialist League refused to disband. Headed by the Boston lawyer Moorfield Storey, the League remained a noisy center for anti-imperialist arguments until 1920, sporadically attacking U.S. interventions in Latin America and colonialism everywhere. After 1902 anti-imperialists lacked a reliable constituency and a wide listening audience. But they remained fixed on a cause that they felt would last across the century.

Incredibly, leaders of the organized peace movement provided only partial support to the anti-imperialist crusade. In large measure, their help was limited because of intramural differences over U.S. imperialism. Several joined Lyman Abbott and Edward Everett Hale in backing McKinley's policies. Others like Trueblood openly opposed the U.S. drive toward conquest. Individually, several peace activists assumed active leadership in the anti-imperialist movement; and a number of influential figures—notably Jane Addams, Stanford University President David Starr Jordan, and the Boston uplifter Edwin D. Mead—used the anti-imperialist struggle as a springboard into longterm service in organized peace seeking.[36] But there was no simple coincidence in 1898 between peace activism and anti-imperialism.

Generally, the country's best-known peace leaders viewed imperialism with an equanimity bred from their overpowering optimism. One month after the outbreak of war, for instance, Trueblood asserted that "No sadder, no more shameful page has ever been written in American history than that which is now being written in the Philippine islands." At the same time, however, he could not repress the certainty that he felt in the triumph of the larger cause. Wars in Cuba and the Philippines were "only temporary disturbances," the APS leader explained, while the peace crusade was "a great, abiding movement" which would eventually secure "permanent institutions which will be as enduring as human society."[37] Seemingly, the peace movement's failure to assess the full implications of Washington's imperial wars reflected a fatal flaccidity. But contemporaries did not think so. More than anything, cosmopolitan peace reformers moved through their experience with war and imperialism to believe even more firmly in the violent irrationality of the masses and in the necessity for Great Power harmony and control of the underdeveloped world. Together, cosmopolitan peace leaders straddled the question of imperialism because of their agreement on the prerequisites of peace: elite education of the masses at home and the Christian disciplining of backward peoples abroad.

While differing over imperialism, cosmopolitan peace workers rallied as one to the support of the First Hague Conference. Called by Russian Czar Nicholas III in August 1898 to consider arms limitation, the First Hague Conference met early in 1899 in an attempt to move the powers to deal with the questions of international arms, the rules of war, and an international court of justice. American peace leaders showed immediate interest in the meeting. After overcoming their initial distrust of the Czar's intentions, peace activists carefully observed and then strongly approved of the Conference's work. They supported The Hague's prohibition on certain types of weaponry as another step in the humanizing of warfare. They applauded its success in establishing the Permanent Court of Arbitration as an available instrument for the settlement of disputes. And they looked forward to a Second Hague Conference that would create a permanent court of international justice with binding powers in the settlement of selected disputes.[38]

Exuberantly, peace workers maximized the limited achievements worked at The Hague even as war racked the Philippines. Robert Treat Paine, president of the APS, announced that the Conference "transcends any human event which has taken place. It is the first Parliament of Man; it is the first step towards the federation of the world." "This union of the nations of the earth is an event of the first historic importance," agreed participants at the Sixth Lake Mohonk Arbitration Conference, "fitly rounding out a great century, and giving promise of immeasurable good for the centuries to come."[39] Happily, the world verged on even greater successes.

The fact that organized peace seeking advanced during America's first wars for overseas empire, while anti-imperialist activism skyrocketed and then fizzled, testifies both to the immovable optimism and the remarkable resilience of the cosmopolitan peace reform. Despite ongoing violence overseas, cosmopolitan peace workers cheered recent peace progress and predicted that the peace movement had "yet wider sweeps of triumph before it." Private dueling had ended. Civil wars had ceased. "Only international wars and those for territorial or commercial expansion still remain"; and the new alliance of Christianity and industrial interdependence promised their extinction.[40] With hopes unbroken, cosmopolitan peace reformers entered the twentieth century as an ambitious— and increasingly respectable—array of world-minded Americans who aimed to spread order at home and abroad. They believed that their reform was within reach of realization. They knew that they had fashioned a movement which was helping to make the world safe "for the international emergence of a virtuous America."[41]

Chapter Five
The Practical Reform

In the first years of the twentieth century, peace seeking became a most practical reform enterprise. Glowing with unprecedented social respectability, the peace reform passed to the leadership of lawyers and businessmen whose identification with success galvanized the support of a broad range of educators, interdenominational Protestant clergymen, and social progressives. These "practical peace advocates" constructed a newly national movement on the old cosmopolitan faith in human reason, progress, Christianity, Great Power harmony, and the need for working peacekeeping mechanisms.[1] Developing several new organizations, practical peace workers raised the peace reform to unparalleled levels of influence. Then the outbreak of the Great War in 1914 undercut their first assumptions and opened the way for the creation of the modern American peace movement.

Between 1901 and 1914, 45 new peace organizations appeared in the United States in a growth spurt unequaled in the history of the peace reform. Essentially, these new organizations represented extensions of the "domestic and professional priorities" of those functional economic elites who presided most visibly over the ordering of American industrialization.[2] Several innovative business leaders, for instance, who were directing the country's corporate consolidation, turned to the peace reform out of an interest in the extension of order at home and abroad. Similarly, lawyers and law professors promoted the peace issue as they championed the importance of courts, while clergymen urged the pursuit of Christian service, and educators saw harmony in the international spread of right reason. Converging from different concerns, practical peace advocates joined forces as they recognized in the peace cause a most "prestigious and proper" calling.[3]

Primarily, practical peace leaders were distinguished by their solid social credentials and their commitment to some kind of international peacemaking machinery. They were people of status who aimed to regularize order in the industrial age. Mostly, they were centered in a northeastern metropolitan collection of lawyers, government officials, and industrialists. But they reached into nearly every part of American life. Some like Elihu Root slid easily along the inner rims of U.S. foreign policy making. Others like Andrew Carnegie and Jane Addams commanded attention because of their wealth and reputation. A few like David Starr Jordan gained influence because of the force of their arguments. Speaking for different constituencies, they were joined in a "tenuous consensus" that felt optimistic faith in progress, Christianity, human reason, Anglo-American cooperation, and the extension of world order through America's rise to international power.[4] Positive-minded conservatives, they believed that their peace movement was not "a mere revolt at the horrors of war—an anti-war movement—but a pro-law movement" that would secure at least arbitration and courtroom justice and at most world federation.[5]

Temperamentally, practical peace reformers approached world affairs with a combination of hopefulness and apprehension. Preoccupied with Great Power relations, most supported U.S. hegemony in the Western Hemisphere and tended to ignore the colonial world. But they worried much about Europe. Disturbed by deepening Old World tensions, prewar peace leaders moved along two salients in an attempt to maintain European stability and preserve the international capitalist order. They established peace societies that were designed to consolidate public opinion behind governmental steps toward stronger international peacekeeping mechanisms. And they pressed the U.S. government to assume the lead in taking those steps.

The first serious drive toward organizing the practical peace reform took place between 1902 and 1906, when a combination of recent converts and veterans began arguing for more permanent forms of international organization. Encouraged by the American Peace Society, the journalist Raymond Bridgman initiated in 1902 a campaign in favor of a periodic world congress. One year later the New York lawyer Hayne Davis wrote a series of articles on a U.S.-modelled world federation that won Hamilton Holt (1872–1951), the editor of the influential *Independent*, to a lifetime of service in the peace cause. In 1904 the Interparliamentary Union met in St. Louis, the home district of its foremost American supporter, Richard Bartholdt. Gathering legislators from throughout Europe, the meeting of the Inter-Parliamentary Union brought new visibility to the international peace movement and moved President Theodore Roosevelt to issue a call for a second Hague Conference. Building upon this momentum, Bartholdt and Columbia University President Nicholas Murray Butler (1862–1947) organized in early 1906 the American Association for International Conciliation (AAIC) as a branch of the French-based Conciliation Internationale for the purpose of employing "private initiatives" among the world's policy-shaping elite.[6] In the same year, Andrew Carnegie assumed the presidency of the re-energized New York Peace Society (NYPS).

Despite the failure of the anti-imperialist crusade, Carnegie never lost interest in the peace reform. Beginning in 1903 the master philanthropist contributed millions to the construction of peace buildings in Washington and at The Hague, and freely subsidized the operation of several old and new peace societies. As importantly, Carnegie brought power to the peace movement by virtue of the fact that he was one of the few public figures in Progressive America "who could be sure of receiving attention when he spoke."[7] With his help, the NYPS grew within four years from a small fellowship of peace educators into the second largest (next to the APS) peace society in the country. His money brought notice to the peace movement. His participation made it respectable.

Adding another dimension to the new respectability of the peace reform was that constellation of legalists who gathered after 1905 around Elihu Root (1845–1937) and his interests. The dream of a world court and the progressive codification of international law had intrigued American peace seekers from the time of William Ladd. But the ethos of legalism—"the attempt to convert international conflicts into cases and to supplement diplomatic negotiations by judicial decisions"—did not really grip organized peace activists until the early twentieth century, when Root and his followers sought to advance beyond The Hague system of arbitration into the judicial settlement of disputes.[8]

Root not only gave force to the legalist approach; he personified it. An unflappable Wall Street lawyer who had helped mastermind the country's surge toward economic concentration, Root was a classic conservative who had a passion for order and a fear of the democratic masses. A smooth conciliator and expert administrator, he was a Republican partisan who had headed the departments of War (1899–1904) and State (1905–1909) in the administrations of McKinley and Roosevelt. He also possessed real personal magnetism. Despite an austere and aloof public image, Root's personality attracted a following of Republican internationalists— including James Brown Scott, Henry Stimson, and Harvey Bundy—who shaped U.S. diplomacy for nearly a half-century.

With Root's encouragement, legalists worked after 1905 to organize the peace reform upon the principles of courtroom justice. They wanted to invest in judges the responsibility for international order. Organizing from a base in the Lake Mohonk conferences, the Columbia University law professor George Kirchwey and the long-time law school administrator James Brown Scott prompted in 1906 the formation of the American Society of International Law (ASIL) as a "scientific" center for the study of international law and as a means of familiarizing the country's world-minded elite with the importance of judicial means of keeping peace. One year later Secretary of State Root instructed members of the U.S. delegation (which included his protégé and departmental solicitor Scott and the prominent peace advocate Joseph Choate) to press at the Second Hague Conference for an international court, as the next logical step toward world order. Undeterred by failure at The Hague, Root helped organize the Central American Court of Justice, an achievement which contributed to his receipt in 1913 of the Nobel Peace Prize. In the meantime, the millionaire Baltimore publicist Theodore Marburg and the New York mining magnate John Hays Hammond presided over the formation in 1910 of the American Society for the Judicial Settlement of International Disputes (ASJSID). Dominated by lawyers and law school professors, the ASJSID promoted the idea of an international court and provided one more select center for spreading an understanding of peace as the product of impartial judicial decisions.[9]

The legalists' concern for the primacy of international law and courts meshed with their larger determination to maintain an independent judiciary as the first domestic defender of private property rights and Anglo-Saxon political power. With other practical peace seekers, they furthermore valued military power and swung easily from positions of prominence within the country's top peace

societies to similar positions within militant preparedness organizations. At one time, in fact, eleven notable prewar peace leaders
served simultaneously as officers of the Navy League. Typically,
John Hays Hammond combined his support of the ASJSID with the
sponsoring of a trophy "for accuracy in bomb-dropping" at a
Boston-area flying meet in 1910.[10] Hardly hypocritical, practical
peace workers made no secret of their conviction that peace would
come through law and order, and that law and order would come
through the extension of Anglo-American power. They disdained
the term "pacifism" and the prewar connotation of passivism that
it conveyed.

Operationally, the most advanced achievement of the practical
peace movement took place in 1907, when over 1,200 delegates (including U.S. cabinet officers, senators, and Supreme Court justices)
from 39 states and 18 nations met at the four-day National Arbitration and Peace Congress in New York. Subsidized by millionaires
like John D. Rockefeller and organized by Carnegie, the Congress
aimed to generate popular support for an advanced American position at the upcoming Hague Conference. Privately, however,
Carnegie had larger hopes. "We mean," he told one English supporter, "to form a *National* Peace Society of distinguished men including practical men of affairs to a greater extent than usual and
stand for 'the abolition of War as a Means of Settling International
Disputes.'"[11] His dream did not seem exaggerated. Secretary of
State Root personally addressed one gathering of the group, while
over 40,000 people attended the Congress's seven meetings in
Carnegie Hall. It was the largest and most respectable peace rally
in American history.

Encouraged by the Congress and the Second Hague Conference,
the practical peace reform expanded impressively after 1907. The
Association of Cosmopolitan Clubs, which originated in 1903, advanced in its work of promoting international friendship and understanding among university students. Preaching a "pacific-
minded internationalism," the Cosmopolitan Clubs enjoyed
the support of university presidents like Cornell's Jacob Gould
Schurman and the leadership on over twenty campuses of students
like Louis Lochner and George Nasmyth.[12] In the same spirit, the
schoolteacher Fannie Fern Andrews formed the American School
Peace League in Boston in 1908 to extend international understanding among schoolchildren. One year later a group of prominent

Chicagoans formed the Chicago Peace Society, the first major peace organization established beyond the movement's traditional geographic rim along the northeastern Atlantic seaboard. At the same time, the APS entered on a remarkable growth cycle that brought about internal reorganization (including the shift of its headquarters from Boston to Washington) and its appearance for the first time as a truly national peace society.

Inevitably, the rapid expansion of the peace reform produced demands for improved organizational coordination. Determined to pass beyond moral preachments, practical peace advocates began in 1909 to call for a more efficient peace-seeking apparatus. Sensitive to "the new watchword" of organizational efficiency, delegates at the 1909 Lake Mohonk Conference authorized Nicholas Murray Butler to seek ways of aligning the activities of the enlarging peace movement.[13] And Edwin Ginn acted. A trained lawyer and early participant in the Mohonk conferences, Ginn was a wealthy Boston textbook publisher who had long been interested in educating people to the necessity of peace through more businesslike procedures. After failing to persuade other businessmen to join him in endowing a major peace organization, he decided in July 1910 to contribute $50,000 toward the formation in Boston of an International School for Peace. Five months later the School became the World Peace Foundation (WPF).

Organized on the model of a prewar university, the WPF was directed by an eminent board of trustees that was packed with educators like David Starr Jordan and influenced by publicists like Edwin D. Mead. Functionally, the Foundation aimed to strengthen the international peace spirit through research and education. Seeking to move peace workers from "sentimentality to rationality," WPF officers arranged for the production of study materials for dissemination at a price to individuals and libraries.[14] Ginn refused to fund the spread of free peace information, insisting rather that people pay for Foundation materials as a way of learning that peace was a business proposition which had to be organized, sold, and secured.

In the same month that the WPF took shape, Carnegie contributed $10 million in U.S. Steel Corporation bonds toward the formation in New York of the Carnegie Endowment for International Peace (CEIP). It was by far the best-subsidized undertaking in American peace history. It also epitomized the prewar movement. Formally, Carnegie directed Endowment officers to "hasten the abolition of international war, the foulest blot upon our civilization," and then proceed to determine "what is the next most degrading remaining evil or evils whose banishment . . . would most advance the progress, elevation and happiness of man, and so on from century to century without end. . . ."[15] Practically, he operated most cautiously. At his insistence, Root became president of the Endowment and directed its operations with the help of a prestigious board of trustees that included prominent businessmen, politicians, and educators. Their concerns were distinctly businesslike. Organized into separate divisions of education, international law, and history and economics, the CEIP assiduously sponsored "scientific" studies of the cause and cure of the war menace. It aimed to organize reason and help administer progress.

Detached and deliberate, CEIP leaders were sharply sensitive to their organizational power. Endowment officers encouraged the research and educational activities of like-minded organizations like the ASIL, APS, and the ASJSID. But they were reluctant to subsidize these organizations too freely, for fear that the very availability of Carnegie largesse would paralyze the fund-raising capabilities of other peace societies and kill them with generosity. In addition, Endowment leaders took care to circumscribe the political scope of their work and avoid unseemly political controversy. After an embarrassing involvement in the 1912–1913 Panama Canal tolls controversy between the United States and Britain, CEIP officers contented themselves with building international relations sections in the country's many Carnegie-endowed libraries and with funding extensive studies of the legal traditions of the Western Hemisphere. Less formally, the Endowment also established a smooth working relationship with the State Department. Helped by figures like James Brown Scott and Robert Lansing, the CEIP developed direct lines of access to top U.S. policymakers. In fact, by the 1920s, the Endowment was operating in Root's words as a virtual "division of the State Department, working in harmony constantly."[16]

While practical reformers tried to rationalize the peace movement, Protestant peace seekers similarly tried between 1911 and 1915 to coordinate their own efforts through the formation of three major organizations. First, the interdenominational Protestant leader Charles Macfarland and Frederick Lynch, a Carnegie confidante and long-time peace worker, moved the Federal Council of Churches of Christ in America (FCCCA) to establish in 1911 a

Commission on Peace and Arbitration. With this organizational lever, Lynch pried from Carnegie a $2 million endowment for the Church Peace Union (CPU). Formed in February 1914, the CPU originated as an interfaith front of prominent religious peace seekers who were interested in building a more systematic and effective crusade against war. Ironically, the Union's first major peace action, an international church peace conference scheduled for Constance, Germany, was literally disrupted by the outbreak of the European war. Fleeing from Constance, members of the conference's Continuation Committee met shortly after in London and formed the World Alliance for International Friendship Through the Churches (WAIFTC). In summer 1915, CPU leaders organized an American branch of the Alliance, seizing one more victory in interdenominational Protestantism's prewar drive toward Christian federalism and international peace. Yet their efforts hardly affected clerical thinking at the grass-roots. "The problem of war had been entirely academic in our infrequent discussions of it," the pacifist minister Kirby Page recalled of the prewar era. "In all those years I had never met an informed and determined pacifist."[17] Even worse, the Protestant effort did nothing to stop European Christians from slaughtering one another after 1914 in the name of tribal salvation.

The tribal attractions of war were nothing new to prewar peace seekers. Stimulated by expanding inquiries into the nature of the subconscious, social commentators speculated increasingly on war's power to enchant the masses and fulfill basic human needs. Their observations took on new sharpness in 1910, when the Harvard University psychologist William James wrote a seminal essay on "The Moral Equivalent of War." Wondering why men in war gave up so much so willingly in the absence of any direct threat, James suggested that the drive for heroism through individual sacrifice for the tribal good represented an elemental expression of human behavior. Modern war lacked any rational validity, James contended. Yet militarism thrived because all people felt an inbred need for the discipline, sacrifice, and challenge that war epitomized. In the face of this need, James believed, peace seekers must substitute a moral equivalent for war's "disciplinary function" in order to pave a peaceable way toward the collectivist future to which industrial peoples were heading.[18]

Personally, James wanted to rechannel the martial virtues of "intrepidity, contempt of softness, surrender of private interest, [and] obedience to command" from military preparations and into peaceable domestic mobilization. In particular, he advocated the conscription of American youth into an army against nature, organizing them to attack and control forests and river systems in order "to get the childishness knocked out of them" and to elicit "their blood-tax" in man's endless struggle to subdue the earth. But most of all James searched for different social conventions that might replace the psychological sinews by which war had historically bound human communities. "So far, war has been the only force that can discipline a whole community," he declared, "and until an equivalent discipline is organized, I believe that war must have its way."[19]

The most imaginative prewar attempt to meet James's challenge emanated from the immigrant slums of Chicago's West Side, where Jane Addams (1860–1935) and her associates tried to transmute the crusading spirit of war into reform campaigns against poverty and disease. Raised in rural Illinois, Addams arrived in Chicago following a round of European travel and bouts of bad health. Joined by Ellen Gates Starr, she established at the decaying Hull mansion a community center that was intended to assist a mixed lot of southern and eastern European immigrants in alternately adapting to and resisting the trials of working-class life in industrial America. Amazingly, their work produced results. Addams and the Hull House staff found jobs for the unemployed, relief for the destitute, and care for the sick. The settlement offered a range of services—from child-care to recreational and occupational opportunities—that created at best an island of harmony in a friction-filled community. In the process, it instilled in Addams a faith in the possibilities of a "communal internationalism" that would extend peace through the operation of an "international welfare community."[20]

Immersed in settlement work, Addams showed no interest in foreign affairs until 1898, when popular enthusiasm for the Spanish-American War swept Chicago. Then she took action and never stopped. Disturbed by the popular fascination with war's violence, Addams tried to uncover some means of redirecting the human drive toward war into more constructive outlets. At first she looked to Tolstoy's exaltation of common labor and simple human solidarity. Increasingly, however, she decided that uncontrolled industrial capitalism fomented the greatest violence at home and abroad with a power far beyond the reach of Tolstoy's preachments. Without foregoing her faith in the peacemaking strength of woman's maternal instinct, she therefore turned to promote the systematic "nurturing" power of the positive state as the best means for controlling capitalism and minimizing the threat of war. Convinced that the war drive could be contained through affirmative action, Addams insisted that a tough-minded new pacifism was displacing the "passive 'dove-like' ideal" of earlier peace sentimentalists. And she resolved to act upon the new fashion. Using her influence as the best-known and most respected woman in the country, Addams argued that the plain wastefulness of war, the general human longing for harmony, and the spread of the modern social welfare state were together moving war toward extinction. Attending national peace meetings, she quickly assumed a significant place within the practical peace reform even as she espoused a pacifism that was somewhat sentimental, surprisingly empirical, and "above all democratic."[21]

Throughout the prewar years, Addams maintained a polite distance from the country's dominant conservative peace organizations and international law societies. Partly, her detachment resulted from the exclusionist practices of the movement's male leadership. Even more, however, she remained apart because she perceived peace as a social—and not national—dynamic that subsisted more in organized acts of simple decency than in the collaboration of nation-states. In this regard, her thinking more fully resembled the peace ideals of prewar American socialists (who ignored her) than it did the work of conservative peace leaders (who lionized her). Hers was a strange position that developed out of her actions and commitment in Progressive America. Few doubted the mildness of Addams's pacifist vision. But then few foresaw the radical direction that vision would take when the country slid after 1914 toward war.

If they could not accommodate Addams's pacifism, practical peace workers did achieve some success in the years 1908–1914 by creating a political climate that induced Washington policy makers to devise some peacekeeping mechanisms. In 1908 Secretary of State Root concluded a series of 24 bilateral arbitration conventions, each of which excluded questions of national honor and vital interests. Two years later, President William Howard Taft surprised a typically genteel party of peacemakers by declaring his interest in securing a bilateral arbitration treaty with another power (but implicitly Britain) that would provide for "the adjudication of an international arbitral court in every issue which cannot be settled by negotiation, no matter what it involves."[22] Encouraged by favorable public reaction, Taft and Secretray of State Philander Knox opened diplomatic negotiations that culminated in August 1911, when the administration concluded with England and France two separate arbitration treaties that were "revolutionary when compared with previous agreements for the pacific settlement of disputes."[23] Unusually inclusive, the pacts provided for arbitration in all matters deemed "justiciable," and authorized the creation of a Joint High Commission of Inquiry to determine the "justiciability" of various disputes. Predictably, however, the Senate resisted the treaties' challenge to the national sovereignty and senatorial prerogatives. Led by former President Roosevelt and Senator Henry Cabot Lodge, Senate nationalists passed the treaties only after attaching reservations that limited their applicability in matters ranging from the Monroe Doctrine to Confederate war debts. Taft was utterly frustrated. Appalled by the Senate reservations, he quietly dropped the treaties and halted diplomatic proceedings in early 1912.

Tellingly, prewar peace advocates backed Taft's arbitration treaties with an unsettling ambivalence. Encouraged by the Carnegie Endowment, the APS and the ASJSID urged ratification of the treaties without Senate amendments. Yet Endowment president and U.S. Senator Root openly agreed with Roosevelt and Lodge on the need for certain reservations, while other practical peace reformers grumbled about potential challenges to the national honor and vital interests. The peace seekers' equivocal reaction to the Taft treaties reflected in some ways a realistic appreciation of power realities, particularly the need to adapt to senatorial pressures. More importantly, however, their well-contained enthusiasm suggested the power of the nationalist impulse that had sustained the prewar peace movement but now proved its fatal flaw.

The ambivalence among prewar peace seekers between their concern for international arbitration and their commitment to independent American nationhood proved even more worrisome in April 1914, when President Woodrow Wilson's meddling in the Mexican Revolution produced a crisis that resulted in an armed

U.S. intervention at Vera Cruz and the likelihood of major war. Top peace leaders immediately called for the arbitration of Mexican-American differences. But they announced with equal vigor their determination to support the President and the national honor in this time of trial. With prominent peace advocates containing their own complaints, the mainstay of antiwar agitation shifted in the spring of 1914 to a collection of feminist groups and to the Socialist Party.[24] Practical peace seekers might have wished to lead the way toward international arbitration, but they proved more successful at following the flag.*

The outbreak of world war in August 1914 finally drove the great majority of prewar peace workers from their interest in practical peacekeeping mechanisms to their first commitment to American nationhood. Ten million men perished in international testimony to the failure of prewar peace efforts. And, as they did, the U.S. government shuddered, equivocated, and then intervened in the war in an attempt to salvage a reconstructed European order. Organized peace seeking interestingly proceeded along a parallel path. Pressured by the war, peace leaders faltered, divided over the question of preparedness, and then split and reassembled, following the U.S. intervention, into a remarkable new constellation of activists who fashioned the modern American peace movement. Peace after 1915 no longer signified the "stability, restraint, and order" preferred by the practical peace advocates of prewar America. It rather connoted "democratization, the preservation of social reform, and even the acceleration of social change."[25] It meant a search for equity and justice.

The crisis that forged the modern peace movement took place in two phases. The first occurred between 1914 and 1916, when the limitations of the practical peace reform became plain and opened the way to an antipreparedness (or antimilitarist) campaign that

*Also during 1913–1914, Secretary of State William Jennings Bryan concluded twenty bilateral "cooling-off" conciliation treaties that required signatory states to submit all disputes to a fact-finding commission and to refrain from war until the commission issued its report. Although a genuine achievement, the treaties allowed too many exceptions for independent national action to serve as adequate peacekeeping mechanisms. As if to emphasize their irrelevance, most were concluded while the Great European War raged on. Merle E. Curti, *Bryan and World Peace* (Northampton, Mass.: Smith College Studies in History, XVI, nos. 3–4, 1931; New York: Octagon edition, 1969), pp. 143–53; and Paolo E. Coletta, "William Jennings Bryan's Plans for World Peace," *Nebraska History* 58, no. 2 (Summer 1977): 193–217.

was led by a progressive coalition of feminists, social workers, and Social Gospel clergymen.* The second phase took place during 1917–1918, when U.S. intervention in the war broke the progressive coalition into two parts. A body of liberal internationalists supported the U.S. intervention out of their desire to help in the construction of a democratized and reformed postwar world order, while a contingent of liberal pacifists withdrew into a lonely peace witness out of their certainty that war itself was the enemy. Between them they proceeded to fashion a new peace movement.

Leaders of the practical peace reform first reacted to the outbreak of war with a combination of frustration and resignation. "All the world has gone mad," the Rev. Frederick Lynch wrote from England in August 1914. "There is no other way to explain it, everybody we met in Europe on our way home was crazy. Nobody wanted war and yet nobody could stop it."[26] Carnegie and Trueblood tried to stop the slaughter through prayers and petitions; and leaders of the Carnegie Endowment quietly offered their mediatory services to the warring governments. But practical peace seekers generally refrained from visible peacemaking efforts and declined to support efforts on the part of domestic progressives to move Wilson into brokering a settlement. Top legalists viewed the war as an Old World affair and as further evidence of the need for judicial means of settling disputes. Out of this belief, the CEIP continued the "scientific" study of international law and supported the APS in promoting a world court and periodic congresses of nations after The Hague precedents. Hoping to establish a united front, several legalists combined in 1915 to create a World's Court League in an attempt to advance the court ideal and a third Hague Conference. But their effort seemed a sad response in view of the magnitude of the European crisis, and it underscored the limitations of practical peace seeking.

The limitations of the practical peace reform and the urgency of the war combined to force forward a new—indeed, the modern— peace movement. Emerging from domestic progressivism, leaders of the new movement comprehended peace more in terms of social

*Gathering force at the turn of the century, the Social Gospel signified "a sub-movement within religious liberalism" that sought in a spirit of optimism to infuse Christian morality into the drive toward the planned elimination of institutionalized social evil. It proved vital to the peace movement during and after World War I. Sydney E. Ahlstrom, *A Religious History of the American People* (New Haven: Yale University Press, 1972), p. 786.

reform than order. They understood international justice more as the amelioration of social wrongs than the construction of courts. They valued nationalism more for its healthful diversity than its Anglo-Saxon exclusiveness. They saw war more as the product of militarism, imperialism, and frustrated national self-determination than as an irrational outburst due to mass ignorance. And they sought a reformed and democratized international system by which responsible politicians and dispassionate experts would *manage* peace through applied social justice. Ideologically and politically, they made up a movement of the left. More than ever, peace was to be known as a literal social re-formation.

The rise of the modern peace reform occurred in fits and starts as prewar peace leaders alternately clashed and cooperated with proponents of the new movement. The first real if unsteady bridge between the two approaches to peace was the League to Enforce Peace (LEP), which rose to prominence during the summer of 1915. Originating among northeastern metropolitan Republicans, the LEP leadership claimed a range of personally conservative but politically adventuresome peace seekers. Some like ex-President Taft and Harvard University President (and WPF leader) A. Lawrence Lowell were relative newcomers to active peace work. Others like the diplomat Oscar Straus and Hamilton Holt were proven veterans. But they all agreed upon the need for an international league "of all the great nations" that would require its members to submit their disputes either to a "judicial tribunal" or "a judicial Council of Conciliation." In addition, LEP leaders made a decisive advance toward a firmer world order by demanding that league members "jointly use their military forces to prevent any one of their number from going to war" before submitting its dispute to some form of settlement. Clearly, LEP organizers believed that peace would prevail when the Great Powers deterred warmaking states through a collective threat of overwhelming retaliation. LEP activists did not oppose the legalist preference for courts. As Warren Kuehl has observed, they "simply wanted to go farther."[27]

Oddly, the LEP failed to win the support of either prewar legalists, who disliked the organization's power-political orientation, or progressive peace seekers, who disliked the LEP preference for the international status quo. Yet the new group worked a tremendous impression upon public opinion. With 23 full-time staff workers and a budget of nearly $300,000, the nonpartisan LEP became by 1916 the most powerful wartime pressure group on behalf of the ideal of a postwar league of nations. League leaders organized state affiliates and dispatched squads of speakers across the country. They established ties with prewar organizations like the CPU and the WPF, and collaborated with sympathizers overseas in order to create an international climate of support. Rallying popular enthusiasm, LEP activists even succeeded in moving President Wilson in May 1916 into publicly announcing his desire for a postwar league of nations. Typically, however, Wilson refused to endorse the LEP program and avoided any precise definition of his league ideal. He refused throughout the war to mortgage his future policy alternatives to any formula or pressure group.

While the LEP mobilized mass opinion behind the league ideal, domestic liberals gathered for the first time in industrial America in pursuit of organized peace. Meeting in September 1914 at New York's Henry Street settlement, a collection of social workers that had never before evinced serious interest in the peace question resolved itself into a pressure group committed to the defense of domestic reform in the face of the international crisis. Headed by the settlement leader Lillian Wald and the social worker spokesman Paul Kellogg, the informal "Henry Street Group" quickly formed the cutting edge of antimilitarist agitation within the United States. It attacked ardent interventionists like Theodore Roosevelt, sidestepped the LEP, and urged Wilson to seek neutral mediation of the war and eventual international reform. Chicago progressives meanwhile showed the same need for action. In December 1915 the pacifist Louis Lochner, executive secretary of the Chicago Peace Society, and Jane Addams convened an Emergency Peace Federation of veteran peace activists, suffragists, and social reformers to press for neutral mediation and oppose preparedness. Convinced that "the real enemy was militarism," urban liberals gravitated toward the peace cause in order to defend reform opportunities at home that would be killed by war abroad.[28]

In the first years of the war, progressive peace seekers worked hardest to convene a continuing conference of neutral mediators, a proposal most cogently developed by the University of Wisconsin English professor Julia Grace Wales. Feminists, especially, rallied behind the idea. Prompted by the suffragist champion Carrie Chapman Catt, nearly three thousand leading women met in Washington in January 1915 and formed the Woman's Peace Party (WPP)

in a dramatic attempt to mobilize the political consciousness of
international womanhood against the war.[29] Joining a wide range of
women's organizations, the WPP concentrated popular attention
upon the need to establish a continuing conference of available
neutral mediators. The Party also provided a powerful springboard
for the ever-present Addams and the indefatigable Hungarian pacifist Rosika Schwimmer in the spring of 1915, when they helped the
International Congress of Women, meeting at The Hague, try to
end the war through neutral mediation.

After some discussion, The Hague conferees agreed to call for a
peace built upon national self-determination, international organization, and democratic control of foreign policy. Neatly, they tied
together the three top tenets of wartime international liberalism.
Less successfully, several top feminists tried to travel directly from
The Hague to the capitals of the major belligerents in order to draw
from their leaders support for mediation by a conference of neu-
trals. Some, like the Wellesley College economist Emily Greene
Balch, felt that the entire effort was ridiculous; "but even being
ridiculous is useful sometimes," she decided, when it brought
about actions that the most hardened warmaking governments
were afraid to chance.[30] The International Congress of Women did
not stop the war, but it established at The Hague a base for neutral
mediation that was available throughout the war. And it proved
the source four years later of the Women's International League for
Peace and Freedom (WILPF), the first feminist-pacifist organization
to emerge in modern times in the transnational drive toward peace
through justice. "Never," says Sondra Herman, "was American
feminism more militant than in its pacifist crusade."[31]

The idea of a continuing conference of neutral mediators took on
dramatic new form later in 1915. Encouraged by Rosika Schwimmer
and Louis Lochner, the industrialist Henry Ford decided in the fall
to charter the *S.S. Oscar II* for the purpose of transporting a delegation of citizen-mediators to Europe in order to concentrate the
strength of neutral opinion against the war. It was a worth-
while—if misconstrued—enterprise. Ignored by the warring governments and ridiculed by the press, over fifty volunteer peace pilgrims plus a large retinue of supporters and reporters reached
Christiana, Norway, in December and proceeded on to Hamburg,
Copenhagen, The Hague, and Stockholm. The unpredictable Ford,
who poured nearly $500,000 into the enterprise, left the expedition

in late December and returned to the United States. Only Lochner and Schwimmer saw the effort through to its conclusion, establishing in Stockholm in January 1916 a Neutral Conference for Continuous Mediation. Their achievement was both frustrating and unique. "Never before," Barbara Kraft has written, "had a gathering of neutral citizens, acting in the name of the people, asked warring nations to stop fighting and settle their disputes, not on the basis of military conquest, but according to the principles of justice and humanity."[32] But the belligerent states had no interest in their pleas. Every man that died added more justification to the need for a war to the knife. And the men died wholesale.

Appalled by Europe's carnage, a group of Social Gospel clergymen, Quakers, and YMCA officials met in Garden City, New York, in November 1915 to consider ways of applying a pacific Christian solution to the suffering. Inspired by the newly formed British Fellowship of Reconciliation and its leader Henry T. Hodgkin, over forty Christian activists agreed to form an American Fellowship of Reconciliation (FOR) as an expression of their commitment to Jesus's primary injunction to love and of their refusal to sanction war in any form. They adopted absolute pacifism as the means toward human healing. "I was a long while coming to it," the young minister Norman Thomas wrote in expressing a sentiment typical of early FOR members, "but finally became convinced that so far as I could see war and Christianity are incompatible; that you cannot conquer war by war; cast out Satan by Satan; or do the enormous evil of war that good may come." Other Christians might consider his views as "extreme and unwarranted," Thomas conceded; "but I cannot fail to record the faith that is in me."[33] At first, the Fellowship was not an action agency, mainly because most liberal Protestants were unfamiliar with the pacifist ethic. Yet it proved in time the first nerve center of modern liberal pacifism. It became the meeting ground of those social progressives who discovered in pacifism an active instrument of reform and those traditional sectarian pacifists (mostly Quakers) who realized that peace could not subsist without larger social change.

But the country's Calvinist President had little use for Christian love as an instrument of policy. After showing an early interest in the peace seekers' proposals,[34] Wilson shifted in the fall of 1915 toward a policy of active preparedness. In November he submitted to the Congress a request for expanded military expenditures, including plans for a 400,000 man "Continental Army" and a naval building program that would bring America into a position of parity with Britain by 1925. The President's proposals ignited a long and bitter public debate over the adequacy of national defense preparedness and provoked the formation of a broad antimilitarist opposition. The erratic but influential William Jennings Bryan, who had resigned as Secretary of State in May because of his opposition to the President's hard-line policy toward Germany, criticized Wilson for "joy-riding with the jingoes" and catering to munitions-makers.[35] Socialists attacked the administration's plans as consistent with capitalist America's practice of nationalizing the blood and money of working people for the private interests of the property holding few. Conservatives like Nicholas Murray Butler (who was Taft's Republican running mate in 1912) helped form the American League to Limit Armaments. And liberals grew restless.

Sparked by Wald and the vivacious Crystal Eastman, the liberals' antipreparedness effort grew to new strength in April 1916, when members of the Anti-Preparedness Committee (heir to the Henry Street Group) established the American Union Against Militarism (AUAM) as the foremost center of opposition to the administration's military requests. With at least 1,000 members organized in 22 cities, the AUAM generated contributions of $50,000 in a year-long fight against plans for conscription and in an attempt to reinvigorate a domestic reform crusade. Activists in the AUAM distributed literature, petitioned legislators, and dispatched luminaries like David Starr Jordan and Oswald Garrison Villard, the pacifist editor of *The Nation*, to rallies across the country. Organizing and agitating, the AUAM not only checked the influence of militant interventionist groups; it also helped calm Mexican-American relations in the summer of 1916, when General John J. Pershing's military intervention nearly precipitated major war. Yet neither the AUAM's organization nor its arguments could halt the government's rearmament campaign. In May 1916 the Congress approved the administration's preparedness program in almost every aspect, eliminating only the proposal for a "Continental Army."[36]

Incredibly, however, the progressives' long fight against the President's preparedness program did not move them to desert Wilson in the 1916 presidential election. Negatively, they felt little attraction to the Republican nominee, Charles Evans Hughes. Positively, they felt genuine enthusiasm for Wilson following his shift toward advanced reform. Beginning in January the President backed the Congress in concluding a series of landmark progressive legislative achievements, including laws regarding rural credits, workmen's compensation, child labor reforms, and fuller autonomy for the Philippines. Within months, Wilson worked a change in his political coloration that was maximized at the Democratic convention in June, when Bryan extolled him as the candidate of peace and reform. Powerfully, Wilson's re-election campaign pounded forward for the next four months upon those allied themes.

The President's shift to the left made him irresistible among the proponents of change. Jane Addams, who had seconded Theodore Roosevelt's presidential nomination at the 1912 Progressive Party convention, declared her support of Wilson in a move seconded by many former "Bull Moosers." The fractious New York intellectual community, including Villard, Columbia University philosopher John Dewey, and the influential Herbert Croly, editor of *The New Republic*, backed the President with the same determination shown by the Non-Partisan League, a collection of Populist stalwarts in the upper Mississippi Valley. Even Marxists like the economist Scott Nearing and revolutionary socialists like the writer John Reed voted for Wilson over the Socialist Party candidate Allan Benson, who had accepted the nomination in place of the ailing Eugene V. Debs. Plainly, Wilson returned to the White House upon the strength of a progressive-peace coalition that, as Arthur Link has observed, constituted "the most important phenomenon" of the election.[37]

Wilson reached the peak of his popularity among progressive peace seekers in January 1917, when he called for "a peace between equals" secured by "some definite concert of power" committed to self-determination, free trade, and arms limitation.[38] Two weeks later, he discarded that popularity when he broke diplomatic relations with Germany over Berlin's decision to unleash its submarines against any ships afloat in British waters. For Germany, it was a desperate gamble to isolate and destroy British power. For Wilson, it was the last straw. Outraged by Germany's unilateral renunciation of past pledges of restraint regarding submarine warfare, the President pressed Berlin to reverse its decision even as he prepared to arm U.S. merchantmen and prime the country for war. Frantically, peace seekers scrambled to prevent violence. After a tense meeting in February with prewar peace advocates (who refused to interfere with Wilson's policy-making prerogatives), progressive peace reformers argued for diplomatic restraint and a popular referendum on any decision for war. But their shouts were overcome by the clamor of events. On April 2 the Congress declared war and threw the country into an international civil war that worked profound changes at home as well as abroad.

Fired by the national emergency, conservative nationalists moved forward after 1917 to attack both anticapitalist radicals and liberal reformers. Backed by government officials at all levels, right-wing militants seized on the symbols of American nationhood, starting with the flag and the national anthem, in order to cast left-wing critics as enemies not only of the American economic order but of the country itself. Advancing fast, they shoved domestic progressives into defensive bunkers, especially after the Bolshevik Revolution in November 1917, from which the left did not escape until the New Deal. In the meantime, Wilson's war for international liberalism was obliged to proceed without large parts of the left; and the new peace movement shriveled along with other reform impulses.

Virtually every prominent prewar peace advocate supported the U.S. military effort. Legalist leaders of the ASIL simply suspended their work, explaining that the world chaos made the study and extension of international law quite irrelevant. More aggressively, the CEIP set aside its low keyed peace preachments and research in favor of the slogan, "Peace Through Victory," while the APS endorsed Wilson's campaign "to secure recognition of the claims of justice and humanity" through force of arms.[39] The LEP flung money, organizers, and pamphlets into a massive campaign to persuade the public that the war was being waged for the sake of a league that would protect the future peace against potential aggressors. Protestant peace spokesmen in the CPU, FCCCA, and WAIFTC gravely blessed the U.S. intervention. Even more, church peace leaders joined LEP activists in forming the National Committee on the Churches and the Moral Aims of the War in a sustained attempt to give moral gloss to the American war machine.

Progressive peace seekers and antiwar socialists meanwhile fractionalized over the war issue. The Woman's Peace Party shrank precipitously as Carrie Chapman Catt and other suffragists seized on the war emergency as a means of affirming women's patriotism and winning their first objective—a constitutional amendment granting women the vote. Other feminists equivocated. Jane Addams and Lillian Wald, for example, each refused to endorse the war; but both toured the country in support of administration efforts to improve national food and health policies for the sake of the war effort. Organized socialists likewise split. At a special April convention in St. Louis, the Socialist Party bravely declared its opposition to the U.S. intervention. But the Party foundered badly when several of its best-known supporters, including Upton Sinclair and John Spargo, joined Samuel Gompers and the American Federation of Labor craft unions in supporting the war in return for unprecedented governmental assistance to organizing labor.

The AUAM, backed by Lochner's Emergency Peace Federation, immediately attacked Wilson's declaration of war and rallied antiwar activists in different parts of the country. Then intensifying preparation for war—and rising resentment toward the war's opponents—broke the will of AUAM leaders like Paul Kellogg and cleanly split the organization. Regrouping in September 1917, half of the AUAM leadership backed the young pacifist and social worker Roger Baldwin in forming the Civil Liberties Bureau (forerunner of the 1920 American Civil Liberties Union) as a means of protesting conscription, protecting the rights of conscientious objectors, and defending First Amendment freedoms in the face of the war crisis.[40] In the same month the second half joined Kellogg and Wald in forming the cryptically titled "Committee on Nothing At All."

The Committee on Nothing At All, which became the League of Free Nations Association in November 1918 (and, three years later, the Foreign Policy Association), gave organizational force to a new strain of liberal internationalism that supported U.S. intervention as the quickest way toward major international reform. Liberal internationalists cared little about courts, but much about science, industry, economics, and administration. Concerned more with ordering change than enforcing order, they believed that peace was a rational social process that evolved most efficiently under the direction of international experts and administrators who planned systematically for industrial reform and ameliorative justice. Certainly these thoughts were well represented at the Committee's first meeting in New York, which was dominated by social workers like Wald and Kellogg, publicists like Croly, and liberal academicians like Dewey and the Columbia University historian

Charles Beard. All believed in the necessity of pragmatic but expert social planning and economic democracy. All felt uneasy with the LEP's understanding of peace as order enforced through Great Power deterrence. And all felt hope in Wilson's liberal promises.

Intrigued by the chance to use the war to energize the national government, liberal internationalists wanted to help Wilson and liberals everywhere in moving through the world crisis to construct a postwar international organization that would sustain peace through planned reconstruction, liberalized trade, and social democratization. Stubborn rationalists, they viewed war as a social atavism favored by a fading class of irresponsible autocrats; and they resolved to displace it through a systematized international structure of administrative experts and regulatory agencies that would manage peace as efficiently as they would direct other aspects of the world's emerging order of industrial interdependence. Liberal internationalists wanted not only to create a new league of nations but also to reform the world social order beyond the reach of reactionary conservatives and revolutionary socialists. "The sword won't do the job any more!" Beard proclaimed. "The old talk about sovereignty, rights of man, dictatorship of the proletariat, triumphant democracy and the like is pure bunk. It will not run trains or weave cloth or hold society together."[41] But progressive experts would, and they would bring peace in the process.

Hastily, liberal internationalists converged from several directions in 1917 to support Wilson in his war for international reform. Some like Raymond B. Fosdick, a New York lawyer and former settlement house worker who became an Assistant Secretary of War, directed a corps of progressives in keeping military training camps free of alcohol and prostitutes and thus keeping the men "Fit to Fight." Others like the Columbia history professor James T. Shotwell and the Harvard law professor Manley O. Hudson joined the Inquiry, a secret White House study group organized by Walter Lippmann and Colonel Edward M. House for the purpose of equipping the President with the rational building blocks of a scientifically planned peace. Drawn by the war into their first serious peace commitment, they and their sympathizers saw the European cataclysm as a matchless opportunity to twist world history at this "plastic juncture" in a more progressive direction.[42]

Other leftists, however, felt less confidence in the liberals' power to turn the war to serve their ends. Challenging the self-proclaimed "realism" of the liberal internationalists, the acerbic Randolph Bourne questioned how prowar liberals could seriously think that they were equipped to channel "the fierce urgencies" of the war into positive democratic outlets. Speaking for a tribe of cultural radicals that John Diggins has aptly termed "the lyrical left," Bourne turned upon prowar internationalists with Deweyan logic. "If the war is too strong for you to prevent," he asked disingenuously, "how is it going to be weak enough for you to control and mould to your liberal purposes?"[43] Wisely, Dewey and other prowar liberals declined to respond to Bourne's challenge. Intellectually, they had no response.

In the meantime, the active antiwar opposition in America narrowed to a hard core of antiwar socialists, FOR-related liberal pacifists, and scattered urban intellectuals who wanted an immediate, negotiated peace without annexations or indemnities. Although they maintained a noisy press and persuasive arguments, most antiwar activists operated with an acute sense of personal loneliness and without any real success in restraining the U.S. war effort. Yet they appeared to prowar enthusiasts to present a dangerous rallying point for the latent antiwar sentiment that pockmarked the country. Many German- and Irish-Americans had little interest in fighting against the Fatherland or for Great Britain. Unorganized migrant workers in western mining and lumber camps thought that there was more reason to attack their class enemies at home than strangers overseas. One-time southern Populists like Tom Watson denounced what he felt was a war to save the world for Wall Street, while antiwar voters cast their sentiments at ballot boxes. Standing as the only antiwar party, socialists recorded impressive gains in the off-year elections of 1917, receiving between 20–50 percent of the vote in a string of municipal contests between New York and Chicago. The antiwar opposition did not need to raise a movement. It had only to activate it.

And activation was precisely what government officials, business leaders, and prowar progressives and trade unionists were determined to prevent. Moving briskly, government leaders joined vigilante organizations like the American Defense Society or prowar groups like Gompers' American Alliance for Labor and Democracy in smashing both antiwar dissenters and sideline doubters through a combination of legal, extralegal, and illegal means. In the process, the forces of authority set off a three-year reign of intimidation, racial violence, political jailings, police attacks, vigilante lynchings, and alien deportations that came later to be known as the Red Scare. It was more truly the White Fright. And it worked its effect. "The years 1917 and 1918," says John Chambers, "represented both the peak of dedication by a relative handful of pacifists and the nadir of the scope and impact of the peace movement as it withered under the forces of alienation and repression."[44]

Upon the national level, the White Fright began in the spring of 1917, when the Wilson administration prepared to compel national war loyalty through statutory law. In May the President signed the Selective Service Act, which required the registration for conscription into the armed forces of all American males between the ages of eighteen and thirty-five. One month later, he approved the Espionage Act, which among other things prescribed stiff punishment for anyone who made "false statements" regarding American military operations or caused or did "attempt to cause insubordination, disloyalty, mutiny, or refusal of duty" in the armed forces or obstructed the conscription program.[45] Federal officers failed to snare a single German spy or saboteur under the dragnet power of the Espionage Act. But they found in it a singularly successful means of silencing the antiwar opposition.

Tactically, the Wilson administration first moved against antiwar activists by singling out leading socialists and officers of the Industrial Workers of the World for highly publicized arrests and trials. On September 5, 1917, federal agents raided IWW headquarters in 33 different cities between Chicago and Los Angeles. Three weeks later, 113 IWW leaders were arraigned in a Chicago federal court on charges of obstructing the war effort. Within one year, 96 were tried, convicted, and jailed, most following a giant showcase trial during the summer of 1918. At the same time, several members of the national executive committee of the Socialist Party were arrested on similar charges. Most went the way of the IWW leaders. By spring 1918 about one-third of the Party's hierarchy was in—or on its way—to federal prison, while those who remained free lost any means of affecting war politics. With Wilson's encouragement, Postmaster General Albert S. Burleson barred from the mails socialist and other publications that criticized the U.S. intervention. With one swing, the administration cut the intellectual lifeline of organized socialism in America and the largest single source of antiwar dissent.

Along another salient, federal authorities quietly minimized the visibility of those men who refused for reasons of conscience to participate in the war. Under a policy restricted at first to members of the Historic Peace Churches, conscientious objectors were given a choice of noncombatant military service or confinement under military authority. Either way they were to be inducted and isolated. At first, nearly 65,000 of the country's 3 million draft-liable men laid claim to CO status. But fewer than 4,000 adhered to their position to the point of suffering assignments to army encampments. Most were scriptural literalists who rejected military service as contrary to their deepest religious beliefs. But a significant number were Christian social reformers, like Evan Thomas and Roger Baldwin, who viewed conscription as central to the whole war system and destructive of the absolute value of the individual human being. Gravely, they attacked conscription as the most egregious symptom of the growing power of the nation-state, and wondered "whether the state which considers it necessary for its own security is worth the price."[46]

Under direct military control, those COs confined to army camps experienced treatment that ranged from distant respect to beatings and abuse, and the death through neglect of at least two. Gradually, however, government officials adjusted to the liberal pacifists' demands for some positive alternative actions. Spurred by the Quaker historian Rufus Jones, Philadelphia-area Friends formed the American Friends Service Committee (AFSC) in April 1917 for the purpose of engaging young Quaker noncombatants voluntarily in the work of war relief and reconstruction. The Wilson administration proved surprisingly supportive. Aiming to spread *"the irresistible and constructive power of goodwill,"* AFSC volunteers grew crops in wartime France and rebuilt villages; and, after the war, they battled disease and famine from Russia to Austria.[47] Organizationally, the Committee marked one more step in the fusion of individual renunciation of violence with a commitment to systematic social reform, a fusion that defined liberal pacifism. But its achievements and promise were eclipsed during the war by the country's preoccupation with military victory and domestic conformity.

While the national government moved on one level, state and local authorities helped in other ways to silence the antiwar opposition. Their effectiveness was most visible in the experience of the People's Council of America for Peace and Democracy. Organized during the spring of 1917 by pacifists like Lochner and radical socialists like Scott Nearing, the People's Council pressed for an immediate negotiated peace, the repeal of conscription, the defense of civil liberties, and (later) support of the Bolshevik Revolution. Radical and pacifist, the Council proved a standing challenge to conservative America as well as to the national war effort. Yet the disposition of the organization was left to state and local—and not federal—power.

In September 1917 Minnesota Governor J. A. Burnquist disrupted Lochner's attempt to convene a constituent assembly of the People's Council in Minneapolis, considered friendly territory because of the power of the local Non-Partisan League. Moving to Fargo, North Dakota, Lochner was summarily driven from town by an orderly mob of respectable patriots and local police. He received the same treatment soon after in Hudson, Wisconsin. Fleeing to Chicago, Lochner finally gathered a small group of supporters at the city's seedy West Side Auditorium at the sufferance of the flamboyant Mayor William Hale Thompson, before Illinois Governor Frank O. Lowden ordered four companies of state militia to Chicago to disperse the gathering. It was the first time since the 1894 Pullman Strike that the Illinois militia had been mobilized to overcome a menace to the public order.

Antiwar activists were flabbergasted. Even the Socialist Party leader Eugene V. Debs, who had led the Pullman strikers and had endured much public abuse for acting in pursuit of his beliefs, expressed shock over the government-sanctioned attack upon the People's Council and the larger suppression of civil liberties. "I cannot yet believe," he wrote early in 1918 to one socialist convicted of violating the Espionage Act, "that they will ever dare to send you to prison for exercising your constitutional rights of free speech, but if they do . . . I shall feel guilty to be at large."[48] Six months later, Debs drew a ten-year jail sentence for an antiwar speech in Canton, Ohio.

Abetted by government authorities and influential citizens, the White Fright rubbed the rawest nerves of white racism, antiunionism, and nativism. In July 1917, random white attacks on blacks in East St. Louis, Illinois, produced an outburst of racial rioting that left 38 blacks and 8 whites dead and hundreds injured. It was the worst explosion of interracial violence in American history, and a mere prelude to similar violence that erupted two years later across the country in towns between Texas and Boston. In the same month, top managerial officials in the Arizona copper fields joined local vigilantes and police in attacking IWW miners who were agitating for higher wages and better working conditions. Branding the dissident miners as pro-German sympathizers, masked mobs in Jerome and Bisbee rounded up over 1,000 miners, packed them into sealed railroad cars, and shipped them miles into the desert without food, water, or means of return. It proved an early symptom of what later came to be known as the "deportation delirium."

Predictably, practitioners of the White Fright also turned during the war upon social dissidents and ethnic aliens, especially German- and Scandinavian-Americans. Extending the country's long tradition of middle-class vigilante violence, local figures of respectability and power unleashed a veritable "reign of terror" across the nation against dissidents and in defense of conservative nationalism.[49] Generally, they were satisfied with tactics of harassment and intimidation; sometimes they were violent. Over sixty people were hanged or burned to death by mobs in wartime America, most often by southern white vigilantes habituated to a regional method of racial control. But many were victims of the domestic bloodlust stirred by the war. In April 1918, for instance, Robert Prager, a young German-born baker in the strife-torn coal town of Collinsville, Illinois, was seized by patriots who stripped and beat him, wrapped him in an American flag, and unceremoniously hanged him. Prompted by national expressions of concern and the local jury's acquittal of Prager's accused murderers, President Wilson finally issued a public condemnation of mob actions. But his words blew away in the winds of xenophobia that his war had generated.

In a larger way, wartime xenophobia also blew apart the formative foundations of the practical peace reform and cleared the way for a new peace movement. Between 1901 and 1914, practical peace advocates had established the most socially respectable and politically influential private peace agencies in American history. But their narrow class vision, political conservatism, and optimistic nationalism left them incapable after 1915 of proposing and pursuing a peacemaking U.S. approach toward the Great European War. Instead, the war shouldered them aside as it forced its way into American politics with a power that obliged social progressives to face frontally, for the first time since the Civil War, the relationship of war to domestic reform. The result was the birth of the modern American peace movement. Practical peace advocates persisted in their preferred approaches after 1915. But peace activism gained fresh significance and momentum as two vibrant new modes of action—liberal internationalism and liberal pacifism—appeared after 1915.

Although both emanated from a common source in progressivism, liberal internationalists and liberal pacifists were initially opposed in several ways. First they differed over the war. Liberal internationalists in the early Foreign Policy Association supported U.S. intervention as the best means toward a reformed world order; liberal pacifists in the FOR opposed the intervention on the grounds that the means of war invariably determined an end of more war. They also differed over the possibilities of social change. Liberal internationalists remained reform gradualists, confident in the planned beneficence of enlightened capitalism. Liberal pacifists, on the other hand, proved more receptive to socialist analyses of the systemic nature of capitalism's failings and more radical in their prescriptions for its overhaul and displacement. Finally, they differed over methods for effecting peace. Liberal internationalists believed that independent nation-states cooperating voluntarily through international mechanisms could best sustain a lasting peace. Liberal pacifists saw peace as a transnational process that subsisted in individual and group cooperation in the outworking of common values and institutions.

Yet liberal internationalists and liberal pacifists held more in common than in opposition. First of all, both had roots in the country's prewar liberal tradition, which blended the sensibilities of Social Gospel Christianity, a socialist mode of social analysis, and a pragmatic concern with ends and means. Imbued with this tradition, both therefore treated peace as a social process. Peace was in their eyes an ongoing process of reconciling peoples by means of democratic structures developed through self-conscious human planning. It was a condition that was made and lived, and not ordered and enforced. Moreover, both peace persuasions were dominated by a generation of well-educated young men and women who had been radicalized by their confrontation with war as was no other generation in American history before Vietnam. Eclectic, individualistic, and energetic, liberal internationalists like Raymond Fosdick and James Shotwell and liberal pacifists like

John Nevin Sayre and Norman Thomas emerged from the Great War to spearhead American peace activism for the next quarter-century. Driven by a new postwar urgency, the pursuit of peace would never again stand merely as a desirable or even as a practical reform. It had become a simple necessity.

Chapter Six
The Necessary Reform

The World War of 1914–1918 devastated Europe, subverted colonialism overseas, abetted the Bolshevik triumph in Russia, and strengthened America. It also fired the formation of the most dynamic peace movement in American history. Driven by the new-style pacifists and internationalists who had organized after 1915, crowds of feminists, educators, reform lawyers, liberal Protestants, and progressive activists surged forward after 1919 in an attempt to convert America's new international power into the driving wedge toward a lasting peace. At first they tried to build the peace. Gathering in new combinations, postwar peace seekers pressured national policy makers toward the Washington Disarmament Conference of 1921–1922, World Court membership, and a series of new arbitration agreements capped in 1928 by the Pact of Paris. By the early thirties, however, peace workers were driven from the task of building peace by the need to prevent new war. And by the late thirties they divided over the question of American involvement in that war.

Throughout this period, peace seeking in America passed through a painful process of frustration and vindication, fulfillment and fragmentation. Operating on many levels, peace reformers pursued a variety of individual but overlapping concerns. Antimilitarists protested the spreading influence of the armed forces in American life. Feminists promoted disarmament and peace education, and pacifists urged the necessity of a conciliating nonviolence. Anti-imperialists attacked U.S. intervention in Latin America. Legalists talked of outlawing war, while internationalists exalted the League of Nations and World Court. Alternately clashing and cooperating, peace workers came into sharp conflict with each other, first over America's relationship to the League, and then over plans to resist German and Japanese expansion in the 1930s. Plainly, there was no single American search for peace between 1919 and 1941. Yet there was an extraordinarily active peace movement.

Peace activists moved forward after 1919 as they were joined together by one slender but tough tendon of common conviction: they believed that peace was the necessary reform. Having confronted the enormity of modern total war, peace reformers felt sure for the first time that peace was not only morally right and practically desirable. It was necessary. It was necessary if modern industrial man were to survive his own capacity to deploy the incalculable and uncontrollable power of modern science and technology. The war had clarified the terms of human survival. Unless controlled, the same forces of science and industry that had given life to the modern world would bring it, through war, certain death.

Between 1919 and 1925 peace seekers organized along three main salients, producing within one brief span the most durable peace agencies in modern America. Internationalists committed to some supranational housing for international relations formed the League of Free Nations Association in 1918 and the League of Nations Non-Partisan Association in 1923.* Pacifists dedicated to the nonviolent realization of transnational social justice gathered in the Women's International League for Peace and Freedom in 1919 and the War Resisters League in 1924. Liberal reformers who oscillated between internationalism and pacifism organized the National Council for Prevention of War in 1922 and the National Conference on the Cause and Cure of War in 1924.

Gearing for the long haul, peace reformers wanted to impress the American electorate with the necessity of peace. More immediately, they tried to recharge national policy with some peacemaking potency. Their first opportunity in this effort came early in 1919, when the victorious Allied leaders met at the Paris Peace Conference to give form to the postwar world. But liberal peace seekers found the experience more sobering than encouraging. Supporting Woodrow Wilson, they were shocked when the President's plans for the peaceful integration of Germany into a stable European order (which isolated the Soviet Union) collided so

*The latter retitled itself the League of Nations Association in 1929, and then underwent several name changes during World War II, until it emerged as the United Nations Association of the United States of America.

forcefully with the more punitive intentions of Britain and France. Citizen peace workers were demoralized by the victors' tawdry quarreling over the spoils of war, and they felt positively dissatisfied with the negotiated League of Nations formula. Fixed in Article I of the Versailles Treaty, the League Covenant figured as one more compromise among the victor states. Setting aside French fears of a renascent Germany, Wilson and British Prime Minister David Lloyd George devised a League system that combined British plans for regular Great Power assemblies with the President's preference for voluntary cooperation in times of crisis. Returning to America, Wilson promoted the Covenant as the capstone of the Treaty and his peacemaking efforts and Article X as the capstone of the Covenant.*

Surprisingly, peace reformers provided little help at home for Wilson's League crusade. Conservative legalists opposed the President's work. Pacifists ignored it. And internationalists split. After declaring its full support for Wilson in early 1919, the Republican-dominated League to Enforce Peace divided over the need to add reservations to the Covenant in order to secure Senate ratification, and disintegrated as an effective pro-League agency. Liberal Protestants in the FCCCA and WAIFTC proselytized actively for the League cause. But neither they nor feminists organized in groups like The Woman's Pro-League Council (Non-Partisan) could shake nationalist suspicions of indeterminate overseas commitments or affect the deadlocked parliamentary process. Wilson rejected reservations to his Covenant. Most Republicans required them. A bipartisan coalition of anti-League Irreconcilables would have neither reservations nor the Covenant. And neither is what the country got.

Liberal internationalists in the LFNA did not even try to affect the political struggle in Washington, mostly because of their own internal divisions. Some, like the dynamic young lawyer Raymond Fosdick, who served with the American delegation at Versailles, conceded that the Treaty was illiberal "from every standpoint, and

---

*The crucial Article X obliged League members to "undertake to respect and preserve as against external aggression the territorial integrity and existing political independence of all Members of the League. In case of any such aggression or in case of any threat or danger of such aggression the Council shall advise upon the means by which this obligation shall be fulfilled." Ray Stannard Baker, *Woodrow Wilson and the World Settlement*, 3 vols. (Garden City, N.Y.: Doubleday, Doran, & Co., 1922), III, p. 179.

there can be no hope of permanent peace under its auspices."[1] Yet he insisted that the League was necessary to correct the Treaty's failings and to effect gradual global reconstruction. Others, like the philosopher John Dewey and the journalist Walter Lippmann, wrote off the League as a Great Power combine designed to impose a retrograde peace. Renouncing Wilson's work, Dewey joined a Chicago lawyer named Salmon O. Levinson in a crusade to bring about the Outlawry of War. Winning the support of other progressives, Dewey and Levinson urged the United States to lead the other nations in declaring war a crime, codifying international law, and establishing a world court free of League control. They wanted to reform world politics under law without risking foreign entanglement.[2]

With its membership split, the LFNA leadership declined Wilson's personal request for help in his campaign and pressed instead for the greater democratization of the League and the liberalization of the Versailles Treaty. Activists in the LFNA argued for greater free trade, against re-intervention in Mexico, and for the recognition of the Soviet government in Russia. In 1921 Association leaders retitled the organization the Foreign Policy Association (FPA) to convey more smoothly the image of a reliable fact-finding and educational agency. But the organization's liberal priorities remained clear and steadfast. It valued international reconstruction and reform over the heedless imposition of order.

Pacifists had even less use for Wilson's work. *The Nation*'s Oswald Garrison Villard attacked the punitive aspects of the Versailles settlement and urged complete nonentanglement in European politics. The New York preacher John Haynes Holmes condemned the League as an alliance of victor states, and enlisted in the Outlawry of War campaign. In a more positive spirit, Jane Addams, Emily Greene Balch, and other female pacifists called for a reformed League, as they presided early in 1919 over the formation of the WILPF at Zurich. Relocating soon after to Geneva, WILPF leaders attacked the Allied food blockade of Germany, criticized the coercive bases of the Covenant, and promoted economic reconstruction. They wanted the League to work, but more for people than governments. Organizing in national sections throughout the world, WILPF pacifists believed that people must eat before they could make peace. They believed that peace came primarily through nonviolent action against hunger, hurting, and injustice.

Liberal pacifists in the Protestant clergy felt the same way. Caught up in the country's postwar industrial crisis, newly awakened pacifists like Kirby Page joined workers in defending wartime advances in wages and collective bargaining against a combined government-business counterattack. Organizing in 1921 in the Fellowship for a Christian Social Order (an extension of the FOR), liberal pacifist clerics assumed an active role in several labor conflicts that scarred the postwar years. Some, like Norman Thomas and A. J. Muste, left their churches in pursuit of the workers' cause. Others like Page remained to crusade within American Protestantism. But none showed any interest in helping Woodrow Wilson save the world for democracy through the League. They were too busy seeking to secure simple justice within industrial America.

Lacking the support of peace seekers and other organized liberals, Wilson tried to bulldoze his Treaty without reservations through a Senate dominated by the opposition party. The surprise was not that he failed but that he even came close. Paralyzed from a stroke suffered in September 1919, the President clung to his position as the Senate rejected two attempts at the unreserved ratification of the Treaty in September 1919 and March 1920. Eight months after the second vote, Ohio's Warren G. Harding rode to a landslide presidential victory in a contest that the stricken Wilson had billed as a national referendum on the League. With the Republican victory, the League cause gradually expired as a serious issue in American politics. The Democrats could not win with it. The victorious Republicans did not need it.

With the League issue in limbo, a determined coalition of feminist, Protestant, and internationalist groups assembled in the spring of 1921 to drive the Harding administration toward disarmament. Impressively, they worked some tangible results. At Harding's request, representatives of the Great Powers gathered in Washington over the winter of 1921–1922 and agreed upon a new security framework for the Pacific that opened the way toward naval arms reduction and a holiday on new construction. By any measure, the Washington Conference signaled the finest achievement of positive citizen peace action in the interwar period. If the League fight bared the limits of citizen peacemaking, the campaign for the Washington disarmament treaties demonstrated its continued importance: citizen peacemaking strengthened politicians in pursuit of their better instincts.

Invigorated by success, leaders of the disarmament coalition agreed in 1922 to support the Quaker activist Frederick Libby in forming the National Council for Prevention of War (NCPW) as an umbrella agency of constituent groups that ranged from the National League of Women Voters to the Veterans of Foreign Wars. The NCPW aimed to build peace through the construction of an overwhelming popular consensus against war. Practically, Libby believed, the first problem with organized peace seeking was that, while left-wing elements designed the best strategies, right-wing leaders directed the great mass of workers. Therefore, the job of the NCPW was "to keep just a little ahead of the right wing" so as to consolidate a slow but steady advance toward the strategies of the left: disarmament, the World Court, and, eventually, the League of Nations.[3]

At first glance, internationalists could use the help. After the LEP disintegrated during the Treaty fight, internationalists lacked any effective means for promoting the League cause. With Harding in the White House, Republican internationalists like George Wickersham (a former attorney general in the Taft administration) felt satisfied in entrusting the League issue to the new administration. Democratic internationalists felt less confident. Goaded by Fosdick and Hamilton Holt, Democratic and independent internationalists demanded that Republicans join in the formation of a national pro-League pressure organization. After months of bickering, the two sides succeeded in January 1923 in establishing the League of Nations Non-Partisan Association (LNNPA) under the joint direction of Wickersham and John Hessin Clarke, a Wilson appointee who had recently resigned from the Supreme Court in order to fight publicly for the League. Within weeks, the LNNPA became the most muscular pro-League organization in the country. Membership climbed to 20,000. Money poured in from most parts of the country. Even the Harding administration paid mute tribute to the effectiveness and potential of the new internationalist combine in February, when the President called for U.S. accession to the League's Permanent Court of International Justice, or World Court, on the basis of four conditions. Internationalists were ecstatic. With America headed toward the Court, its attachment to the League again seemed a real possibility.

Actually, Harding's decision in support of the Court—and the opposition that decision generated among anti-League activists—

created a dilemma that gripped peace activists until the Senate finally rejected the Court bill in 1935. On the one side, most serious analysts agreed that American accession to the Court constituted only a minor step toward an organized peace. Yet the very insignificance of the Court proposal magnified the need to secure it, for failure would reveal the real weakness of postwar peace seeking. Trapped between the meagerness of the Court gesture and the implications that would result from its failure, peace leaders waded into battle in its behalf. Feminists and mainline Protestant peace activists took particular interest in the cause and shrewdly turned the issue into the broadest common denominator of direct peace action. Seeing that the Court's very insignificance left it noncontroversial, feminist and Protestant peace leaders championed the cause among those uncommitted millions of Americans who favored tokens of international cooperation. Libby and the NCPW became the driving center for pro-Court activism, while a broad band of moderate church groups and women's organizations coordinated supporting sentiment.

Women provided both animating force and mass audiences to the necessary peace reform. With the suffrage cause secure, feminists turned in force after 1920 toward peace activism for a number of reasons. Most like the Ohio Supreme Court Justice Florence E. Allen, who lost two brothers on the Western Front, simply hated war. Several believed that the peace cause offered the most natural outworking of the maternal instinct. Others held that women's political freshness would bring new vitality to the peace reform. Less openly, top feminists also conceded that the peace cause was vital to the unity of the women's movement, which was threatening to fractionalize in the absence of a unifying issue. The peace reform needed women activists, but the women's movement also needed the healing peace reform.

As the two causes converged, female pacifists took the lead in organizing women in pursuit of the necessary reform. In 1919 Addams and Balch established the U.S. Section of the WILPF in Philadelphia in an attempt to move American women into cooperating with their sisters overseas in behalf of the interrelated goals of peace and social justice. Two years later the 77-year-old Fanny Garrison Villard, daughter of William Lloyd Garrison and mother of Oswald, organized the Women's Peace Society as a non-resistant cadre committed to the literal living out of Christ's peace preachments. In a schism soon after, Elinor Byrns and Caroline Babcock Lexow formed the Women's Peace Union of the Western Hemisphere as a means of mobilizing women behind a campaign for a constitutional amendment that would prohibit the Congress from voting for war. After much searching, WPU leaders finally won South Dakota Senator Lynn Frazier to the public sponsorship of their proposal. But the idea failed to make any more headway than did Frazier's aspirations for higher office.

In 1924 the veteran feminists and antimilitarists Tracy Mygatt, Frances Witherspoon, and Jessie Wallace Hughan combined a cross section of pacifists into the American branch of the War Resisters League (WRL), an international group that had been recently founded in London for the purpose of joining nonviolent resisters in public pledges against participation in future wars.* While not an explicitly feminist enterprise, the WRL was the high-water mark of pacifist leadership in the postwar women's peace movement. It also marked the first major breakthrough in modern war resistance. Crossbred from philosophical anarchism and pacifism, war resistance appeared during and after World War I among men and women of conscience who invented "a revolutionary movement" that aimed at "the abolition of war, not merely its rejection," and the construction of a global society upon the transnational values of democratic socialism. Ideally, war resisters planned to stop the next war through a massive general strike. In practice, they gathered a membership that topped 19,000 by 1942 around the simple individual pledge "not to support any kind of war, international or civil, and to strive for the removal of the causes of war." They held unflinchingly to the belief that war was nothing less than "a crime against humanity."[4]

Also in 1924 Carrie Chapman Catt assembled the National Committee on the Cause and Cure of War as an organizational clearinghouse for an annual conference of independent women's groups. Hoping to mobilize feminist peace action through a strategy of consensus, Catt invited delegates from nine of the country's largest women's organizations, ranging from the National League of Women Voters to the General Federation of Women's Clubs, to an annual Conference on the Cause and Cure of War that would

---

*The FOR, WPU, and Women's Peace Society each sent representatives to the organizational meeting, and each affiliated with the larger War Resisters International on an independent basis.

specify the country's top peace priorities. Faithfully for the next twelve years, hundreds of representatives from these organizations met annually in Washington to introduce, debate, and establish peace objectives that had a decidedly internationalist flavor. The conferences failed, however, to meet Catt's hope of building a consensual women's coalition against war. There were too many divisions within the women's movement—and too few areas of agreement—to permit a replication of the suffrage victory.

Yet popular peace sentiment percolated in the early 1920s through other sources. In June 1923 the millionaire Philadelphia publisher (and editor of the popular *Ladies Home Journal*) Edward M. Bok offered a $100,000 prize for the best brief plan that would involve the United States in the maintenance of a cooperative international peace. He called it the American Peace Award. Denying any partisan purpose, Bok gathered a distinguished collection of judges, including Elihu Root, Colonel Edward M. House, and Henry Stimson, for the purpose of selecting the winning plan. While they conferred, over 22,000 plans swamped the Award's New York City offices (staffed in large part by Eleanor Roosevelt) over the next six months. But then the campaign sputtered slowly into the new year, a victim of Washington's indifference and the spreading suspicion—which proved to be true—that the contest was adjusted to favor a pro-League formula. In early February 1924 Bok announced that the longtime peace activist Charles Levermore was the author of the winning plan and recipient of the first $50,000-half of the award. The 69-year-old Levermore died without collecting the second half, which was to be issued when the U.S. government adopted the winning plan as official policy.[5]

More strikingly, popular peace enthusiasm swelled as organized Protestantism rose in the early twenties to its highest level of influence in recent American history. Beginning in 1924 various denominational meetings and student YMCA assemblies produced powerful antiwar statements. The editorial offices of *The Christian Century*, liberal Protestantism's most influential weekly, overflowed with demands for peace action from anxious readers. The brilliant young Reinhold Niebuhr affirmed his pacifist faith and support of the FOR, while the YMCA's premier evangelist, Sherwood Eddy, professed his conversion in 1924. Plainly, as Robert M. Miller has observed, pacifism became the "'party line' of liberal Protestantism" in the early twenties.[6]

Excited by popular demands for action, pacifists, Protestants, feminists, and internationalists seized upon the World Court cause after 1924 as the most promising route toward an early peace success. Both major parties and almost every major interest group were on record in its favor. Few could find good reason to oppose it. The Court campaign furthermore gained force in October 1925, when France, Germany, and Belgium agreed at Locarno, Switzerland, to several nonaggression compacts that were underwritten by Britain and Italy and supported by a number of arbitration conventions. Rather suddenly, the Locarno pacts worked a dramatically sharp break away from the bitterness of the recent past and toward some promising harmony. American peace seekers were exultant. Three months later, the U.S. Senate added to their high spirits when it approved the administration's World Court bill with only five reservations.[7]

The peacemakers' enthusiasm was muted after 1925, however, by the contradictions that they encountered as America rushed headlong through fuller economic modernization. Combining the world's most modern industrial plant and the best credit facilities, America exported its products, loans, technology, and organizational skills overseas in the late twenties with a power that promised to transform the societies of host nations. U.S. economic expansion introduced new goods and new techniques, but it did not succeed in pacifying the world through shared self-interest in growing material betterment. On the contrary, American economic dynamism threatened to change old values in host societies, intensified nationalist resentment, and turned on its head liberalism's traditional faith that peace would be promoted by industrial interdependence. Perversely, increased material interchange was breeding more tribal animosity than goodwill. In the same way, U.S. economic dynamism accelerated at home the power of American nationalism and turned Americans more inward as they effected tremendous international achievements. The power of these twin contradictions—of the growing international involvement and interdependence that bred instability and insularity—understandably puzzled peace seekers as they worked in the late twenties to effect peace through America's influence. In some it only produced wonder. In others action.

Both pacifists and internationalists showed concern over the instability that America's economic dynamism was producing overseas and particularly in less-developed countries. Reviving anti-imperialist arguments that had lain dormant for a generation, Kirby Page protested America's deepening involvement in Near Eastern oil politics and demanded the liberation of the country's Philippine colony. Emily Balch and other WILPF leaders conducted an expert investigation of America's informal control of Haiti. In a final report drafted by the University of Chicago economist Paul Douglas, the WILPF task force attacked the U.S. neo-colonial role in the Caribbean and worried "that America may well be at a point where it must decide whether it shall be an empire or a democracy."[8] Internationalists like Catt similarly urged their followers to examine the economic sources of war and social unrest, while Foreign Policy Association leaders warned that the sudden "vastness of American foreign investments" threatened to trap the country "unknowingly and unwillingly in the mazes of economic imperialism."[9]

Most impressively, pacifists and internationalists rose up early in 1927 in an anti-imperialist coalition that proved the single most successful antiwar undertaking of the decade. Stirred by Washington's military intervention in Nicaragua in December 1926, a broad collection of peace activists lobbied Congress for the withdrawal of U.S. forces and demanded the peaceable settlement of persisting Mexican-American differences. For several reasons, Congress welcomed the anti-imperialist outburst and conveyed its own cautionary warnings to the White House. Surprised by the strength of the opposition, the Coolidge administration softened its hardline position in Nicaragua and eased its demands upon Mexico. Gently but firmly, peace workers helped to realize what historians often overlook: an episode that precluded violence and preserved calm.

Yet peace seekers failed to solve the larger problem of converting America's economic dynamism into more peaceful pursuits. In fact, the peacemakers' efforts in this direction only aggravated their differences with those right-wing nationalists whose power grew in the cultural confusion that accompanied postwar modernization. Led by the Ku Klux Klan and the American Legion, a new coalition of conservative forces emerged after 1919, dedicated to empowering the state in defense of private property and social order. Whether called "activist-repressionists" or "statist conservatives," the new rightist coalition pressed for the fuller militarization of American society at home and of its policies abroad. It also cooperated happily with the government in attacking peace reformers as subversive of the public good.[10]

The armed forces helped most to amplify right-wing power. In 1922 General Amos A. Fries, head of the War Department's Chemical Warfare Service, publicly charged the disarmament concerns of Libby and the NCPW to Communist sympathies. One year later, Fries distributed the so-called spider web chart, a broadside that graphically traced the interconnections of peace, social welfare, and religious organizations and their leaders in an inventive attempt to demonstration that "The Socialist-Pacifist Movement in America Is an Absolutely Fundamental and Integral Part of International Socialism."[11] Armed with Fries's chart, Legionnaires, Klansmen, and R.O.T.C. officers worked in the late twenties to exclude peace activists from speaking out in several parts of the country. In 1926 the University of Oklahoma banned the FOR leader John Nevin Sayre from speaking on campus after a U.S. infantry officer complained that Sayre's pacifism made him "more dangerous than an open communist." Jane Addams was vilified at nearly every one of her public appearances, while Kirby Page struggled against attempts to silence him on campuses and in churches from West Virginia to Oregon.[12]

Page's resistance exemplified the peace seekers' growing willingness to oppose spreading military influence actively. In 1924 the NCPW waged a long and successful fight against War Department plans for a national mobilization day. One year later Nevin Sayre, E. Raymond Wilson, and other FOR leaders organized the Committee on Militarism in Education (CME) to resist pressure for compulsory military training programs in the nation's schools. Although its concerns were broad, the CME position was simple: compulsory military training was by definition subversive of democratic principles. The compulsory nature of the proposed military training would override the sovereignty of the individual conscience; and drilling young men in obedience and death-dealing undermined the first values of a free Christian society.[13]

Antimilitarist activism constituted the most visible sign of the peace movement's shift to the left in a decade absorbed in bitter cultural conflict. The noble experiment in Prohibition, the Scopes "monkey" trial, the executions of Sacco and Vanzetti, and the presidential candidacy of the Roman Catholic Al Smith all marked skirmishes in a decade-long confrontation between the traditionalist defenders of native Protestant America and the modernist champions of industrial and international democracy. Standing with the forces of change, peace activists engaged traditionalists in a protracted struggle over the very custodianship of the nation's values. The conservative and CEIP leader Nicholas Murray Butler led the criticism of the Volstead Act. Oswald Garrison Villard and John Haynes Holmes argued vigorously in defense of Sacco and Vanzetti, while pacifist clerics chided Willian Jennings Bryan for his Old Testament intransigence during the Scopes trial. Undeniably, peacemakers felt real pride in American nationhood.[14] But they insistently flavored that pride with the values and issues of the left.

As they shifted more firmly left, peace reformers wielded progressively less influence in Republican Washington. President Coolidge and Secretary of State Frank Kellogg did defer in policy matters to prewar peace leaders like Elihu Root. But they discreetly avoided pro-League internationalists, who talked like Wilson and who threatened G.O.P. party unity. And they politely sidestepped the church leaders, feminists, and pacifists who wanted them to pursue more actively disarmament and arbitration opportunities. Seeking to solidify the administration's peace appeal, Coolidge did initiate a Geneva Naval Disarmament Conference in August 1927, but the gathering collapsed after three weeks of fruitless discussion. In the same way, Kellogg concluded early in 1928 a round of arbitration conventions with several nations. Substantively, however, the pacts did nothing more than extend the life of the Root agreements of 1908.

Pressed by peace activists and French Foreign Minister Aristide Briand, the administration opened negotiations early in 1928 toward the Pact of Paris (or Kellogg-Briand Pact). Discussions sped forward until August, when representatives of the powers agreed in an elaborate public ceremony to renounce war as an instrument of national policy and to seek only pacific means in resolving their disputes. Official Washington expressed full satisfaction with Kellogg's achievement. But peace leaders felt skeptical. While publicly backing the Treaty, most viewed the document—which took form at the same time as U.S. troops occupied Nicaragua and the Congress passed the largest naval appropriations bill in peacetime American history—as mere affirmative gesture at best and as a hypocritical one at worst. Drily, WILPF leader Dorothy Detzer reported that it was "almost impossible for the Peace Movement to go in with great and wide enthusiasm [for the Pact] when Kellogg continues his policy in Nicaragua and says that it should not at all interfere with a big Navy." "I think we should force him on this," she added, "but it is awfully hard to get people to accept his sincerity."[15]

The sincerity of the Republican effort became irrelevant, however, after October 1929, when the Great Wall Street Crash plunged the country into severe economic depression. Although dogged by the pressure of domestic priorities, peace leaders emphasized the need for peace education, disarmament, and the development of the Paris Pact into a means of cooperation between the United States and the League. The AFSC took the lead in educational work. Headed by Ray Newton, the AFSC Peace Section organized institutes of international education, sponsored a string of student peace caravans through the Midwest, and subsidized the pacifist writer Devere Allen in forming the No-Frontier News Service (subsequently, the Worldover Press) in 1933. The WILPF and FOR meanwhile advanced disarmament. In April 1931 pacifist leaders from these and other organizations established the Emergency Peace Committee as "a board of strategy" for the purpose of mobilizing left-wing pacifist opinion on disarmament and related issues.[16] At the same time, CEIP leaders Nicholas Murray Butler and James Shotwell organized a special internationalist committee that developed plans to strengthen the Paris Pact by committing all signatories to join in economic sanctions against an aggressor state. Pressing a point that they had first raised in 1924, internationalist leaders worked resolutely to adjust American neutrality to the needs of the League system and an organized peace.[17]

Gradually, however, the peace seekers' first concerns broke before that combination of economic catastrophe and international violence which pervaded the thirties. Crowded by the two crises, peace leaders plotted, organized, and agitated for reform at home and restraint abroad. But war mercilessly stalked them on both fronts. At home, they pressed for drastic economic reform at the same time as President Franklin D. Roosevelt rallied the nation against the Depression through the rhetoric and mechanisms of a pseudo-war emergency. Abroad, they tried to come to terms with fascist regimes that valued war both as a means toward desired national objectives as well as the vindication of life itself. On all fronts, the rapid pace of unpleasant events sped peace workers toward the realization that the opportunity to make the necessary peace reform had passed. Now all they could do was to try to prevent another Great War.

Early in the thirties, the peace movement molted into an antiwar movement that operated behind the leadership of internationalists, pacifists, and radical leftists. Inspired by Fosdick and the League of Nations Association, internationalists remained committed to international economic reform and the prevention of aggression through collective action against aggressor (or revisionist) states. Pacifists in the FOR and WILPF, on the other hand, remained committed to their former pursuit of reform at home as well as abroad. Most maintained their allegiance to the primacy of the nonviolent ethic, but many questioned the effectiveness of nonviolence as an instrument for social change and drew closer to those socialists and Communists who talked of peace as the "overthrow of privilege." Inevitably, as Charles Chatfield has shown, the more deeply pacifists became involved in immediate struggles for social justice, the more they wondered whether, "if violence were necessary to end oppression, could socially concerned pacifists counsel peace?"[18] A few eventually accepted the righteousness of class conflict as propounded by the radical left. But most just puzzled over the larger questions that troubled people of conscience throughout the thirties. Could the American industrial order be humanized without massive violence? Could pacifists invest the class conflict with a nonviolent ethic? Could international fascism be checked as domestic reform progressed?[19]

While internationalists played down domestic reform efforts, pacifists moved in the early thirties into working cooperation with the radical left in general and the Socialist Party in particular. Ideologically, pacifists and socialists had much in common. Practically, they were joined even more in the person of Norman Thomas (1884–1968). Born to a minister's family in Marion, Ohio, Thomas studied at Princeton University and at New York's Union Theological Seminary before he assumed the pastorate of an impoverished immigrant church in east Harlem. Radicalized by his pastoral experiences, the young Presbyterian joined the Socialist Party before World War I moved him a step further into the FOR. In 1918 he assumed the editorship of the FOR monthly, *The World To-*

morrow, and became more actively engaged in socialist and pacifist affairs than he was with the church, although he did not resign his ministry until 1931. In the twenties, Thomas rose rapidly in Party affairs; and, after 1928, he rallied the organization through a growth spurt that peaked in 1932, when he polled nearly 900,000 votes as its presidential nominee. Within two years, however, the Socialists' new-found strength evaporated because of internal quarreling and growing popular support for Roosevelt's New Deal. Yet the Party remained a bulwark of antiwar sentiment throughout the decade.

The Communist Party similarly tried to operate as a peace-seeking agency in the thirties, particularly among discontented college students. But the Party's transparent subservience to the Soviet Union robbed it of any value as a means toward working peace. Between 1929 and 1935, Communists promoted Stalin's plans for independent revolutionary action. Out of this commitment, they formed the American League Against War and Fascism in September 1933, as an instrument for promoting a Soviet-style peace revolution and attacking anti-Stalinist socialists. The conclusion in 1935 of the Franco-Soviet security pact ended Russia's diplomatic isolation, however, and opened the four-year Popular Front era. At Moscow's direction, Communist parties everywhere promoted cooperation among anti-Nazi elements and supported the League of Nations and collective security. In the United States, the American League Against War and Fascism became the American League for Peace and Democracy, and adopted the slogan, "Keep America Out of War by Keeping War Out of the World."[20]

As the Communists shifted according to Moscow's dictates and socialists like Thomas clung to their pacifist faith, a few radicals like A. J. Muste (1885–1967) briefly discarded their nonviolence in hope of achieving revolutionary social change. Born in the Netherlands and raised in Grand Rapids, Michigan, Muste attended Hope College and Union Theological Seminary, before the Great War and the everyday suffering that he encountered in working-class New York converted him to pacifism and socialism. Active in the postwar years as an FOR leader and labor organizer, he headed the Brookwood Labor College between 1921 and 1933, when he dropped his pacifism in favor of several attempts to build a "democratically organized revolutionary party" among industrial workers.[21] Tirelessly, Muste helped organize workers in a number of strikes during 1934–1936, and became absorbed in the endless factional in-fighting among revolutionary Trotskyites. But in the end he found nothing in Marxism-Leninism to meet his personal need to live according to the principles of peace and justice. In 1936, while on a visit to Paris, he underwent a conversion experience and returned to Christianity. Four years later, he became executive secretary of the FOR and one of the country's most influential pacifist spokesmen.

Pacifists not only ranged across left-wing politics in the thirties; they also clarified their beliefs and purpose. In 1934 a Harvard-trained lawyer named Richard Gregg published a remarkable book on *The Power of Nonviolence* which served for the next generation as the virtual manual of action for practitioners of nonviolent change. A labor relations expert who quit his practice to study the work of Mohandas Gandhi in India, Gregg explained in full context the historical, practical, and philosophical assumptions of nonviolent coercion as the necessary mode of conflict resolution. With other liberal pacifists, Gregg viewed peace as a dynamic social process in which power was redistributed in order to reach among contestants "a mutually satisfactory approximation of justice."[22] The job of pacifist actionists was therefore to employ coercive— but explicitly nonviolent—techniques in an effort to persuade the oppressor of the futility of violence and the desirability of conciliation with his victim. Specific tactics would vary according to the distribution of power within the conflict situation. Some pacifists might fast. Others might organize mass protests. But none could ever sanction violence, for the simple reason that the means of social change invariably shaped the ends to be achieved.

Equipping pacifists with a pragmatic ethic of action that excluded violence, Gregg's analysis appealed powerfully to pacifists who needed a working pattern of realizable reform action. But Gregg's text worked no impact in national politics, where Franklin Roosevelt struggled to rally the country toward economic recovery through the metaphor of war. As William Leuchtenburg has brilliantly shown, the Roosevelt administration deliberately deployed the "analogue of war" against the Depression in a conscious effort to permeate the country with a spirit of devotion and sacrifice customarily known only in war. Repeatedly, New Deal spokesmen compared the economic crisis to the war emergency of 1917, when selfish personal and class interests were supposedly subordinated to the national need. In addition, they crafted their foremost programs upon bases established during the Great War. In March 1933 Roosevelt unilaterally declared a bank "holiday," an action that he justified on the strength of presidential powers granted in the 1917 Trading with the Enemy Act. The National Industrial Recovery Administration, which served as the keystone of the early New Deal, was fashioned on the example of Bernard Baruch's War Industries Board of 1917. The Civilian Conservation Corps gathered young men in forestry camps that were directly patterned upon military models (and initially under military control), while farm price supports drew inspiration from the wartime Food Administration.[23] Palpably, early New Dealers used the war metaphor and World War I precedents to achieve domestic reform, just as they later used World War II to realize, finally, economic recovery. In either case, the fact that wartime models were employed so deliberately reform for the sake of reform was ominous for the future of liberal activism in America. Put briefly, could twentieth-century American liberalism realize its goals without war?

The resort to reform through the war analogue disturbed several peace leaders in the early 1930s. But nothing frustrated them as much as the course of overseas developments. Beginning with Japan's invasion of Manchuria in September 1931, peace activists showed a greater and more sophisticated interest in foreign affairs than did any other segment of the American population. They showed a much sharper sense of the futility of the Great War and were much more aware of the inequities of the Versailles Treaty system. They became alert earlier to the unlimited aggressiveness of Hitler's Third Reich, and they suffered more than others in their anguished realization that the expansion of fascism could not be stopped by anything short of another World War.

Starting with the 1931 Manchurian crisis, American peace workers split over the basic question of how far they might try to modify the Versailles and Washington treaty systems without encouraging Germany and Japan in further assaults upon the existing world order. At first, their intramural differences were scarcely noticeable. In 1931 pacifists in the FOR and WILPF denounced Japan's flagrant use of force in Manchuria and urged Washington to cooperate with the League of Nations in efforts to move the Japanese back. Helped by LNA leaders, several pacifists and socialists pressed the Hoover administration to invoke sanctions against Tokyo, and to work through the League toward an effective program of international economic justice that guaranteed Japanese access to raw materials. No American peace leader spoke of U.S. intervention in defense of China. But most called for greater U.S. cooperation with the League powers in reversing the Japanese advance. And all agreed that peace could not endure in the face of national economic want.[24]

They also knew that peace could not endure in the face of international arms competition. Disturbed by the spiraling arms race, representatives from 28 different organizations, ranging from the WILPF to the CEIP, agreed in April 1931 to establish the Interorganization Council on Disarmament (ICD) as a means of concentrating their demands for general disarmament. Led by pacifists, the ICD showered Washington with appeals and petitions. But the Council's internationalist and pacifist spokesmen differed heatedly over such questions as dealings with Japan, inter-Allied war debts, and America's precise relationship to the League. Failing to agree upon a specific program of political action, the ICD disintegrated at the start of 1933 in an early sign of the internationalist-pacifist split that would deepen across the decade.

The collapse of the ICD did not, however, diminish the peace seekers' concern for disarmament. In December 1933 the national board of the WILPF voted to highlight the need for a regulated arms industry. Prompted by Dorothy Detzer and other pacifists, Republican Senator Gerald Nye of North Dakota opened an investigation early the next year of the arms industry and its relationship to war. Merging with the antibusiness sentiment that had rolled with the Depression across America, Nye's investigation caused a national sensation. Committee investigators documented the extraordinary profit levels reached by American arms manufacturers during the World War, the industry's corruption of public officials, its lobbying for larger military budgets, and the collusion between American and British arms manufacturers in price-fixing and marketing. More than ever, the fatuity and futility of America's intervention in Europe's last war seemed plain. It had benefitted only armsmakers. It certainly—as Hitler's and Mussolini's posturings daily demonstrated—had not brought peace.

Moved by the signs of a fresh European conflict, waves of antiwar sentiment struck the United States in the early 1930s. Protestant preachers renounced their support of Washington's last war and declared their refusal to sanction another. Veterans' organizations warned against entrapment in another Old World struggle, while hundreds of thousands of college students swore to the American version of England's Oxford Pledge that they would not "support the United States government in any war it may conduct." On April 13, 1934, young socialists and Communists joined in a rare united effort to produce a massive student strike against war. At 11:00 a.m., nearly 25,000 students across the country left classes in protest against the gathering war clouds. Stunned by their success, radical organizers succeeded the next year in mobilizing over 150,000 protesters on 130 campuses throughout the nation.[25]

Clearly, however, the burst of antiwar feeling in the early thirties reflected the popular anxiety to avoid involvement in European politics rather than any positive peace commitment. It strengthened isolationism, not peace activism. Although exploited by the radical left for factional purposes, the country's generalized antiwar sentiment did little to reinforce the pacifists' commitment to peaceable international reform. It likewise did nothing to advance internationalist plans to promote American cooperation in defense of a collective world peace. Yet peace workers persisted in their attempts to transmute antiwar opinion into alternative national policies that might check the rising momentum toward another Great War.

In August 1935, peace leaders hit upon one alternative policy. Pressed by the impending Italo-Ethiopian War, members of the Nye committee pushed through the Congress the Neutrality Act of 1935, which required the imposition by the President of an impartial arms embargo upon all belligerent states. The bill also authorized the President to warn Americans traveling on belligerent ships that they did so at their own risk, and established a National Munitions Control Board to license and supervise U.S. arms exports. The first Neutrality Act granted some discretionary powers to the President; but its key provisions effectively abrogated Washington's traditional defense of neutral rights and constricted the White House's need for diplomatic flexibility.

The Congress's legislation of neutrality and restricted executive authority laid the groundwork for the conflict among peace workers over what constituted proper U.S. policy in the face of Europe's worsening tensions. Pacifists clung to a "committed neutralism."[26] Persuaded that there were no definitive moral differences among the European powers, pacifist leaders supported the neutrality legislation and urged Washington to work toward the peaceable revision of the Versailles system in the hopes of meeting German and Italian needs. Internationalist leaders were less sanguine and more determined to invest the President with broader discretionary authority in expectation of greater international crises. Convinced that Hitler and Mussolini intended to disrupt the Versailles system through war, top internationalists pressed U.S. officials to cooperate more fully with the League powers in defending the existing European order.

As if in microcosm of the larger conflict, the growing differences between pacifist-neutralists and internationalists cut through the infant Catholic peace movement, which had appeared in the early thirties with the formation of the Catholic Association for International Peace (CAIP) and the Catholic Worker Movement. The CAIP, which had organized in 1927 out of the National Catholic Welfare Conference at the inspiration of the Reverend John Ryan, was the first Catholic peace organization in American history. Gathered among an elite group (it never numbered more than 500) of respectable Catholic social actionists, the CAIP criticized prevailing isolationist tendencies among U.S. Catholics, and teamed with other internationalists in promoting the League of Nations and World Court. Rejecting pacifism, it advanced the Church's traditional just war position and backed attempts in the early thirties to help the anti-Nazi powers. The Association proved mute, however, before the conscience-wrenching spectacle of the Spanish Civil War. Deferring to Rome's pro-Franco position, it quietly accepted strict American neutrality in the war and the consequent fascist victory. The CAIP did not regain its antineutrality voice until 1939, when Franco's triumph freed it to demand fuller U.S. action in support of France and Britain.[27]

In contrast, the Catholic Worker Movement held tenaciously to an "evangelical pacifism" whose spirit had informed the fellowship since its formation on Manhattan's lower East Side early in 1933.[28] Conceived by the itinerant French mystic Peter Maurin and the Catholic convert and journalist Dorothy Day, the Catholic Worker Movement was less an expression of theoretical pacifism than the living application of Christ's working love. Catholic Workers were lay apostles who fed the hungry, tended the sick, and clothed the naked. Consumed by this commitment, the Movement did not develop an explicitly pacifist position until 1935, when it renounced war in principle as well as practice. Despite heavy pressure from the Catholic hierarchy, the Workers maintained their witness throughout the Spanish Civil War and urged a policy of pacific neutralism upon Washington throughout the decade. Active Christian literalists, Workers viewed the idea of a just war as a contradiction in terms and asserted the right of Catholics to conscientious objection. Late in 1936 a handful of members formed PAX as the first organization of Catholic COs, reorganizing four years later as the Association of Catholic Conscientious Objectors. Remarkably, the Workers' unprecedented radical actions and pronouncements frayed but never broke their ties with the official Church. The Movement rather assumed for Catholicism in America the Church's prophetic role, striving in various hospitality houses and farms to make real in most personal ways the life-giving love that Christ said must animate His followers in this world.[29]

But their love never affected the concerns of national policy makers. Instead, Europe marched relentlessly after 1935 toward new war; and American peace seekers writhed in continuing attempts to form political coalitions that might save America from the violence and help to organize the postwar peace. Progressively, however, the ugly successes of the dictators made the prospect of war less repugnant to many peace reformers and deepened the growing division between the pacifist proponents of neutrality and internationalists who favored intervention. As fascism swept from Spain through Czechoslovakia and Japanese troops invaded China, the irony of the thirties became complete. In no other decade in the century did peace seem so imperative. Yet no other decade found war so necessary. Indeed, by the start of the 1940s, war had for all practical purposes replaced peace as the necessary way toward reform. War alone promised the salvation of those ideals of international organization and liberal humanism that peace seekers hungered most to make real.

For peace advocates, the last half of the decade opened bleakly in January 1935, when the Senate rejected the administration's World Court bill. Shocked by the Senate decision, top internationalists, like Shotwell and former Secretary of War Newton Baker, met in New York in an attempt to revitalize the pro-League cause by cooperating with pacifist leaders. The internationalist strategy of combination was simple. *"A peace movement without the pac-ifists would be an absurdity,"* explained Shotwell, *"but a peace movement based upon pure pacifist doctrine can never achieve its aim."*[30] Promising money and organizational assistance, inter-nationalists therefore tried to draw pacifists like Page and Nevin Sayre into a common front that would weld the pacifists' grass-roots power to the internationalists' preference for collective security and fuller discretionary authority for the President in war situations.[31] Pacifists responded politely and positively. Meeting in October, leaders from the two sides agreed to form a working combination under the direction of the veteran Protestant peace seeker Walter Van Kirk. Operationally, the new coalition enhanced the strength and reach of the National Peace Conference, a shaky pacifist clearinghouse that had first appeared in 1932. Pro-grammatically, it aimed at bolstering the League of Nations and liberalizing international economic practices.[32]

Sadly, however, the new coalition collapsed within a few months because of inadequate funding and recurring differences between the pacifist-neutralist defenders of mandatory arms embargoes and the internationalist proponents of discriminatory arms legislation. But the recurring differences did not preclude continuing action. In December 1935 Kirby Page and Ray Newton rather re-energized the NPC when they established within it an action arm, the Emergency Peace Campaign (EPC), that sought to promote international eco-nomic justice and keep a neutral America out of foreign wars. It marked "the supreme effort" of organized peace makers in prewar America.[33] Aided by the NCPW and the FOR, the EPC took off in April 1936 with an astonishing $130,000 budget and the support of the broadest peace *assemblage* of the interwar period. Page organ-ized study conferences and public meetings in nearly 200 cities. Over 200 volunteers—including ministers, educators, and femi-nists—undertook lecture tours through nearly every state in the Union. More than 3,500 clergymen pledged to deliver five peace sermons each in support of the Campaign, while separate organ-izational departments tried to move legislators, farmers, workers, and racial minorities behind the EPC's specific foreign policy goals: a defense policy limited to American soil, governmental control of the munitions industry, cooperation with the League of Nations in nonpolitical matters, and membership in the International Labor Organization and the World Court.

Along a parallel track, student groups contributed creatively to the antiwar surge. In April 1936, Princeton University students formed the Veterans of Future Wars and demanded "adjusted service compensation" of $1,000 for every male citizen between the ages of 18 and 36. Gravely, they insisted that the compensation be paid immediately so that those destined for future casualty lists would enjoy "the full benefit of their country's gratitude" while they were yet alive. Within months, the new-style VFW claimed to represent 30,000 members organized in 375 college posts. It also included several ladies auxiliaries, which sprang up demanding immediate pensions for future war widows and a trip to Europe "in holy pilgrimage" for all mothers of future soldiers.[34] In a more serious vein, large-scale student peace agitation also hit stride in April, when an estimated half-million youths left their classrooms across the country to join in mass demonstrations. Some gatherings were ad hoc; others were sponsored by the EPC. And still others were organized jointly by the EPC and the Communist-led American Student Union, though pacifists refused to cooperate with avowed Communists.

Invigorated by student support and receptive audiences, EPC leaders began long-range planning toward a more sweeping No-Foreign-War Crusade. Formulated by Page, the new Crusade hoped to connect established peace organizations into a broad national political movement which would join together all citizens who favored strict continentalist defense policies and opposed overseas adventures. Opening on April 6, 1937, (the twentieth anniversary of U.S. intervention in the Great War), the new campaign sponsored a national radio broadcast that featured the antiwar views of Admiral Richard E. Byrd, Eleanor Roosevelt, and the Rev. Harry Emerson Fosdick. Immediately after, volunteer workers and local committees spread the Crusade's message through some 2,000 towns and cities and on 500 college campuses, as well as among farm and labor organizations.

The message of the No-Foreign-War Crusade mirrored the neutralist commitment of its pacifist sponsors. Hardly indifferent to overseas developments, pacifists viewed the international crisis of the thirties as systemic in nature. They believed that the European power struggle was an imperial conflict of the basest sort; and they felt that, besides proposing international economic reforms, the United States must maintain a continentalist defense strategy to avoid being sucked into the coming bloodbath. Obsessed with the futility of World War I, pacifists demanded strict U.S. neutrality, as the only way of escaping Europe's unregenerate politics and preparing for a functional postwar international system that would provide people with necessary food, shelter, and work. Neutrality was the only means by which America could ride out the storm and build a new world in the ruins of the old.

The No-Foreign-War Crusade raised pacifist influence in the antiwar movement of the thirties to its highest level. Then it collapsed with the rest of the EPC in the last half of 1937. Member pacifist organizations like the WILPF quit the Campaign on the grounds that their principles were being diluted in the coalition's consensual strategy. Internationalist sympathizers resented the Campaign's insistence on strict neutrality and its opposition to providing the President with greater discretionary authority in foreign policy matters. Local student groups fell apart. Friendly ministers drifted in other directions.

With the EPC's collapse, several pacifists followed Libby and the NCPW into the fight to require a popular referendum prior to a declaration of war. Supporting Congressman Louis Ludlow (Rep.-Indiana), pacifists joined a broad band of neutralists and right-wing isolationists in an attempt to secure a constitutional amendment which would require a national referendum before Congress could declare war, except in case of an invasion of the United States. Seemingly, the Ludlow amendment signified the most ambitious attempt to democratize peace in American history. Certainly many peace workers thought so. Lecturing and distributing literature, several worked to mobilize public support for the measure until January 10, 1938, when the Ludlow bill reached the House floor upon a crest of antiwar enthusiasm. The Roosevelt administration was mortified. Exerting every bit of pressure at their command (including the opposition of leading internationalists), administration forces beat back the amendment in the House by a count of 209–188. A change of eleven votes might have effected what majority leader Sam Rayburn called "the most tremendous blunder since the formation of our government under the Constitution."[35]

The defeat of the Ludlow amendment precipitated a rapid erosion of remaining pacifist influence within the antiwar movement. Yet pacifists did not quit the struggle. Some like Nevin Sayre worked through the National Peace Conference with Clark Eichelberger and other internationalists in pressing for the convocation of an international economic conference. Others like Libby and Detzer joined Norman Thomas in the neutralist "Keep America Out of War" campaign. Linking pacifists and socialists, the campaign opened in February 1938 and mushroomed within three months into a formal Keep America Out of War Congress (KAOWC). Popularly, the Congress conveyed its purpose in the slogan: "The maximum American cooperation for peace; the maximum isolation from war."[36] Practically, it served as a non-Communist antiwar front on the left that tried to connect the pacifists' resources and legislative contacts with the mass political orientation of the Socialist Party. But the Congress could never overcome its financial weakness or internal divisions. While it sponsored several mass meetings and a few student strikes in 1938, the KAOWC failed to function as a politically influential force.

Yet it was the only national antiwar coalition alive when the European war broke out in September 1939. Eight months later, Nazi forces rolled across western Europe in a shocking blitzkrieg; and the KAOWC crashed into action. Protesting Roosevelt's bold assistance to the Allies, the Congress struggled to revitalize a progressive antiwar bloc until September 1940, when the right-wing America First Committee arose to resist interventionist pressures. While pacifists withdrew, the KAOWC fell gradually under the influence of antiwar socialists and behind isolationist plans for a Fortress America concept of defense. Then the Japanese attack at Pearl Harbor suddenly hurled the United States into war on two fronts. Hastily, the America First Committee disbanded, and its members hurried to back the national war effort. Despondently, the rump executive committee of the KAOWC dissolved the organization and created in its place a Provisional Committee Toward a Democratic Peace. Emulating the People's Council for Peace and Democracy of World War I, the Provisional Committee worked to promote civil rights at home and to distribute more equitably the costs of the war. Taking no position on the war, it aimed simply to regroup progressive internationalists and anti-imperialists behind the need for a just and lasting peace.

Other pacifists meanwhile turned inward in the late thirties and prepared for another lonely defense of the peace witness during wartime. Fearing a repetition of the hostility that surfaced during World War I, FOR leaders began in 1935 to organize local and denominational cells designed to support individual conscientious objectors and promote nonviolent action toward social justice.[37] Small fellowships of COs took shape soon after within mainline Protestant denominations. The Historic Peace Churches reaffirmed their commitment to nonresistance, while the Association of Catholic Conscientious Objectors gathered under the aegis of the Catholic Worker Movement.

Their preparations were quite necessary. In 1940 the Roosevelt administration began planning for massive military conscription, prompting denominational Protestant leaders to start pressing for some recognized nonmilitary status for any conscientious objector. After much discussion and debate, the administration agreed to classify as a CO any person "who, by reason of religious training and belief, is conscientiously opposed to participation in war in any form."[38] It was an improvement over the traditional exemption of only members of the Historic Peace Churches. But it fell far short of the pacifists' demand that the government respect equally the scruples of nonreligious objectors. And it said nothing about selective conscientious objection to participation in certain wars.

While neutralists faltered and pacifists turned inward, internationalists swung after 1938 into an interventionist force bent on involving the United States in the anti-Nazi cause. They became— as one undergraduate student wrote recently in an expression of naive brilliance—"intervenationalists." After the Italo-Ethiopian War, Shotwell, Eichelberger, and League of Nations Association leaders were unable to conceal any longer Geneva's utter failure to maintain a progressive international system. They accordingly drew back from their first concern for American cooperation with the League and moved in other directions. At first, internationalists tried to use the National Peace Conference as a means of mobilizing mass peace sentiment behind their ideals. Although the heavy influence of pacifists and neutralists within the NPC inhibited their larger ambitions, Shotwell and Eichelberger worked tirelessly under its name to promote fuller international economic cooperation, revision of the League Covenant, and the expansion of the President's discretionary authority in implementing the Neutrality Acts. And more than ever they talked of collective security. Indeed, they made the very term a euphemism for American cooperation with the anti-Nazi powers.

In January 1938 Eichelberger, a World War I veteran and indefatigable organizer, formed the Committee for Concerted Peace Efforts, in an attempt to move beyond the limitations of the proneutrality position favored by pacifist leaders. Centered about an internationalist core in the LNA, Eichelberger's committee supported the Roosevelt administration in its fight against the Ludlow war-referendum amendment. After the narrow victory there, Eichelberger, Shotwell, and their supporters turned to demand repeal of the mandatory arms embargo provision that lay at the heart of the Neutrality Acts. Insisting that a mandatory arms embargo discriminated unfairly in favor of the fascist powers, internationalists opened a long campaign to bring about neutrality revision and fuller U.S. support of the anti-Nazi forces. In the process, they discarded the dream of a unified peace movement. "I have come to the conclusion," Shotwell wrote in April 1939, "that the effort of many years to try to bring into a single body those who hold divergent views concerning not only the way to get peace but the nature of peace itself, is fruitless and simply leads to confusion and ineffectiveness."[39]

Advancing fast, internationalist leaders picked up the support of several former neutralists and pacifists, including the influential Reinhold Niebuhr and the evangelist Sherwood Eddy. Encouraged by these gains and by the White House, Eichelberger and his allies formed the Non-Partisan Committee for Peace through Revision of the Neutrality Act in September 1939. Joining the LNA organization with White House pressure, they finally tasted a bite of success. In early November 1939 the Congress voted to renew the 1935 Neutrality Act, but to replace the mandatory arms embargo provision with a provision allowing all belligerents (but presumably Britain and France) to purchase and ship arms from the United States on a "cash-and-carry" basis. Formally, America retained its neutrality. Actually, it listed heavily toward the Allied side.

Following the outbreak of the European war, internationalists shifted their cause into high gear along two other routes. First, Shotwell convened in November a group of notable international authorities, including John Foster Dulles, Owen Lattimore, and Max Lerner, into an organization called the Commission to Study the Organization of the Peace (CSOP). Gaining the support of the Church Peace Union, the CSOP conducted several round-table discussions and issued on Armistice Day, 1940, its first annual report, in which it called upon the American people to cooperate in the destruction of fascism and to help create a postwar international security system empowered to suppress future aggression. Although they shrank from the prospect of a world superstate, Commission members insisted upon the establishment of a new security system equipped with effective police powers. In particular, Shotwell and the University of Chicago political scientist Quincy Wright called for the creation of an international air force—with bases scattered around the world—for the purpose of deterring aggression through the assured application of immediate punishment to the aggressor. They called it collective security, but it smacked more of a determination to compel world order through an intimidating Great Power consensus. Manifestly, liberal internationalists were moving further from the reform-minded visions of the early Foreign Policy Association.

Along a second route, Eichelberger worked openly to place American resources at the disposal of the Allied powers. Building from a base in the LNA, he and his fellow interventionists delicately pressed for aid to the Allies until the spring of 1940, when the Nazi blitz brought German troops to the Atlantic and shook the American electorate with an unprecedented sense of physical vulnerability. Stirred by the Nazi success, Eichelberger moved the well-known midwestern Republican journalist, William Allen White, to assist him in establishing the Committee to Defend America by Aiding the Allies. With the help of LNA branches in over 300 cities, the White committee quickly became the dynamic center of pro-Allied agitation in the United States. It also provided the main housing for those who favored a postwar league of democracies which would keep the peace through the collective deterrence of aggression. Already, internationalists were insisting that they would not permit America to lose the second peace.

Yet the quarreling that split so many antiwar coalitions in the thirties did not spare the White committee. Late in 1940 White resigned his chairmanship, complaining that pro-Allied interventionists had moved the Committee from campaigning for all aid short of war to advocating outright military involvement. Eichelberger did not deny the charge. Imperturbably, he and other internationalists rather entered into an uneasy but working partnership with militant interventionists, who had gathered in a group called Fight for Freedom. Together, these "intervenationalists" called for the convoying by U.S. vessels of supplies to Britain, advanced U.S. patrols in the Atlantic, the imposition of an economic embargo upon Japan, and the repeal of all neutrality legislation. Ambitiously, they intended to organize all supporters of collective security into an overpowering Washington lobby for war.[40]

Less dramatically, a Missouri-born journalist named Clarence Streit published in 1939 a book called *Union Now* that rapidly became the most popular proposal for the future organization of peace. Streit called upon the world's fifteen leading democratic nations to join in a loose confederation of states that would gradually tighten the bonds of global union, just as the American states had done on a national scale in the generation after the American Revolution. Predictably, the America-centered orientation of Streit's plans generated sharp interest in the United States. Within two years, *Union Now* sped through fourteen printings and sales of at least a quarter-million copies. In 1940 devotees of Streit's ideas organized the Federal Union, Inc., in an attempt to realize his plans. Within one year, they claimed to have organized sixty chapters across the country.[41]

Then in June 1941 Hitler invaded Russia, throwing Stalin into the arms of Churchill, and the cause of Anglo-American democracy into confusion. The war was no longer an unambiguous contest between Western liberalism and fascist totalitarianism. Six months later, a Japanese attack force destroyed large elements of the U.S. Pacific fleet at Pearl Harbor and drove the country into war on two fronts. The peace reform that seemed so necessary in 1919 became immediately dispensable. The imperative nature of the modern pursuit of peace did not cease in 1941. But the pursuit did become postponable. And out of the costly delay would come a refashioned reform.

Chapter Seven
The Subversive Reform

The most profound development within American politics between 1941 and 1961 was the rise to pre-eminence of national-security concerns. Justified by the threats of Nazism and then Communism, a counter-subversive constellation of governmental agencies and private interests organized, in the name of state security, for the purpose of extending U.S. military power abroad and minimizing dissent at home. The necessity for such a movement was felt to be incontestable. "There can be no tampering with the national security," one government committee declared in 1954, "which in times of peril must be absolute. . . . Any doubts whatever must be resolved in the interests of the national security."[1] With the United States suddenly vulnerable to external attack and even annihilation, national leaders strove to achieve complete security through military preparedness in a world of hostile powers and revolutionary ferment. And, as interest in military-based security increased, citizen peace seekers who emphasized nonmilitary cooperation toward a more just world order appeared as threats to the American way of peace. Private peace seeking in the national-security state seemed not only a dispensable reform; it came also to be viewed as subversive.

The Japanese attack at Pearl Harbor and Washington's abrupt entrance into a two-front war in December 1941 cracked the organized peace movement along its most prominent fault lines. Religious sectarians and radical pacifists refused war service and passed either into noncombatant service, Civilian Public Service (CPS), or federal prisons. Pacifists in the FOR and WILPF aided conscientious objectors, protested saturation bombing, and criticized the Allies' failure to propose specific peace terms or pursue a negotiated settlement. And internationalists cheered the Allied war effort as the basis of a new international organization.

Actually, pacifists first met the war's challenge in 1940, when Congress passed the first peacetime conscription bill in American history. Following provisions written into the 1940 Selective Training and Service Act, over 25,000 conscientious objectors joined the armed forces as noncombatants between 1941 and 1945. In addition, 6,000 absolutists (nearly three-fourths Jehovah's Witnesses) were jailed for draft resistance or nonregistration, while another 12,000 entered the novel experiment in CPS. In origin, CPS derived from the pacifists' past experiences with voluntary work camps and the government's satisfaction with the Depression-era Civilian Conservation Corps. The CPS program was intended to blend the two successes. Supervised by the military-dominated Selective Service Administration and subsidized by participating churches and pacifist organizations, a wide variety of COs—ranging from quiescent members of the Historic Peace Churches to restless Catholic anarchists—lived between 1941 and 1947 in forestry camps and public hospitals across the country, where they served as soil conservationists, roadbuilders, health-care aides, and volunteers in medical experiments.

But problems quickly outpaced the reach of the program. Neither the men nor their families received compensation for their service. The work was sometimes dangerous, and usually meaningless. The military asserted growing control over the camps, and the cooperating churches buckled beneath its pressure. Disturbed by these developments and an "overpowering sense of alienation," social activists organized collective protests in various camps during 1943.[2] But the protests fizzled, and disaffection festered. The CPS was a pathbreaking experiment. But few peace seekers chose to take the path again. "What began as an experiment in tolerance," observed the program's two leading historians, "ultimately demonstrated in unmistakable terms the deep and inherent contradiction between the American demand for national security and the claims of individuals for personal liberty and conscience."[3] Participants like Gordon Zahn were less generous. The CPS "was punitive in practice and intent," he maintained, "an experiment in the democratic *suppression* of a dissident religious minority in time of war."[4]

With COs isolated, antiwar activism centered during World War II among those pacifists affiliated with the FOR, the WILPF, and the WRL. Prompted essentially by religious concerns, top pacifists like A. J. Muste and Evan Thomas organized relief services for war refugees and for the families of interned COs. They denounced the forced internment of West Coast Japanese and attacked Allied saturation bombing of civilian targets. More positively, they called for an immediate military armistice and global reconstruction through functional international agencies that specialized in the satisfaction of essential human needs, starting with food and health. Pacifists showed little interest in any postwar collective security system. They wanted people instead to practice cooperation through functional administrative agencies on the grounds that "our ultimate goal is peace—not some particular type of world organization."[5]

Politically, however, the antiwar movement possessed only a tiny base of support. Membership in the U.S. section of the WILPF slipped by half in 1941, while the anti-interventionist Socialist Party shrank to a hard core of 6,000. A few radical pacifists tried to take direct action against U.S. war policy. In the spring of 1943 the 28-year-old David Dellinger formed the short-lived Peace Now Committee to demand an immediate end to the war. Shortly after, the Columbia University sociologist and WRL leader George Hartmann and the Quaker Dorothy Hutchinson organized the Peace Now Movement in a more modest attempt to move the Allies to enunciate a negotiable set of "fair and reasonable" peace terms.[6] But other pacifists showed little interest in either group, and both sank beneath a combination of popular indifference and congressional harassment.

Yet peace militants did not quit their struggle against war and injustice. In November 1943 the veteran AFSC leader E. Raymond Wilson and some eastern seaboard Quakers established the Friends Committee on National Legislation (FCNL) to press Washington policy makers on matters involving civil liberties, racial justice, and relief and reconstruction. Proudly, they identified themselves as "the first Protestant lobby."[7] Other pacifists meanwhile adopted more innovative tactics. Borrowing nonviolent social action techniques pioneered by Mohandas Gandhi in India, FOR activists like Bayard Rustin and George Houser helped form the Congress of Racial Equality (CORE) in Chicago in 1942, and superintended in 1943 a series of nonviolent interracial actions that succeeded in desegregating public accommodations in cities between Detroit and Denver. With the encouragement of FOR leaders, Rustin also assisted the black labor leader, A. Philip Randolph, in the wartime work of the March on Washington Movement (MOWM). Inspired by the several massive direct action demonstrations that had occurred in the thirties, the MOWM marked the first attempt to mobilize the black masses in the nonviolent pursuit of racial justice through threatened street action. It also formed the first link in the connection between pacifists and black activists that would give driving force to the postwar civil rights movement.[8]

Internationalists in the meantime supported the U.S. war effort in the hope of establishing through military victory a new international organization that would keep the peace. Working under the slogan, "Win the War, Win the Peace," the wartime internationalist coalition combined old-line Wilsonians, one-world federalists, and sympathetic Protestants (like John Foster Dulles) from the Commission to Study the Bases of a Just and Durable Peace. The most experienced were those at the top of the League of Nations Association and the Commission to Study the Organization of Peace. Headed by Eichelberger and Shotwell, these Wilsonians believed that wars originated when military aggression erupted from longstanding economic conflict. They therefore centered their postwar plans upon a reinvigorated League that would ease international economic tensions and check aggression through the deterrent threat of collective military counteraction, particularly by an international air force.

Functionally, Wilsonians enjoyed close ties with Washington policy makers. In 1943 Eichelberger directed a national campaign of sympathetic congressional speakers, including J. William Fulbright (Dem.-Arkansas) and Albert Gore (Dem.-Tennessee), that operated through a network of local CEIP and LNA contacts. As military successes accumulated, Washington became even more eager to please. In October 1944, after preliminary plans for a new United Nations were drafted at the Dumbarton Oaks Conference, the Roosevelt administration "did all in its power to supplement the work" of organized internationalists.[9] Happily, their union produced the most welcome result. In June 1945, Shotwell, Eichelberger, Dulles, and other top Wilsonians served as State Department consultants attending in San Francisco at the birth of the UN.

More advanced hopes for a world federation centered in The Federal Union, Inc., which was formed in New York in January 1941 by several people who had been impressed with Clarence Streit's two-year-old argument in *Union Now* for the federation of the

Western democracies. Glistening with celebrities like Dorothy Thompson, Clare Boothe Luce, and Robert Sherwood, the Union leadership announced the establishment of sixty chapters across the country and plans for sixty more. Hurrying to organize behind an idea whose time seemed ripe, federalists promised that the democratic federation would eventually expand into a more inclusive organization. In the meantime, they held, America offered the best working model for an evolving world federation. The world could not do better than to emulate a country that had organized upon a common defense force, a customs-free economic union, common communications and monetary systems, and respect for the autonomy of member-states.

In 1942 Federal Union leaders adapted to the imperatives of the Grand Alliance and decided to expand their projected world federation to the Soviet Union and all anti-Axis states. The decision did not seriously alter the Anglo-American coloration of the various federalist and internationalist plans. Yet internationalists as a whole played down their Anglo-American sympathies, and tried to win popular support in one of two ways. They emphasized a sense of human community by employing the term "One World"; and they paid tribute to the "lost peace" of the martyred Woodrow Wilson. Bringing home the reality of One World was easy. Shaken by years of foreign crises that struck home at Pearl Harbor, Americans proved highly susceptible to the internationalist attacks upon isolationism and to their emphasis upon the immediacy of modern global interdependence. Encouraged by the popular interest, internationalists blanketed the country with speakers, pamphlets, and radio broadcasts. But none achieved the singular power of Wendell Willkie's *One World*.

Issued in 1943, *One World* was essentially an anecdotal account of Willkie's recent world travels that closed with a moving "sermon on internationalism."[10] Convinced that America must help maintain global freedom, Willkie urged his countrymen to lead the way toward a new international order based upon an inclusive United Nations Council. Though short on detail, the message of the former Republican presidential nominee was long on appeal. The first printing of *One World* sold out in two days, and 200,000 copies were snatched up within one week. In a few months, Willkie's testimonial to world interdependence enjoyed the most fantastic sales in American publishing history.

Alongside the popular fascination with One World, internationalists nurtured a revival of interest in Woodrow Wilson. The Woodrow Wilson Foundation, which had been established in honor of the ex-President's ideals in 1923, distributed pamphlets that virtually attributed World War II to the success of Wilson's enemies in 1919. More subtly, the diplomatic historians Thomas A. Bailey and Ruhl Bartlett rued the "lost peace" of 1919–1920 and warned against repeating the nationalist error by rejecting membership in a new international organization. But it was typically left to Hollywood to magnify Wilson's struggle into an uncomplicated drama of high heroism. Operating upon the second largest budget in film history to that time, Darryl F. Zanuck produced the technicolor epic, *Woodrow Wilson,* which opened to excited crowds and mixed reviews in August 1944. In theaters across the country, history was rewritten in behalf of the internationalist cause with a popular power that scholars could not challenge for a generation.

Heightened by the internationalist agitation, popular interest in the organization of the postwar peace peaked over the winter of 1943–1944. But it was too diffuse to force President Roosevelt in any single direction. Instead, the President chose, characteristically, to conceal his precise postwar preferences. A one-time Wilsonian, FDR had lapsed from the faith in the 1920s and ignored it altogether in the 1930s. During World War II he professed a vocal but vague internationalist commitment. In August 1941 he and British Prime Minister Winston Churchill publicly agreed upon the need for a postwar general security system. In January 1942 he led Stalin and other members of the anti-Hitler alliance in a general pledge to act in concert toward a postwar United Nations. One year later, he authorized the State Department to initiate planning— with the help of prominent internationalists—toward a postwar peace organization.

Consistently, however, Roosevelt refused to detail his plans for the projected UN. He politely dismissed the Wilsonians' neo-League proposals and ignored the federalist alternative. Instead, he talked of enforcing world order and guaranteeing national security through the interregional cooperation of the world's foremost police powers—America, Britain, Russia, and America-assisted China. FDR had no doubt that peace must be enforced. And he felt equally sure that the enforcement of peace could not be entrusted to a new international organization. It was a matter best left to the informal cooperation of the Great Powers.

Perhaps the best evidence of FDR's limited faith in the postwar UN lay in his attitude toward the wartime development of the atomic bomb and his relationship with the scientists who manned the super-secret Manhattan Project. From the start, Roosevelt demanded absolute secrecy in the bomb's development. Inevitably, his insistence upon secrecy for the sake of unilateral development disturbed atomic scientists working at other sites between Oak Ridge, Tennessee, and Los Alamos, New Mexico. Although determined to beat the Germans to the bomb, atomic scientists (who were influenced deeply by European emigrés) felt real concern over the future use and control of nuclear energy. True members of an international community, they realized clearly that the bomb could not long remain a national secret or monopoly. They also knew that it signaled a profound revolution in weaponry and warmaking.[11]

Beginning in 1944 atomic scientists called upon Washington policy makers to initiate a more cooperative atomic policy. The renowned Danish physicist Niels Bohr personally asked FDR to share information of the bomb's development with Moscow as a sign of Allied solidarity and as a step toward investing in the postwar UN multilateral means of controlling atomic weaponry and preventing a nuclear arms race. Later, as the workability of the bomb became more manifest, scientific humanists like James Franck and Leo Szilard urged Washington officials to arrange a demonstration test for Japanese leaders and to push more aggressively for international controls. In both ways, they held, America could show the world the bomb's power even as it helped prevent a nuclear arms race and avoided the moral stigma of being the first country to "release this new means of indiscriminate destruction upon mankind."[12]

The muted but emphatic concerns of the atomic scientists established them as a potent new element in the country's evolving peace movement. With the old vision of a Protestant America giving way to a triumphant technological-rational order, scientists emerged in wartime America as a new priesthood that backed its moral sensibilities with practical achievements. "No group has a greater appeal to the public," one expert observed, "and none has greater potentialities for producing change in public opinion."[13] Conversely, the prowar preachments of religious leaders—liberal and otherwise—cost them precious moral influence in their claims to peace leadership. Among churchmen, only a minority of clerics protested the terror bombing of enemy civilians; and only the Roman Catholic hierarchy criticized, as being contrary to the tenets of the just war, President Truman's decision to atomize Hiroshima and Nagasaki.[14] Along with organized womanhood, religious spokesmen lost force as a propelling element in the American peace movement. They liked the war too much and thought of peace too little.

Yet the peacemaking power of the atomic scientists was limited by their support of the national-security state, the one phenomenon whose wartime growth most dramatically affected the environment in which they and other peace seekers worked. Faced with external crises and fearful of internal subversion, government leaders assembled a many-sided security apparatus that came eventually to constitute the axis of the American state.[15] The Federal Bureau of Investigation, for instance, expanded tremendously during the war. While its annual budget increased eightfold in the decade after 1939, the FBI undertook to check espionage, sabotage, subversion, and the loyalty of federal employees for the overall "internal security of nation."[16] The military services and defense-related civilian agencies likewise enjoyed a "stunning growth" during the war.[17] Between 1939 and 1945, while the federal budget expanded from $9 billion to $95 billion, defense expenditures zoomed from less than $1 billion to over $81 billion; and the number of military personnel shot from less than one-third of a million men to over 12 million.* As significantly, the number of civilians employed in the executive branch on defense-related matters increased between 1939 and 1945 from less than 200,000 to more than 2.6 million, a tenfold increase at a time when the total civilian federal workforce barely tripled.[18] Adopting an "ideology of preparedness" which assumed that military power "could deter or subdue future troublemakers," national leaders prepared the country to secure the postwar peace through a bureaucratized state-security system that required surveillance at home and pre-emptive action abroad.[19]

Ineluctably, the rise of the national-security state complicated

*The number dropped in 1948 to a postwar low of 1.4 million, then rose again during the Korean War to over 3.6 million, and never dropped below 2 million after that point. *Historical Statistics of the United States: Colonial Times to 1970*, Part 2 (Washington: U.S. Bureau of the Census, 1975), p. 1141.

beyond measure the peacemakers' attempts to establish a cooperative peace outside of the reach of Great Power predominance. And
so did the very sweep of history. On June 26, 1945, delegates from 55
nations met in San Francisco to sign the Charter of the new United
Nations, pledging to "unite our strength" in the common pursuit
of justice and security. Seven weeks later the atomic devastation of
Hiroshima and Nagasaki helped end the war in Asia and brought
America to a new level of armed pre-eminence. Peace seekers generally disliked the modest scope of the new UN. Yet they valued
the UN as an essential step toward the kind of international cooperation that was all the more vital with the dawn of the Atomic
Age. With Russia devastated, Britain depleted, and China divided,
the peace of 1945 signaled the peace of an America triumphant. But
what kind of peace that would entail—as peace seekers well
knew—remained still open. Would it be a cooperative peace upheld
collectively by the powers and legitimatized through the UN? Or
would it be a peace of deterrence and death, imposed unilaterally
by the reviving powers and sanctioned through a cluster of independent nuclear arsenals?

For the next fifteen years, American peace activists struggled to
secure an organized peace in the face of the worsening Soviet-
American Cold War and the expanding national-security state. It
proved a frustrating fight. Atomic scientists and world federalists
made impressive advances until the end of 1947, when international and domestic Cold War pressures converged to drive them to
the defensive for a decade. Radical pacifism in the meantime
seemed frankly anomalous in a society that had gained so much
from war. Neither sympathetic Protestants nor political liberals
could comprehend the second failure within a generation to bring
peace through war. And no one could fathom the enormity of the
Holocaust. Peace activists who grew up believing in man's elemental decency could in no way account for the Germans' systematic
annihilation of 12 million captured innocents. Unable to accept
Hiroshima or the Holocaust, peace workers of most persuasions
rather persevered in the belief that the international control of
atomic weaponry and a neo-orthodox appreciation of human sinfulness would carry the world beyond the past and through the
menace of a potential World War III.

After 1945 several prominent atomic scientists moved into active
peace seeking for the first time, determined "to act into history as

they once acted into nature."[20] Appalled by the bomb's destructiveness, concerned scientists struggled to familiarize the public
with the revolutionary significance of atomic power to safeguard
further nuclear development against military domination, and to
construct international controls against the bomb's proliferation
and use. Leading atomic scientists refused to apologize for their
discovery. Yet they hurried to broadcast the first political message
of the Atomic Age: no people could devise a defense against nuclear annihilation. *"The nations can have atomic energy, and
much more,"* promised the Federation of American Scientists. *"But
they cannot have it in a world where war may come."*[21]

Convinced that they were "the naturally appointed guardians" of
peace in the Atomic Age, scientists and engineers led by Leo
Szilard and Eugene Rabinowitch formed the Federation of Atomic
Scientists in November 1945 (it became the Federation of American
Scientists early in 1946), in order to impress the public with the
bomb's significance and promote international controls.[22] Organized mainly in four local associations, the FAS claimed a peak
membership of 3,000 in 1948, before it slipped to a stable constituency of 2,500 in 1950. Programmatically, the Federation first
fought to assert civilian control over the U.S. atomic energy program and to establish an international control system. Backing
Connecticut Senator Brien McMahon, the FAS supported the creation in 1946 of the Atomic Energy Commission, which was charged
with managing atomic development under the direction of a
nine-member General Advisory Committee that included eight
civilians. For the scientists, the AEC marked a real if limited victory
both over uncontrolled private atomic entrepreneurs and secretive
military domination.

But they encountered greater frustration on the international
plane. Promoting a U.S. plan identified with the New York finan-
cier Bernard Baruch, the scientists pressed at the UN in 1946 for an
International Atomic Energy Authority that would control nuclear
development and preside over the phased destruction of existing
(i.e., U.S.) atomic stockpiles. The Soviet Union balked, however, at
the plan's prohibition of further nuclear development and its temporary protection of the U.S. arsenal. When Russian representatives
presented an alternative plan in July 1946, the UN fell into dead-
lock over the crucial question of international control; and each
power accelerated plans for independent nuclear preparedness.

The failure of the Baruch plan struck the atomic scientists' movement at a time when its unusual postwar unanimity and influence were already waning. The scientists' public credibility first suffered a serious reverse in July 1946, when the U.S. Bikini tests did not prove as devastating as scientists had predicted and satisfied the American public that the bomb was simply a conventional—if highly destructive—new weapon. The scientists' movement lost even more strength during 1947–1948 as the Cold War intensified and as President Truman prepared to contain the Soviet Union militarily and domestic dissidents politically. The President's commitment to Russia's containment required the imposition of restraints through the deterrent threat of atomic attack. His commitment to the containment of dissent required the formalization of a domestic security apparatus that extended a network of control and a shadow of intimidation across scientific policy critics.

The final crack in the scientists' postwar peace power took place over the winter of 1948–1949, when the movement fractured over the question of committing the United States to the creation of a hydrogen (or thermonuclear) bomb. With scientists divided, the President authorized the development of an H-bomb in the fall of 1949. Truman's decision, coupled with Russia's first atomic explosion in September 1949, killed the scientists' last lingering hopes that an atomic arms race could be checked through international controls and national safeguards against military influence. With the race on, concerned scientists broke confusedly into three factions until June 1950, when the outbreak of the Korean War drove most back into the work of strengthening a militant America. Once more, the scientific community provided major research and development support to American military power. In February 1951 the United States exploded a hydrogen bomb of awesome destructiveness. Thirty months later Russia matched the American achievement and stung Washington into rushing the deployment of airborne H-bombs, a feat that it accomplished in May 1956. The atomic arms race sped past several scientific milestones, and well beyond international control.

The achievements of the scientists' postwar search for peace were real but limited. Peace-minded scientists did establish *The Bulletin of the Atomic Scientists,* in order to familiarize the public with the significance of nuclear energy and scientists with the mysteries of national and international politics. And they maintained a ready reservoir of talent and arguments to further action toward arms control. But there was no disguising the fact that scientists had failed in their highest ambitions at the moment of ripest opportunity. They who had derived untold powers of destruction from the physical universe could not move human politics beyond the reach of catastrophe. They could affect governments, but not move them. They could acquaint citizens with the danger of nuclear war, but never drive home its full meaning.[23]

Other Americans thought that they could succeed where the scientists had failed. Certain that atomic weaponry had changed the very nature of international politics, a coalition of world federalists organized in the immediate postwar period for the purpose of establishing either through or beyond the UN some democratic world government that would operate directly on individual citizens. World federalism claimed special strength among student activists like Harris Wofford, Jr., academicians like University of Chicago President Robert M. Hutchins, respected Establishment figures like the New York lawyer and longtime preparedness advocate Grenville Clark, and war veterans like Cord Meyer, Jr. Spread at first over several organizations, federalists divided over the pace and reach of their cause. Some favored a gradual approach toward an international federal structure, while others preferred the immediate creation of an operational system. Some supported a regional approach, starting from the Atlantic community, toward a world government whose powers would be restricted to the work of preventing war. Others demanded a constitutional regime fully capable of providing for justice and the common defense. Divided by temperament and aspirations, federalists agreed upon very few things except the need to preserve peace through a world government that would operate as a supranational sovereign authority. They wanted more than the existing UN.

Determined to save America and the world, representatives from five separate federalist organizations met at Asheville, North Carolina, in April 1947 and formed the United World Federalists (more accurately, the United World Federalists for World Government With Limited Powers Adequate To Prevent War) as a pressure group dedicated to moving the United States toward leadership in the work of ensuring "world peace through world law." The new group boasted impressive frontline leadership. Headed by the dynamic Yale graduate and Pacific War hero Cord Meyer, Jr., the UWF won the support of atomic scientists like Harrison Brown, influential Wall Street figures like the lawyer (and later Air Force Secretary) Thomas Finletter, publicists like *The Saturday Review's* Norman Cousins, and youth leaders like California's Alan Cranston. More importantly, the UWF showed remarkably broad mass support. At its peak in 1949, the organization included 720 local chapters in 31 states, with a membership of 45,000 men and women who succeeded in moving 17 state legislatures to pass resolutions urging Congress to begin planning toward world government.[24]

But federalists could not escape the submergence of all liberal causes beneath the rising Cold War. Oddly, the world government movement grew strongest at the very time that international tensions aggravated U.S. security fears, facilitated the expansion of the national-security state, and compromised federalism's first beliefs. In March 1947 Truman announced his determination to defend Greece, Turkey, and all "free peoples who are resisting attempted subjugation by armed minorities or by outside pressures" that seemed Communist in origin. Simultaneously, the administration established in the 1947 National Security Act and related legislation the bureaucratic means for streamlining the President's power as military commander-in-chief and preparing the country for protracted struggle. Almost in counterpoint, the Soviet Union tightened its stranglehold over occupied areas of East-Central Europe, engineered a coup d'etat in Czechoslovakia in January 1948, and, six months later, threw an overland blockade around Berlin which required a massive, eighteen-month Allied airlift to overcome. In September 1949 the USSR exploded its first nuclear device, a shattering achievement that was followed three weeks later by the final success of Mao Tse-tung's Red Army in China and, nine months later, by the North Korean attack on South Korea.

As world politics froze into two great bipolar blocs, the UWF campaign for a democratic world government sputtered and failed. Federalist leaders criticized the aggressiveness of Washington policy makers, but they also felt real concern over Stalin's ambitions. Trapped between their liberal One-World ideals and their fear of revolutionary Communism, top federalists agonized over the workability of their principles in the postwar war. Their belief in the need, for instance, of a democratic system of enforceable world law seemed meaningless in the face of Russia's heavy-handed control in East-Central Europe or before Washington's transparent indifference toward the UN. At the same time, the federalists' operational assumptions coincided all too easily with the Cold War premises of the emerging American national-security state. Federalists believed sincerely in the indivisibility of peace. So did Truman. Federalists believed that totalitarian aggressors possessed insatiable appetites. So did the State Department. Federalists believed that the United States must undertake "unlimited competition for influence in every corner of the globe."[25] So did the Pentagon.

The federalist cause grew even weaker as it became identified along with the entire peace reform as an instrument of Communist subversion. In 1948–1949, a series of Soviet-sponsored "peace offensives" among Western leftists devalued the political currency of the peace cause in America and left liberal peace seekers even more vulnerable to conservative charges of disloyalty. World federalists never regained the offensive. Attacked from without and confused within, the UWF shrank in membership through the early months of 1950, until the outbreak of the Korean War moved the organization to rally behind the U.S. intervention in the name of a UN "policing" action. But the UWF's unanimous support for the U.S.–UN role in Korea failed to save the fast-fading dream of world government or smooth over differences among its foremost leaders. Some like Cord Meyer, Jr., who resigned the UWF presidency in 1952 in order to join the Central Intelligence Agency, concluded that the cause of world order would best be realized through a global U.S. police role. Others like Norman Cousins, who succeeded Meyer to the organization's presidency, resolved to stand by their original principles, resist the anti-Communist sweep of American politics, and work toward those conditions most supportive of world government. With a remnant of atomic scientists, Cousins and the remaining world government activists maintained through the 1950s an emphatic opposition to any and all atomic war. Confirmed "nuclear pacifists," they nurtured a spirit of species "survivalism" that gave impetus in 1957 to the formation of the National Committee for a SANE Nuclear Policy and renewed liberal interest in controlling the nuclear menace.[26]

The third major postwar peace element consisted of those various pacifists who worked at living peace. Organizationally, liberal pacifists in the FOR and WILPF emerged from the war with small but committed constituencies. Most opposed the UN's collective security aspirations, although they valued the new organization's functional administrative agencies (such as UNRRA and UNESCO) as the sinews of an expanding world order that flourished as it served vital human needs. Pacifist veterans like the WILPF's Emily Greene Balch attacked Great Power pre-eminence at the UN and dismissed the possibility of enforcing peace. But they held fast to their belief that peace would best penetrate human relations with the spread through the UN and other agencies of organized benevolence.

The country's new cluster of radical pacifists was much less optimistic. Hardened by their experiences in wartime resistance to racial segregation and government authority, Gandhian activists like David Dellinger and Jim Peck moved after 1945 to attack war and injustice through disciplined cadres that combined democratic socialist politics and a nonviolent spiritual vision. They were revolutionaries who despised "the traditional revolutionary tendency to think of people as mere instruments to be used for bringing about a future revolution."[27] Instead, radical pacifists sought first to work an "inner transformation" within peace-minded individuals as the way of organizing a popular revolution against war and institutionalized violence. Seeking mutual support and a means of action, several moved between 1945 and 1948 to create a number of autonomous groups like the Committee for Non-Violent Action and Peacemakers, which was patterned after Gandhi's Indian *ashrams*. Decentralizers and disobedients, radical pacifists furthermore organized income-tax resistance and mass protests against Washington's reinstitutionalization in 1948 of military conscription. They resolved on individual resistance as mankind's "best hope" at a moment when impersonal social forces were carrying the species toward disaster. "To insist on acting as a responsible individual in a society which reduces the individual to impotence may be foolish, reckless, and ineffectual"; thought Dwight Macdonald, "or it may be wise, prudent and effective. But whichever it is, only thus is there a chance of changing our present tragic destiny."[28]

Radical pacifists failed to sustain any organizational momentum by 1950 or to work any major effect. Yet neither they nor other pacifists considered making peace with the warmakers. Pacifists knew, with all other peace seekers, that they had to end the nuclear menace and reconstitute a general faith in the possibility of realizing peace with justice. But they also knew that the Holocaust and the bomb had enormously intensified global fear and made people more dependent on governments which were prone to violence and indifferent toward injustice. More avidly than anyone, pacifists battled for the next generation to overcome injustice and end preparations for World War III. They refused to deal either in the politics of appeasement or of the apocalypse.

The one figure who managed to link the concerns of the various pacifist persuasions was A. J. Muste. Frustrated in his wartime attempts to reconcile governing authorities and resisting COs, Muste was positively shocked by Washington's decision to atomize Hiroshima and Nagasaki while Japan was sinking in defeat. "No political or moral appraisal of our age is adequate," he wrote in his last major work, "no attempt to find an answer to its dilemmas and destiny offers hope, which does not take adequate account of that fact."[29] Extolling absolute love as the only alternative to the demands of the modern power-state, the veteran FOR secretary urged pacifists on toward a variety of peace actions in postwar America. He and others practiced tax resistance and refused after 1948 to register for the draft. They publicly burned their draft cards in symbolic protest against renewed conscription and urged atomic scientists to stop their search for more efficient instruments of death. At the least, Muste and other postwar pacifists aimed *"to leaven academic, scientific and religious institutions with pacifist values."* At most, they tried to build an effective non-Communist left "that must be nonviolent in order that we might be neither victims nor executioners."[30]

Opposed to Communist totalitarianism, Muste and other pacifists held that America could best meet the Soviet challenge by securing model economic and racial justice at home. In April 1947 the FOR assisted George Houser, James Farmer, and other CORE leaders in a two-week "Journey of Reconciliation" through the upper South, in the first biracial attempt to test compliance with recent Supreme Court decisions against segregation in interstate travel. The nonviolent foray against Jim Crow bus trips produced several jailings, some beatings, and a little publicity. Yet it provided "a dramatic high point" that sustained CORE's organizational morale until the remarkable "Freedom Rides" of the early 1960s.[31]

More immediately, the joint FOR-CORE action exemplified

Muste's determination to attack those domestic injustices that Cold War liberals felt obliged to underplay as they battled a resurgent right wing at home and Communism abroad. But the strategy worked little impact. Popularly identified with the appeasing diplomats who helped lead the way to World War II, pacifist leaders rapidly lost influence among anti-Communist liberals, who were rallying to the defense of the national-security state, and among liberal Protestant churchmen, who were turning toward the comforts of neo-orthodox theology. Weakened in their two main constituencies, pacifists tried through internal community-building and symbolic actions to highlight the country's domestic failings and alternatives to the Cold War. It was the most realistic tack for activists who hungered for peace in a country gearing for war.

With pacifism, the larger peace movement fell back after 1948, as its main bases of support became absorbed in the national quarrels over the future of the New Deal welfare state and the Communist challenge. Organized labor, which was struggling to preserve its newly won bargaining rights against conservative counterattack, was riven by division between the A.F. of L. and C.I.O., and anxious to purge itself of racketeers and Communists. The interests of organized women took on a vocational coloration, as middle-class women's groups struggled to preserve the woman's place in the professional work force against a tide of returning veterans. College campuses, crowded by returning GIs, likewise turned away from social activism and toward a career orientation that fit the desires of a generation that had already struggled for its life-cause in Europe and the Pacific. Organized religion ministered to the greater part of the country that was "in a settling-down mood."[32] And political liberalism shattered.

Beginning in the mid-forties, there arose a group of anti-Communist liberals who supported Truman's Cold War policies, greater public works projects through enlarged military spending, and a strong presidency responsible for domestic reform and international stability. Deriving their strength from many sources,* Cold War liberals prided themselves upon their political realism

*The Cold War liberal coalition included New Deal enthusiasts like Eleanor Roosevelt and Chester Bowles, anti-Communist labor leaders like Walter Reuther and David Dubinsky, anti-Popular Front politicians like Hubert Humphrey, and "activist-scholars" like Arthur M. Schlesinger, Jr., and Reinhold Niebuhr. Alonzo L. Hamby, *Beyond the New Deal: Harry S. Truman and American Liberalism* (New York: Columbia University Press, 1973), pp. 161–62.

and their pragmatic opposition to a popular front with Communists. When former Vice-President Henry A. Wallace and the Communist-influenced Progressive Citizens of America argued for a leftist united front and more conciliatory policies toward the Soviet Union, anti-Communist liberals responded by forming the Americans for Democratic Action in January 1947. The infant ADA emphatically supported New Deal welfare programs, the UN, and fuller civil liberties. But it explicitly excluded Communists from membership and opposed calls for a less militant Russian policy. Organizing to full strength, the two liberal armies battled bitterly until November 1948, when Truman squeaked to a presidential victory in a wild four-party campaign that killed Wallace's vague "peace liberalism," ended the last hopes of seriously pursuing American peace interests through the UN, and deferred dreams of a renewed popular front on the left until the 1960s.

The massive fracture of postwar liberalism and the accompanying "defection of the intellectuals" to either apathy or the celebration of Cold War America—coming atop labor's besiegement, the socialists' decline, student uninterest, women's distractions, and Protestantism's passivity—altogether cut peace activists from their traditional sources of support.[33] With the country's progressive coalition in disarray, peace reformers lost their most reliable audiences and strongest sympathizers. And they could not find others. The Congress's dominant conservative coalition of Republicans and southern Democrats existed to oppose domestic reform efforts and attack Communism. Republicans hungered for party unity and presidential victory. Right-wing activists smelled subversive intent in any reform endeavor.

The outbreak of the Korean War in June 1950 demonstrated most fully the humiliating weakness of the peace movement. Pacifists in the FOR and WILPF called for an immediate ceasefire and a UN–negotiated settlement; and the WRL mounted a handful of meager protests. But that proved the limit of opposition. On the other side, one-time pacifists like Norman Thomas and Dwight Macdonald backed the U.S. intervention, while internationalists and federalists approved the combined U.S.–UN action as a vindication of the principle of collective security and a step toward world government. And the national-security state flourished. Between 1950 and 1953, U.S. military expenditures quadrupled, and the number of men under arms tripled. The level of civilian defense-related personnel nearly doubled, while the CIA grew sixfold "into an independent government agency commanding manpower and budget far exceeding anything originally imagined."[34] In this atmosphere, it was understandable that the greatest expression of antiwar dissent took place in April 1951, when Truman fired the joint U.S.–UN commanding general Douglas MacArthur because of the general's demands that the war be widened into China. Incongruously, the loudest opposition to America's first land war in the Atomic Age arose among those who complained that the war was not big enough.[35]

Thus, when Wisconsin Senator Joseph R. McCarthy announced in February 1950 that he had evidence of Communists in high governmental positions, he only loosed a four-year reign of repressive conservative activism that had long been building. Although customarily identified with the Wisconsin Republican, McCarthyism was actually a sensationalized extension of the hypernationalistic anti-Communism that had been the political habit of anti-New Deal conservatives for nearly a generation. It merely worked better in the early 1950s. It worked better because of the desperate nature of Republican political needs, the frustrations of the limited war in Korea, and the domestic conformitarian demands exacted by a national-security state.

Anxious to overcome the doubtful and repel the alien, the Congress passed a series of anti-sedition and immigration control bills after 1950. Officials in the executive branch hounded from office, through security checks and loyalty clearances, hundreds of skeptical or unlucky government employees. The Supreme Court approved the imprisonment of top Communist Party leaders in the 1951 *Dennis* decision, on the grounds that their beliefs constituted a clear and present danger to the republic. Each major party struggled to assert the superiority of its anti-Communist credentials. Unchecked by any offsetting institutional force, politics in Cold War America veered into a fogbank of rightist repression. After the early 1950s only the lonely professed to doubt the need for a vigilant security state and the danger of subversives within and enemies without.

Within this climate, the peace movement tumbled to the lowest point of its twentieth-century influence. Its constituencies were broken and preoccupied. Its leaders were harassed and divided. Some insisted upon standing in defense of the necessary peace reform in a suspicious society. Others chose the immediate work of protecting civil liberties against dangerous encroachment. Yet even in the movement's weakness there appeared signs of revival and regeneration. With both the Cold War and American politics frozen in immobility, peace seekers reflected and acted on alternative ways of coming to terms with an inhospitable world. And out of their reflections and actions came the momentum that carried the peace reform out of weakness and toward social relevance in the last half of the 1950s.

Starting in 1954, peace leaders took advantage of a combination of improving political conditions, promising internal developments, and pressing social concerns to reinvigorate their movement. Political conditions improved following the end of the Korean War, the collapse of Senator McCarthy, and an improvement in Soviet-American relations. Internally, the peace movement gained new intellectual vigor following the publication in 1955 of the AFSC pamphlet, *Speak Truth to Power*, and the concurrent rise of a group of social scientists committed to the creation of a discipline of peace research that would provide the rational bases for a lasting peace.[36] Most importantly, the movement seized new strength in the middle 1950s when two fresh issues—the civil rights crusade and the danger of radioactive nuclear fallout—roused its traditional supporters to renewed opposition to racial injustice in America and to the atomic menace in the world.

Reaching across an unusual cross-section of urban middle-class liberals, rural southern blacks, and atomic scientists, the two issues precipitated the development among peace seekers of two lines of strategic action. One line of strategy, which was pursued by the radical pacifist Committee for Non-Violent Action (CNVA) and Martin Luther King's Southern Christian Leadership Conference (SCLC), emphasized nonviolent direct action toward the social salvation of the oppressed and the spiritual liberation of the oppressor. Alive with spiritual fervor and high drama, direct actionism was intended to serve as the cutting edge of fundamental social change as armies of aroused citizens peaceably attacked racism and armaments. In a parallel way, the more traditional strategy of the liberal nuclear pacifists, who led the National Committee for a SANE Nuclear Policy (SANE) as well as the scientists' Pugwash conferences, involved more familiar techniques of petitioning and lobbying toward the specific end of halting atmospheric nuclear testing and the atomic arms race. Although temperamentally more secular and rationalistic, liberal nuclear pacifists knew with radical direct actionists that they shared the same cause. They realized before anyone that the struggle for human dignity and human survival, civil rights and nuclear disarmament, were one.

Radical pacifists in CORE and the FOR had long been active in resisting racial discrimination through nonviolent direct action. Yet none of their work galvanized blacks and sympathetic whites like the force that swept Montgomery, Alabama, in December 1955, when Mrs. Rosa Parks was arrested for refusing to leave a seat in the "whites-only" section of a city bus. Organizing and improvising, Montgomery black leaders sustained an extraordinarily solid boycott of the municipal bus lines in a classic exercise in non-cooperation that shook the local white establishment, seized international headlines, and catapulted into prominence a charismatic preacher named Martin Luther King, Jr.

The well-educated son of a leading Atlanta Baptist minister, the 25-year-old King had served as pastor of Montgomery's Dexter Avenue Baptist Church for nearly two years when he accepted the chairmanship of the Montgomery Improvement Association and responsibility for the victorious resolution of the bus boycott. Encouraged by money and advisers from CORE and the FOR, King and the MIA began hastily to drill local blacks in the techniques of nonviolent resistance to official abuse, and won national sympathy for their patient calls for Christian justice. Personally, King at the same time re-examined the writings of Gandhi and social-gospel clerics, and underwent a conversion to a faith in nonviolent resistance that fused loving Christianity and peaceable direct action. "Christ furnished the spirit and motivation," he liked later to say of the Montgomery boycott, "while Gandhi furnished the method." Through the whole process, King fired the two welds that connected the peace and civil rights movements for the next ten years. He joined the concerns of middle-class northern whites with the needs of sub-caste southern blacks. And he channeled the "feral outrage" felt by oppressed blacks into a massive but nonviolent crusade that proved the relevance to a modern society of Gandhian techniques.[37]

Yet King realized that the victory of nonviolence in Montgomery did not represent a full victory for the highly-disciplined life of true Gandhian *satyagraha,* or truth-seeking. Anxious to promote the life—and not merely the techniques—of nonviolent resistance, King worked with the clergymen Fred Shuttlesworth and Ralph Abernathy in forming in January 1957 the Southern Christian Leadership Conference (SCLC; originally, the Southern Leadership Conference on Transportation and Non-Violent Integration) in order to mobilize southern blacks for the peaceable overthrow of institutionalized racial segregation. In the same spirit, he worked more closely with northern white pacifists affiliated with CORE and the FOR, and undertook an extended tour of India early in 1959, that was underwritten by the AFSC. Altogether, King's studies, his confrontation experiences, his survival under the constant threat of death, and his growing admiration for Gandhi and Ghana's Kwame Nkhruma steeled him in his deepening determination to act as the loving agent in the liberation of his people. Equally, however, he resolved to realize through black liberation the "soul-truth" of the white Christian oppressor and emancipate through direct action the whole society from its sinfulness. King wanted to show that mass nonviolent resistance was not simply one technique toward racial progress in America, "but the sole authentic approach to the problem of social injustice."[38]

His hopes were soon outstripped, however, by the rapid alteration of race relations in the South and the anxiety that this alteration produced among whites throughout the country. In February 1960 the civil rights struggle entered a new phase when black college students engaged in a passive but unyielding "sit-in" at a segregated dime-store lunch counter in Greensboro, North Carolina. Spreading quickly throughout the South, the "sit-in" tactic set off a surge of fresh militancy among southern students and local civil rights leaders. It also fired a need for further organization. Aided by student activists like Julian Bond, SCLC organizers like Ella Baker, and FOR veterans like Bayard Rustin, King presided in May 1960 over the formation of the Student Nonviolent Coordinating Committee (SNCC). Powered by black and white students, SNCC was originally designed as an organizing instrument for a nation-wide campaign of selective buying against racially discriminatory business firms and as an agency for the disciplining of cadres of nonviolent resisters. Plainly, King helped instill in SNCC an early emphasis upon militant action toward liberation and reconciliation. Yet the depth of his imprint was highly uncertain. Montgomery, SCLC, CORE, and SNCC had shown that Gandhian *techniques* could work in America. What remained at issue at the start of the 1960s was whether the country could accept the Gandhian *way* of nonviolent reconciliation and welcome the liberation through "soul-truth" of the oppressor as well as the oppressed.

Besides the civil rights movement, the issue of atmospheric nuclear testing gave new life to American peace activism in the mid-1950s. Pushed by concerned scientists, the testing issue arose after 1954 with a force that set off "the most passionate politics among scientists since World War II."[39] Disturbed by the fallout danger, the British philosopher Bertrand Russell joined Albert Einstein and nine other renowned international scientists (including seven Nobel Prize winners) in issuing in July 1955 an appeal for governments to acknowledge the suicidal nature of modern nuclear war and to seek only pacific means in settling their disputes.[40] Shortly after, the World Association of Parliamentarians for World Government convened in London an international conference of scientists that was brightened by the unexpected appearance of a four-man Soviet delegation. Encouraged by the Russian presence, organizers of the London meeting scheduled a Conference on Science and World Affairs that met in July 1957 in Pugwash, Nova Scotia, in the first in a series of similar scientific gatherings. In the same month the famed chemist Linus Pauling issued a statement signed by 11,000 scientists, including 2,000 Americans, that called for an early international agreement against atmospheric testing.

The unprecedented cooperation among the world's foremost scientists to limit atmospheric testing heightened the growing concern within the peace movement over the same issue. Early in 1957 New York-area pacifists led by the AFSC's Lawrence Scott and Clarence Pickett formed the ad hoc Committee to Stop H-Bomb Tests. Goaded by Muste and Rustin, Scott convened a larger meeting in April of liberal pacifists from the WILPF and WRL, internationalists from the rump world government movement, and unaffiliated radical pacifists for the purpose of forging an ambitious "tripartite alliance." Linked in common concern, peace leaders agreed to form within their respective constituencies two new organizations that would serve as "the important dual thrusts of the same movement" against nuclear weaponry.[41] Radical pacifists consented to organize the Committee for Nonviolent Action (CNVA; for the first two years, the organization was called Non-

Violent Action Against Nuclear Weapons) and undertake direct action toward unilateral and immediate disarmament. Liberal pacifists and internationalists agreed to develop the National Committee for a SANE Nuclear Policy (SANE) in order to generate pressure through more traditional techniques for gradual general disarmament and international control of atomic development.

In May 1957 Muste and Scott gathered the CNVA out of a few score radical pacifists who were already emboldened by the success of their year-old journal of principled expression, *Liberation* magazine. Deliberately designed as the cutting edge of a revived peace movement, the CNVA organized for the purpose of dramatizing the saliency of war/peace issues through symbolic protests such as tax refusal, trespassing upon atomic testing sites, and international walks for peace and disarmament. Activist in orientation, the group was Quaker in coloration and democratic socialist in its politics.

Between 1957 and 1959 CNVA activists gently invaded U.S. missile installations and nuclear test sites from Omaha, Nebraska, to the Pacific Ocean. In the process, they won jail terms, publicity, and encouraging expressions of larger support. But their actions also forced to the surface serious differences among radical pacifists over crucial tactical issues. Distressed by the Committee's preoccupation with civil disobedience, Quakers like Scott and George Willoughby decided in the summer of 1959 to withdraw from the group in order to pursue their own concerns with peace education and atmospheric testing. In their place, more militant peace seekers like Bradford Lyttle rose to the top of the CNVA and resolved all the more to jolt the American people into considering the twin threats of war and militarism.

At the turn of the 1960s the reconstituted CNVA ambitiously planned more aggressive actions. In September 1960 planning began for a San Francisco to Moscow Walk for Peace, which commenced three months later. Also in September the CNVA challenged the military-industrial extension of the national-security state when it initiated in New London, Connecticut, its Polaris Action, a citywide campaign to urge workers against complicity in the construction of nuclear-missile-bearing Polaris submarines. Pacifist militants combined direct action techniques, such as leaping aboard berthed submarines, with educational attempts to dissuade townspeople from participating in the manufacture of the vessels.

But their gains were minimal. Activists in the CNVA had attacked the national-security state at its most formidable salient—the war economy; and they barely made a dent.

In the meantime, world government leaders like Cousins, scientists like Pauling, and pacifists like Homer Jack organized SANE. First formed in fall 1957, SANE did not gain national prominence until November 15, when it published a *New York Times* advertisement that called for an immediate suspension of atomic testing and the long-term redirection of human loyalties toward the global community. Popular response to the appeal was unexpectedly strong. Requests for 25,000 copies of the statement, along with $12,000 in contributions, flowed into SANE's New York headquarters. By the following summer, nearly 130 SANE chapters were established around the country, with a membership of 5,000 people.

The sudden success of SANE resulted from its position as a moderately liberal, single-issue organization that promised to help the species survive. Within American politics, SANE offered "a retreat bunker for liberals who couldn't find a place to take a stand in the structure of political parties."[42] Within the peace movement, it filled the gap that had opened among liberal peace seekers following the decline of the world government cause and the shift among internationalists to the support of Cold War America's interventionist policies. Strategically, the new organization sought a nuclear test-ban agreement under UN auspices, a goal that it later broadened to include a UN-supervised system of general disarmament. Operationally, it employed traditional means of educating the electorate toward the support of "nuclear pacifism," and avoided any "eyebrow raising" tactics.[43] Leaders of SANE built by their modesty an organization that was most appropriate to liberal peace needs during the Cold War. What was at question was whether liberalism was appropriate for converting the Cold War into a working peace.

That question beset SANE from its inception. Hardly one month before the appearance of the pathbreaking *Times* advertisement, a Soviet Sputnik satellite orbited the earth in a stunning display of Russian technological advancement and missile capability. Shocked by Moscow's achievement, U.S. government leaders urged educators to produce a generation of aerospace engineers and technicians, while intellectuals and scientists rededicated themselves to support the peace that came with the Pentagon's power.

The fragility of liberal peace seeking became even more manifest three years later, when major debate flared within SANE over the generation-old leftist question of whether to accept Communist support. In May 1960, shortly before a giant SANE rally scheduled for New York's Madison Square Garden, Connecticut Senator Thomas Dodd, a former UWF activist and temporary head of the Senate Internal Security Committee, attacked the organization as Communist-influenced. Stung by Dodd's accusation, SANE executive committee president Cousins immediately responded by declaring that Communist Party membership was "incompatible with association with SANE." "We do not think," Cousins and Pickett told local SANE leaders, "it is possible to mount a powerful peace movement in the United States if we take a contrary position on this issue."[44]

Cousins's decision precipitated a major division within SANE and left a residue of resentment that dogged the organization for the next decade. Prompted by Muste, radical pacifists quit SANE in protest, partly because of the craven nature of Cousins's retreat, but mostly because of what they deemed to be a major reversal for the whole peace movement. With most observers, Muste believed that the movement was regaining momentum along a broad leftist front in the early 1960s; and it was, he held, because Dodd and other Washington officials "knew that, *that* they moved when they did."[45] But Cousins and other "nuclear pacifists" believed that the anti-Communist purge was essential in helping SANE to build an independent peace movement in the face of national security fears. Dodging right-wing attacks from the beginning, SANE's dominant liberal leadership aimed to assemble a progressive movement that would "strengthen America's relationship with other peoples through the creation of nuclear policy that can serve as the basis for world leadership."[46] Members of SANE wanted the peace reform to become once more a respectable endeavor; and they felt that it could best become respectable—and effective—as it first met American security concerns through the international control of nuclear weaponry.

Their modesty was reasonable in light of their experiences. Between 1941 and 1960 the dialectic that arose in World War I between war's mounting destructiveness and peace's growing inaccessibility advanced with shattering effect upon the American peace movement. For the sake of security through violence, the United States joined in a war that cost over 55 million lives, developed nuclear and thermonuclear means of extinguishing its enemies, and prepared methods of delivering mass doom with unsurpassed speed. War for the first time became a threat to the literal survival of the species. Yet peace did not appear as anything more than armed deterrence. Almost as depressingly, citizen peacemakers proved little match to a national-security state that aimed to "wage" peace abroad and extend quiescence at home. Challenging the security credo that official America called peace, peace workers seemed by their very efforts to be in the service of a subversive reform. They seemed to their opponents dangerously willing to transcend the claims of military security in order to help peace break out.

Chapter Eight
The Deferred Reform

Gathering strength after 1957, peace activists rode into the 1960s hoping to halt the nuclear arms race and end the Cold War. Brimming with new supporters and confidence, organized citizen peace seeking worked a mixed but promising record of success until 1965, when the sudden expansion of U.S. military involvement in Vietnam ignited outbursts of opposition and drove top peace reformers to the center of an antiwar coalition. For the next ten years, veteran volunteer peacemakers provided the one source of stable strength within an ever-changing antiwar movement. In the process, they helped to contain the war's violence and to identify Vietnam as the logical and costly consequence of Washington's determination to wage peace through military deterrence. Peace workers won some solid educational and political victories through their anitwar opposition; but they also paid a heavy price. Ineluctably, antiwar activism obliged peace seekers to retreat from their first concern with the nuclear arms race and global underdevelopment, and to subordinate the struggle for lasting peace advances to the immediate need to end the war. "Imagine at dawn sometimes," the Rev. Daniel Berrigan once brooded, "I actually dream the war is over and I am free to turn to some of the great questions from which these years are so monstrous a distraction." "What a marvelous century it might have been," he thought. "Imagine what we might have done with our lives!"[1]

The peace movement entered the 1960s with as much strength, variety, appeal, and potential as it had at any time in its history. It claimed in spokesmen like A. J. Muste some highly persuasive leaders. It offered reasonable alternatives to the pressing national issues of atmospheric nuclear testing and endless Cold War. It possessed in SANE (for liberal internationalists), FOR and WILPF (for tra-

ditional pacifists), and CNVA and WRL (for radical pacifists) three
operational bases of action. And it was gaining new centers of support and encouragement.

Beginning in 1959 fresh collections of students, intellectuals, and
women sped into the work of organized peace seeking. Originating
among Chicago-area pacifists and socialists, the Student Peace
Union (SPU) emerged in 1959, committed to working "independently of the existing power blocs" toward the dismantling of the
nuclear arms race and international militarism. It was the first
major student peace organization of the American sixties.[2] In the
following spring a group of high-powered intellectuals, including
David Riesman, Erich Fromm, and Lewis Mumford, gathered
themselves into The Committee of Correspondence, in order to
concentrate their collective intelligence on alternatives to the arms
race and on "the crucial problem facing men today: how to survive
with honor and with human dignity."[3] Early the next year, veteran
federalists fashioned the World Law Fund as an educational branch
of the thirteen-year-old Institute for International Order for the
purpose of catalyzing "new thinking commensurate with the realities of our age."[4] A few months later Dagmar Wilson and other
impatient Washington-area feminists organized several local wom-
en's peace action groups into the national Women Strike for Peace
(WSP) as a means of mobilizing women—and especially mothers—
in protest against the expanding nuclear arms race. Organizationally invertebrate, WSP operated without dues or a formal
membership list. But it did put women peace protestors in the
streets and politicians on notice.

The most ambitious attempt to convert the newly assertive
peace concern into the reform of American foreign policy was Turn
Toward Peace (TTP), a clearinghouse of nearly forty peace, church,
and labor organizations formed in the fall of 1961. Headed by
Norman Thomas and coordinated by the pacifists Robert Gilmore
and Robert Pickus, TTP aimed to attach the peace movement to
established change-making forces in American society in an attempt to divert policy makers from the further militarization of
Washington's Cold War policies. The campaign undertook elaborate
organizational efforts in a score of American communities and
made intensive efforts to win the communications media to a more
sympathetic peace stance. But it failed to establish any devices that
might channel generalized peace sentiment into a force capable of
moving elite policy makers.

Nonetheless, TTP succeeded in emphasizing the entire peace movement's opposition to Cold War America's central strategy of deterrence. Peace leaders felt sure that the superpowers' mutual strategy of maintaining a rough international equilibrium and avoiding major war by threatening each other with annihilation was foredoomed to failure. The policy of deterrence was as fragile as "an egg on a golf tee," one critic complained. "It is stable for small but not large disturbances."[5] Yet the great majority of peace seekers was unwilling to join the radical pacifist minority in demanding a unilateral American renunciation of the entire arms race. Instead, they talked of limited U.S. peace initiatives and the need for graduated, reciprocal reduction in tension.

Not satisfied with forming new organizations and issuing policy critiques, the resurgent peace movement also undertook new actions. In April 1961 SANE and other peace liberals mobilized over 25,000 demonstrators throughout the United States in a show of solidarity with the fifth annual "Ban-the-Bomb" marches in Aldermaston, England. It was the largest American peace demonstration in a generation. Eight months later, WSP rallied 50,000 women in 60 cities against the nuclear arms race and in favor of mutual disarmament. In mid-February 1962 nearly 7,000 student peace activists responded to an SPU call to demonstrate and lobby in Washington against continued atmospheric testing and proposed civil defense programs. The student action proved more than ephemeral. Spurred by concern over the expanding arms race and the viability of an American left, membership in the SPU mushroomed to a peak of 4,000 by 1962, while the formative *Port Huron Statement* of the Students for a Democratic Society made an explicit connection between an end to the Cold War and advancing domestic reform.

Peace liberals meanwhile prepared for electoral action. In the 1962 congressional elections, more candidates ran for office on positive peace platforms than ever before in Cold War America. The electoral results proved disappointing. Yet even this setback was counteracted in December, when WSP activists challenged for the first time the House Un-American Activities Committee's practice of identifying citizen peace seeking with Communist subversion. Testifying in open hearings, WSP militants spoke freely of their individual peace efforts, refused to identify others with their actions, and boldly declared their non-exclusionist intention to welcome anyone—including Communists—to share in their work. The open disdain of the WSP for HUAC did not end the Congress's preference for treating private peace action as subversive. But it did help break the petrified anti-Communism of Cold War American politics and gave heart to those reformers who conceived of peace as more than military preparedness.

Ironically, the very success of the resurgent peace movement tempered its long-term effectiveness. In the fall of 1961 Congress established the Arms Control and Disarmament Agency within the Pentagon as an institutional means of coming to terms with the arms race. Even more strikingly, Washington and Moscow concluded in August 1963 a limited test-ban treaty which prohibited nuclear testing at sea or in the air. While containing a loophole permitting underground testing, the treaty constituted the first significant breakthrough toward arms control among the Great Powers since the 1920s. Peace militants continued to press for an absolute ban on testing and for more active disarmament efforts. But the limited test-ban treaty invested with new credibility the Kennedy administration's promise to wage peace by negotiating through military strength. Playing off of the right-wing passion for "total victory," Kennedy took advantage of a thaw in Soviet-American relations to present himself as the champion of détente. By fall 1963 the test-ban treaty, the improved climate of superpower politics, an accompanying decline in popular fear of atomic fallout, and the distraction of the black civil rights crusade together robbed the peace movement of the momentum that it had briefly gained at the turn of the decade.[6]

Even more devastating was the remembered weakness of the peace seekers' response to the October 1962 Cuban missile crisis. While Moscow and Washington moved along a collision course over the emplacement of Soviet missiles in Cuba, WILPF leaders urged Kennedy to halt the U.S. naval blockade of the island and to submit the entire question to the UN. Activists in SANE similarly pressed the administration to consider the Russian proposal for the joint withdrawal of missiles from Cuba and Turkey. Spontaneous peace demonstrations erupted on various campuses; and a few thousand marchers demonstrated in New York, Washington, and San Francisco, demanding some negotiated alternative to nuclear catastrophe. But altogether the peace movement's response to the world's closest brush with atomic self-destruction was humiliatingly weak. There was no use minimizing the fact, wrote one critic, "that we came near being blown up, and that our almost total impotence to avert the crisis has had its effect on all of us".[7]

The Cuban missile crisis not only exposed the meager political influence of the resurgent peace reform but also gave new force to the criticism raised by emerging New Left spokesmen that the issue of nuclear testing was distracting peace seekers from realizing how America's repressive presence in the Third World was blocking necessary change abroad and progressive advances at home. A product of many forces, the New Left shot forward in the early sixties, as an amalgam of student radicals, civil rights workers, and action-oriented intellectuals who aimed to democratize American society by dismantling the welfare state and decentralizing corporate power. Unlike Old Left remnants of the 1930s, New Left militants valued action over theory, inclusiveness over sectarianism, and institutional decentralization over consolidation. Operationally, they moved South with SNCC in support of the civil rights struggle, battled at the University of California-Berkeley in defense of the Free Speech Movement, and organized community action projects in impoverished ghettoes from Newark to Chicago. They also cared deeply about foreign affairs.[8]

The SDS best typified the early New Left orientation. Established in January 1960 by the socialist League for Industrial Democracy and activated by student radicals like Tom Hayden and Al Haber, SDS was the first action agency to demand "participatory democracy" in America's corporatizing society, attack the sense of personal alienation bred by huge institutions (most importantly, universities), and convincingly connect the persistence of social injustice at home with status quo liberalism. Leaders of SDS claimed no detailed foreign policy program. But they were self-consciously world-minded, suspicious of U.S. interests in the underdeveloped world, and committed to the domestic conversion of the military economy to civilian needs.[9]

With other New Left activists, SDS leaders felt great concern over the Cold War because of their belief that a militarized America stood opposed to necessary radical change at home and abroad. At first, SDS militants worked to demilitarize America by cooperating with TTP and other peace liberals in attempts to link academic peace research to efforts at community organizing and full-employment alternatives to the Cold War. By the start of 1964, however, Washington's tolerance for underdevelopment at home and its resistance to revolutions abroad moved SDS closer to Old Left remnants (most notably, the pro-Maoist Progressive Labor Party, the Trotskyist Socialist Workers Party, and its youth affiliate, the Young Socialist Alliance) in attacking U.S. interventionism in the Third World. Convinced that "A movement against Overkill and Underdevelopment is the social imperative today," SDS leaders like Richard Flacks identified American involvement in Vietnam as "the single most important foreign policy issue which peace groups can act on." There was "a desperate need," he declared, for peacemakers "to forcefully

> articulate an alternative to the policy of counterinsurgency—an alternative based on aid through the UN rather than bayonets and napalm as a means of meeting the problems of the Third World. Are detente and disarmament possible if this issue is not faced?[10]

Like SDS, peace liberals in SANE and FOR recognized Washington's growing interest in the Third World and opposed the official emphasis upon counterrevolutionary military action. Yet radical and liberal peace seekers failed to find common ground for working agreement until they encountered a concrete issue. And that was Vietnam. Peace leaders had long feared that U.S. involvement in Vietnam might produce another Korean War or even worse. But they did not express serious concern until the summer of 1963, when the weakening of the Saigon government produced growing instability within South Vietnam, an expanding American presence, and the first stirrings of antiwar opposition in the United States.

In August 1963 the U.S.-supported government of Ngo Dinh Diem concluded a repressive campaign against South Vietnamese Buddhists which divided the officers corps of the Army of the Republic of Vietnam (ARVN) and bolstered the guerrilla power of the Communist-dominated National Liberation Front (NLF). One month later the National Board of SANE called for American "disengagement" from Vietnam. Three weeks later student radicals from SPU and SDS organized protests against the U.S. visit of Diem's sister-in-law, Mme. Ngo Dinh Nhu, and Washington's general "interference in the revolution in Viet Nam and the continued American support of the Diem regime."[11] For the next several months, demands mounted within the peace movement for an immediate ceasefire in the war between Diem's Republic of Vietnam and the

NLF, and the adoption of the French suggestion for an international conference that would pave the way toward the neutralization of all Southeast Asia and the reconstitution of the 1954 Geneva accords.

In March 1964 Senate Foreign Relations Committee chairman J. William Fulbright (Dem.-Arkansas) gave fuller force to demands for a peaceable U.S. disengagement from Vietnam in a major attack on the "old myths" of Cold War orthodoxy that blinded Washington to the "new realities" of the international system. Early the next month over 200 feminists from WILPF and WSP rallied in Washington to demand an immediate ceasefire and expose "the myth that South Vietnam is being invaded." One month later, a Maoist coalition called the May 2d Movement (M2M) organized 1,000 young socialists in five cities to advertise their refusal to fight "for the suppression of the Vietnamese struggle for national independence." Shortly after, the founding convention of the Communist Party youth affiliate, the W.E.B. DuBois Clubs, resolved to rally "a great popular movement" against U.S. intervention in Vietnam and in favor of a return to the 1954 Geneva agreements.[12]

In August, shortly after the Gulf of Tonkin clash set off deeper U.S. military involvement, over 200 radical pacifists conducted a silent vigil at the Democratic National Convention in Atlantic City in protest against "the immoral nature of U.S. policies in Vietnam." On November 28, 300 peace liberals from SANE and Americans for Democratic Action (ADA) demonstrated at the White House in favor of a negotiated peace. Three weeks later a coalition of WRL, CNVA, and Catholic Worker pacifists opened "a continuing campaign of nonviolent action to end the war in Vietnam." Borrowing a tactic used by French intellectuals in their fight against the Algerian war, the pacifist coalition issued a "Declaration of Conscience," which pledged its signatories to counsel draft resistance and employ any nonviolent action that would "stop the flow of American soldiers and munitions to Vietnam" on the grounds that "what is happening in Vietnam is a crime."[13] The words were strong, but they well conveyed the sense of moral revulsion that first energized a broad range of peace seekers and leftists in sustained antiwar opposition.

Over the winter of 1964–1965 the antiwar movement assumed a lasting triangularity that radiated from its three constituent parts: the anti-imperialist cadres of the sectarian (Old and New) left, the radical pacifist proponents of revolutionary nonviolence, and the string of peace liberals that stretched from senatorial critics to Quaker activists. Each explained the war through different analyses. Each saw in the war a different enemy. And each proposed to end the war in a different way by means of a different strategy.

To anti-imperialists, the war involved a revolutionary struggle for Vietnamese national liberation against American imperialism; the enemy was America's corporate ruling class; and the proper strategy was for radicals to take any action that would move the American people to see in their leaders democracy's real enemies, and thus pave the way toward immediate U.S. withdrawal from Vietnam and subsequent revolutionary change at home and abroad. Radical pacifists shared the first part of the left's analysis. But they defined the enemy as war, and resolved to work through any nonviolent means that would move the American people to demand immediate withdrawal and a re-emphasis upon radical nonviolent change at home.[14] Main-line peace liberals meanwhile explained the war as an error that resulted from Washington's foolhardy attempt to contain China. Identifying the enemy as Cold War zealots everywhere, peace liberals aimed to end the war through traditional means of political pressure that would compel U.S. policy makers to negotiate a settlement that opened a governmental role in Saigon to the NLF and provided for subsequent American withdrawal.[15]

In practice, the triangularity of the antiwar movement was repeatedly misshapen by intramural differences of substance and style. The left lauded Vietnamese revolutionaries, for instance, while radical pacifists wished that the Communists would use nonviolent means, and peace liberals feared that the NLF was no more than totalitarianism creeping in peasant sandals. The entwined questions of revolution and violence proved equally confounding. The left favored both; radical pacifists supported the first but not the second; and peace liberals (who lived in fear of a rightist backlash) liked neither. Tactically, the question of whether or not to include Communists in antiwar actions was a superficial issue, but one that raised old memories and major differences. Vote-conscious liberals disliked the idea; conciliation-minded radical pacifists favored it; leftists insisted on it. When one considers that these differences over substance were mixed with continuing tactical quarrels, clashes in personal style, and personality conflicts, there should be no wonder as to the antiwar movement's limitations. What is surprising is that it organized and persevered.

And that achievement was due essentially to Washington's unyielding prosecution of the war. The three parts of the antiwar movement came together in February 1965, after Lyndon Johnson's bombing of North Vietnam and his plans for major troop increases signaled the start of a massive U.S. intervention and set off a shockwave of opposition. On February 10 Dagmar Wilson led 300 WSP and WILPF picketers in Washington in demanding a negotiated settlement and "dignified" U.S. withdrawal from Vietnam. Eight days later the Rev. Daniel Berrigan told rallying pacifists that they must engage in "peaceable conflict" with the state until the United States quit Vietnam. On March 16 Alice Herz, an 82-year-old WSP member and a refugee from Nazi Germany, burned herself alive on a Detroit street in a display of her anguish over U.S. actions in Vietnam. She died ten days later, two days after the first in an epidemic of campus teach-ins on Vietnam began at the nearby University of Michigan and proceeded to sweep the country.[16]

On April 17 SDS sponsored a joint mobilization that drew over 25,000 demonstrators to Washington to listen to Senator Ernest Gruening (Dem.-Alaska) and the journalist I. F. Stone call for immediate U.S. withdrawal. The SDS action was a landmark in the antiwar movement in two ways. First, the size of the demonstration was unprecedented in wartime American history, far exceeding its organizers' most hopeful predictions. Secondly, it was the first major public demonstration in Cold War America to invite Communist participation—and this on the eve of Johnson's intervention in the Dominican Republic for the purpose of excluding Communists from positions of power.

The demonstration gave impetus to further action. In May, protests organized by the Vietnam Day Committee, which had inherited the supercharged political climate left by the recent Free Speech Movement, swept the Berkeley campus of the University of California. One month later, SANE and other peace liberals gathered over 18,000 people in New York's Madison Square Garden, where they heard the noted political theorist Hans Morgenthau and the famed pediatrician and SANE co-chairman Benjamin Spock call for a ceasefire and negotiated settlement of the war. Leaders of SANE deliberately avoided involving radical pacifists or left sectarians in the Garden rally. Yet the gathering testified fully to the fact that liberals who had voted in 1964 for peace and got war felt compelled to affirm their position through mass action. Plainly, an active antiwar movement was now stretching along a broad continuum in open dissent.

Antiwar activism expanded in the United States during 1965–1970 with such rapidity, diversity, and spontaneity that it seemed to preclude the very existence of an organized movement. One British commentator called the antiwar movement "a formless affair made up of many groups with many attitudes and many leaders, not one of whom can be called representative of the whole." An American activist agreed that antiwar elements were so confused and divided that a real movement existed only in "the fantasies of the paranoid right." Yet antiwar opposition clearly proliferated over these years, prompting perhaps 4 million people (collected in at least 560 organizations) to take different actions at different places at different times toward different ends.[17] And in sustaining a movement, anitwar opposition performed two vital functions. First, it produced awareness of an alternative America that stripped away through dissent and resistance the rational, moral, and political legitimacy of Washington's war in Indochina. Second, it provided in the process a respectable haven for those many Americans who shifted against the war in the late winter of 1968, when the Tet offensive convinced a preponderant body of opinion that the war was unwinnable. Oddly, the antiwar movement served as the domestic counterpoint to the war: it schooled millions in the limits of American power in the world; and it introduced millions to the limits of policy change within America.

The antiwar opposition after 1965 contained two major dimensions. The larger encompassed those peace liberals who resented the immorality and political foolhardiness of Johnson's war. Convinced that a client Saigon regime could not be propped up on bomb craters and burning peasants, peace liberals demanded an end of U.S. bombing as the prelude to a negotiated settlement that would provide for NLF participation in a reconstituted South Vietnamese government and the ultimate withdrawal of U.S. troops. Organized most visibly in SANE and ADA, liberal dissidents declined to challenge the legitimacy of Johnson's authority in fixing policy for Asia. But they did attack his administration's moral obtuseness and political judgment.

The opposition's second dimension surfaced among those radical pacifists and leftists who perceived a systemic connection between Washington's war in Indochina and its failure to overcome poverty and racial injustice at home. In early August 1965, as the black Watts community of Los Angeles exploded in the first major ghetto uprising of the decade, 300 representatives from over 20 peace and civil rights organizations met in Washington in the Assembly of Unrepresented People for the purpose of fusing the two movements into the cutting edge of domestic reform. Led by the civil rights leader Robert Parrish (Moses) and the pacifists David Dellinger and Staughton Lynd, the assembled radicals wanted desperately to stop the war through immediate U.S. withdrawal. But they sought just as anxiously to convert opposition to the war into a multi-issue coalition of radical domestic reformers. Immediately, the radicals' strategy created an incongruity that dogged the larger antiwar movement throughout its existence: while they struggled to stop the war, movement leaders realized that they would not be the determining force in the war's end, and that they must use the ongoing war as an organizing means toward fuller domestic justice and as a basis for preventing future Vietnams.

In practical terms, the Assembly of Unrepresented People succeeded in forming the National Coordinating Committee to End the War in Vietnam (NCCEWV). Based in Madison, Wisconsin, the NCCEWV worked to coordinate the activities of several local antiwar organizations that had sprung up across the country in sudden reaction to Johnson's escalation of the war. With its help, antiwar groups in over 50 communities involved about 100,000 people in demonstrations against the war during the October 15–16 "International Days of Protest." Several rallies featured mass mobilizations and draft card burnings—the last in direct defiance of recent congressional legislation that made the destruction of draft cards a federal felony. The October protests were particularly intense in the San Francisco Bay area, where the Vietnam Day Committee led demonstrations blocking trains carrying troops headed for Vietnam through the Oakland Army Terminal.

Five weeks later, SANE sponsored a more subdued rally that drew 25,000 supporters to Washington. Joining SANE were representatives of two recently formed groups, the pacifist Catholic Peace Fellowship and the interfaith Clergy and Laymen Concerned About Vietnam (CALCAV). The appearance of the two groups not only signaled increasing concern among religious people over Johnson's war but also marked the first important involvement by Jewish and Catholic clergy in American antiwar activism. In all events, the religious presence was needed to meet the peacemakers' mounting moral anguish. In early November a 32-year-old Baltimore Quaker named Norman Morrison doused himself with gasoline and set himself afire on the Pentagon grounds in protest against the war. One week later, the young Catholic Worker Roger LaPorte did the same thing on the United Nations Plaza.

The strategy of building a multi-issue coalition against the war gained fuller expression over the winter of 1965–1966 with the formation in New York of the Fifth Avenue Peace Parade Committee. Assembled by pacifism's master pacifier, A. J. Muste, the Committee served as a nonexclusionist gathering point for any individual or group that was willing to work toward its single goal: "Stop the War Now." With that appeal, the Committee attracted a variety of liberal, radical, and socialist elements into the broadest leftist coalition in America since World War II. It also put people in the streets. Over March 25–26, 1966, the second "International Days of Protest" mobilized the marching support of over 50,000 people in New York and another 150,000 elsewhere in the country and abroad. The costs of Washington's limited war meanwhile mounted. Over 800 Americans and Vietnamese died every week by the spring of 1966, as American military strength approached 380,000 and as American military strategy shifted toward a war of attrition that aimed to emulsify the guerrilla insurrection at its rural base.

The war's growing cost and viciousness prompted Sen. Fulbright to convene the Senate Foreign Relations Committee in February 1966 in open hearings on administration policy and its alternatives. It proved a most visible forum for polite dissent. Contending that Vietnam was diverting strength from America's real strategic needs, prominent policy critics like retired Lt.-Gen. James Gavin and the veteran diplomat George Kennan urged the Johnson administration to limit the U.S. role in Saigon and turn the war over to the Vietnamese. Dismissing any talk of withdrawal, these prestigious dissenters actually had little in common with the great majority of antiwar activists. But their criticisms brought the antiwar opposition fuller public attention and greater respectability. The dissent of one general, as Dr. Spock declared, seemed easily "worth the objection of ten professors or ministers."[18]

Yet whatever respectability the antiwar opposition gained from the Fulbright hearings was offset over 1966 by the increasing attachment of hippies to the peace cause. Generally young and highly experimental in matters of drugs, sex, and lifestyle, hippies poured across the bourgeois American consciousness in the middle sixties. Historically, they represented the latest expression of the country's bohemian sub-culture, which traditionally emphasized personal liberation through the pursuit of alternative lifestyles, along with an ambiguous attitude toward social reform. More immediately, they took pleasure in shocking the surrounding culture. Hippies flaunted formless old clothes, long hairstyles, and a preference for mind-altering drugs and "acid" rock music. They spoke of the need for simplicity and community, love and peace. And they deeply bothered middle-class America.[19]

More cerebral hippie sympathizers offered a sophisticated critique of the cultural *anomie*, personal alienation, and criminal absurdities that inhered in the highly rationalistic, technocratic forms favored by modern industrial-bureaucratic societies. But hippies as a whole failed to translate that critique into an attractive and self-sustaining social alternative. They rather took pride in their appearance as a slouching reproach to the emptiness of the competitive society and the work ethic. Addicted to individualism and sensual gratification, hippies lacked the discipline and dedication needed to serve as patient participants in a prolonged antiwar struggle. Yet they leavened the movement with color and comedy. And they added to it a gentle spirit which attracted young people otherwise put off by the unsmiling militance of student radicals.

The antiwar cause also gained in 1966 the support of leaders of the decade-old civil rights crusade, which was being squeezed between stiffening white resistance and a growing black separatist appeal. Dr. Martin Luther King, Jr., had called for a negotiated settlement of the war in the summer of 1965, before he retreated to answer the immediate demands of his northern urban desegregation campaign. But his younger associates proved less patient. In January 1966 SNCC leaders declared their sympathy for draft resisters and attacked President Johnson for violating international law in Vietnam while neglecting to enforce civil rights ordinances in Mississippi. Six months later SNCC demonstrators took to the streets in Atlanta, encouraging young blacks to refuse military induction and spreading the antiwar sentiments of their electrifying new leader, Stokely Carmichael. Dr. King undertook serious antiwar activism soon after. Moved by a variety of concerns and the need "to break the betrayal of my own silences and to speak from the burnings of my own heart," the 1964 Nobel Peace Prize laureate accepted the co-chairmanship of CALCAV and proceeded—despite the opposition of several long-time supporters—to dispute the rightness of Washington's war. "Somehow," he implored, "this madness must cease."[20]

Perversely, however, the antiwar commitment felt by hippies and civil rights activists intensified the popular opposition to the antiwar movement that constituted warmaking Washington's main source of domestic strength. The Vietnam War was never popular in America. But opposition to the antiwar movement was. Unable to convince many to die for Saigon's generals, the government and prowar leaders turned instead to justify the war by attacking antiwar elements as alien threats to the nation's most valued cultural symbols—including the flag, draft cards, and modest white middle-class appearance. *Time* magazine typically referred to the "Vietniks and Peaceniks, Trotskyites and potskyites" who took to the streets for peace, while right-wing militants frequently assaulted antiwar demonstrators with the tacit approval of local police.[21] Both the Johnson administration and its nominal Republican opposition maintained that the antiwar movement was Communist-controlled, and created the convenient rationale that domestic opposition provided the main source of continuing NFL resistance to American firepower. The power of the politicians' consensus proved compelling. Consistently, the majority of the American people supported the government's defense of the country's traditional values, if not the government's war. Public opinion polls indicated regularly through 1973 that, if there was anything more unpopular than the war, it was the antiwar opposition.[22]

Yet antiwar opposition increased in early 1967 along with U.S. casualties and Vietnam's agony. Mainstream magazines like *Life* and *Saturday Evening Post* began for the first time to question the wisdom of the war, while a band of trade union functionaries organized the National Labor Leadership Assembly for Peace in a brave attempt to modify organized labor's otherwise solid support for the war.[23] Younger dissidents meanwhile moved from protest to resistance. Collecting in loosely affiliated groups like the Resistance, antiwar resistants brought to a boil long-simmering campus resentment toward the unpredictability and inequities of government draft practices. The combined antiwar, antidraft anger spilled over into several campus demonstrations against military recruiters and representatives of the Dow Chemical Corporation, the main manufacturer of the jellied gasoline called napalm. It also threatened the very operation of the whole conscription process. With adults enlisting in groups like Resist, for the purpose of supporting any young man who chose to resist "illegitimate authority," the rate of conscientious objection to military service quadrupled that of World War II, while levels of draft evasion, violations, and exile by flight to Canada or into the domestic underground swelled to record heights.[24]

Unprecedented personal antiwar decisions became commonplace. Thousands of young men tried for the first time in American history to invoke the principle of selective conscientious objection (and thus revived the ancient notion of the just war), in order to avoid participating in one war that could not be reconciled to their personal sense of right. In June 1967 the world heavyweight boxing champion Muhammad Ali was sentenced to five years in jail and a $10,000 fine for refusing induction on the grounds that his Black Muslim beliefs prohibited him from fighting white men's wars. In the same weeks, Army Captain Howard Levy, a physician, went on trial for refusing to train combat teams for action in Vietnam on the grounds that the Nuremberg doctrine of individual responsibility forbade his complicity in their war crimes. For those who did not believe that U.S. forces were committing war crimes in Vietnam, the British philosopher Bertrand Russell convened an International War Crimes Tribunal in Stockholm in May. Still most did not believe.

The years 1967–1970 framed the most volatile period in American life since the early years of the Depression. And the antiwar movement swirled at storm center. On April 15 a Muste-inspired coalition called the Spring Mobilization Committee to End the War in Vietnam rallied over 300,000 people in New York and San Francisco behind UN Secretary-General U Thant's recent three-point peace program, which called for a multilateral ceasefire in Vietnam, negotiations among all warring parties, and the phased withdrawal of U.S. troops. In the same month the ADA leader Joseph Rauh, Jr., and other liberal luminaries launched Negotiation Now! as a means of pressuring the administration into stopping the bombing and negotiating the creation of an inclusive coalition gov-

ernment in Saigon. One month later the Baltimore insurance magnate Henry Niles ran a *New York Times* advertisement that
prompted the formation of Business Executives Move for Vietnam
Peace as another support group for U Thant's peace program. At
the same time Boston-area students and academics organized Vietnam Summer, a nationwide attempt to replay the 1964 Mississippi
Freedom Summer project by sending hundreds of young people into
local communities across the country in order to educate and organize grass-roots America against the war.[25]

Like its model, however, the Vietnam Summer operation was
soon engulfed in a flash flood of violence. But this time the violence was nationwide. After 150 racial riots seared the country in
the first half of 1967, the black ghettoes of Newark and Detroit
exploded in midsummer in the bloodiest urban rebellions of the
decade. In September the National Conference for New Politics
met in Chicago in an attempt to connect black rage and white radical militancy into an effective electoral force. The attempt ended
in humiliating failure when white delegates caved in to the blacks'
insistence that liberation would come only through violence.
There was neither room nor time for the ballot box. One month
later antiwar resistants took to the streets of Oakland in a disruptive "Stop the Draft Week." On October 21–22 the National
Mobilization Committee to End the War in Vietnam (heir to the
Spring Mobilization) conducted a massive "March on the Pentagon
to Confront the Warmakers."

Billed as the turning point in the movement's shift from dissent
to resistance, the March prompted the government to call out federal troops to defend Washington against petitioning citizens for
the first time since the 1932 Bonus March. While a few hundred
SDS-led demonstrators were arrested for breaching the Pentagon,
the vast majority of the 100,000 marchers demonstrated without
untoward incident or visible effect. Yet their very irrepressibility
heightened the electric atmosphere that was pervading the country.
Here were white middle-class Americans staring down the gun-
barrels of their government. Here were marching multiples of the
feeling that the prominent theologian Robert McAfee Brown de-
scribed when he declared that he had "now gone the full route—
from unconcern/to curiosity/to study/to mild concern/to deep
concern/to signing statements/to genteel protest/to marching/to
moral outrage/to increasingly vigorous protest/to . . . civil disobedi-

ence."[26] He was one step short of insurrection. But others were not.

The supercharged atmosphere of late 1967 produced tremendous strains within the antiwar movement. The fractionalizing left quarreled over the effectiveness of violent revolutionary action and the identity of the true revolutionary vanguard. Pacifists argued over the tolerability of revolutionary violence and the mode of America's exit from Vietnam. Radical pacifists were more willing to justify leftist violence and insistent upon immediate U.S. withdrawal; moderates in FOR condemned all violence and urged a phased U.S. withdrawal that would give strength to the Buddhists and other "third force" elements in Saigon. Members of SANE similarly split over the question of cooperating with social radicals in a bitter quarrel that was merely papered over in the early part of 1968. Nor were their differences purely theoretical. On January 8, 1968, a federal grand jury indicted SANE co-chairman Spock and four other antiwar leaders for conspiring to violate the Selective Service Act.[27] Coming as Washington's first overt attack upon prominent antiwar activists, the indictments only aggravated intramural conflicts within the movement. Some looked upon the Spock trial as a matchless opportunity to try the legality of Johnson's war. Others saw it as a costly diversion from the need to apply unrelenting political pressure on the warmakers.

The movement's tension and confusion was compounded in late November 1967, when Senator Eugene McCarthy (Dem.-Minnesota) announced his decision to challenge Lyndon Johnson for the 1968 Democratic presidential nomination with the promise of negotiating a settlement in Vietnam. Leaders of SANE and the ADA raced to McCarthy's support. Students quit school to campaign on his behalf, and liberal money chests flipped open to help. But nothing gave fire to McCarthy's campaign like the NLF's Tet offensive. On January 31, 1968, after months of promises from Washington of impending victory, NLF and North Vietnamese forces launched a surprise offensive over the lunar Tet New Year that resulted in major attacks on thirty provincial capitals, a month-long occupation of the ancient imperial city of Hue, and a brief invasion of the U.S. embassy in Saigon itself. Militarily, the southern-based NLF suffered irreplaceable losses during Tet. Politically, they won a devastating victory.

With incredible volunteer support, McCarthy polled 42 percent of the popular vote in the New Hampshire Democratic presidential primary in March. He lost the vote count, but won an astonishing psychological victory that opened the way for New York Senator Robert Kennedy's decision to enter the race on an antiwar platform. With critical support slipping, Johnson startled the country by announcing on March 31 his decision to withdraw from the upcoming presidential contest. At the same time, the President authorized a drastic reduction in the three-year-old bombing of North Vietnam and succeeded in clearing the way for the convocation in Paris in May of peace talks among the four warring parties. Johnson's March 31 address signaled the end of Washington's attempt to win the war militarily through the open-ended use of U.S. ground troops. But it fell far short of ending the war. On the contrary, the administration's new tack only cut the ground from beneath those peace liberals who had argued for three years against the bombing and for negotiation. Now the question became what was to be negotiated. And the answer was the makeup of the Saigon government and control of South Vietnam. Still unprepared to face that issue, peace liberals retreated into a holding pattern for the next year.

While they did, America burned. Over 200 major demonstrations rocked American campuses in the first half of 1968, with the bitterest occurring at Columbia University and San Francisco State University. In Catonsville, Maryland, the brother-priests Daniel and Philip Berrigan and seven associates gave new momentum to Catholic radicalism and the antiwar resistance when they seized the records of a local draft board and burned them with a napalm concoction that they had discovered in an Army training manual. Racial tensions likewise hit new heights. On April 3 Martin Luther King was gunned down in Memphis. In fiery reaction, black ghettoes across the country lashed out in uprisings that were met with the largest deployment of military force against civilians in American history. Two months later Robert Kennedy was assassinated in a Los Angeles hotel kitchen in a murder that also killed the McCarthy campaign. "The lift, the light, the glee of the campaign disappeared that night in California," one top McCarthy organizer recalled. People worked hard through the summer; but "the innocence of the campaign was tarnished and demolished," and the way was open for the succession of Johnson's vice-president, Hubert Humphrey.[28] The turn of events was incredible, and the war was its generator. "The war is now something which almost *must* obsess sane men," wrote WRL leader David McReynolds,

> and perhaps even turn us neurotic because we cannot keep our health in any other way. Mothers sit down at induction centers. Priests pour blood on draft files. Ministers chain themselves to those refusing induction. And, one and all, we are trying to say, sometimes well and often badly, that what the government is doing is evil. Simply that—evil.[29]

Months of political murder, deepening racial hatreds, Vietnam's unending suffering, and the prospect of a presidential race among Humphrey, Richard Nixon, and Alabama Governor George Wallace moved antiwar militants back to the streets. In August, a mélange of young McCarthy moderates, radicals, and Yippies (politicized hippies attracted to the clown politics of Abbie Hoffman and Jerry Rubin) converged upon Chicago in order to show up the Democratic National Convention as a fraud and sham. They were assaulted for their efforts by the Chicago police in three days of rioting that finally split the Democratic Party and opened the way to victory for Republican candidate Nixon. Within four years, Johnson's war policies had destroyed over 30,000 Americans, 415,000 Vietnamese, countless other Indochinese, and the largest electoral mandate in American political history.

In January 1969, with a peak of 543,500 Americans in Vietnam, Richard Nixon entered the White House, committed to ending the war and winning the peace. Expressing an early concern for domestic reconciliation, Nixon won a respite from popular pressure to halt the fighting. Some peace liberals, anticipating a settlement in Southeast Asia, established the Coalition on National Priorities and Military Policy as a means of redirecting war expenditures toward domestic needs, and went ahead in the struggle against the proposed anti-ballistic missile program and in behalf of arms control efforts. Others moved toward the idea of legislating a date for total American withdrawal from Vietnam. But Nixon moved faster in cutting off the left side of their support. In January 1969 federal prosecutors in Chicago indicted David Dellinger, Tom Hayden, and six other radical leaders for conspiring to cause the Chicago police riot. Already torn by factional in-fighting, the left was poorly prepared to meet the administration offensive. Remnants of the National Mobilization Committee mounted a noisy counter-inauguration in Washington in January to protest continuation of the war, repression of black militants in the Black Panther Party, and the jailing of political dissidents. But they could not recharge an antiwar movement still weakened by Chicago and desperate to believe Nixon's promise to end the war.

By summer 1969 antiwar activism was revitalized by the growing realization that Nixon's plan to end the war by winning the peace (meaning the preservation of a client regime in Saigon) entailed endless war in Asia. Guided by older peace liberals, the former McCarthy campaign youth coordinators Sam Brown, Marge Sklencar, and David Hawk organized the Vietnam Moratorium Committee as the nerve center for a nationwide effort to suspend "business as usual" for one day on October 15 (and increasing one day per month thereafter) in order to compel the earliest possible withdrawal of U.S. troops. Activating liberal, student, and religious support, the Moratorium idea gained impressive momentum in the early fall among traditional as well as previously inactive antiwar elements. At the same time, the reconstituted New Mobilization Committee to End the War in Vietnam (heir to the National Mobilization Committee) prepared for major demonstrations in Washington and San Francisco over November 13–15 in support of immediate U.S. withdrawal, free speech for dissenting GIs, and the freeing of jailed political dissidents. Working in uneasy collaboration, the two groups superintended the largest mass volunteer actions in American history. On October 15 millions of Americans participated in local activities that varied from the massing of 100,000 people on the Boston Common to the tolling of the Bethel (Kansas) College chapel bell once for every American killed in Vietnam. Altogether, the Moratorium exuded the air of a religious folk festival, asking more in sadness than anger for Washington to "give peace a chance."[30]

The November Mobilization was less forgiving but equally subdued. The weekend featured rallies, rock concerts, lobbying, speeches, and one unscheduled attack in Washington by an SDS splinter group on the South Vietnamese embassy. But most unforgettable was the 38-hour "March Against Death." Beginning Thursday evening, participants carried placards with the names of every American killed in Vietnam. They marched from Arlington Cemetery past the White House to the Capitol, where the signs were placed in wooden coffins. "It was one of the most emotional experiences I've ever had," recalled one participant. "I remember one young girl who carried a placard with her brother's name on it through the whole march and then stood for long minutes at the coffins before she could bring herself to put it in with the others. Haunting."[31] Marching with individual candles in apparently endless procession through a night of rain and high winds, the participants presented the most moving sight in the war's history. They also formed part of the largest antiwar demonstration. With 350,000 people gathered in San Francisco and 500,000 in Washington, the November Mobilization figured as the greatest outpouring of mass protest that the country had ever known.

Strangely, the reawakening antiwar opposition gained fuller force in the fall with the national uproar that took place when the Army charged 2d Lt. William Calley, Jr., with the murder of at least 23 unresisting men, women, and children in the South Vietnamese village of Mylai 4 in March 1968. Right-wing partisans condemned Washington for persecuting a soldier who was acting in obedience to orders. Left-wing critics charged that fixing the atrocity on Calley served to protect a chain of more culpable superiors that stretched to the White House. Pressured by the Calley case and the fall mobilizations, on November 3 Nixon emphasized his policy of "Vietnamizing" the war. Essentially, the policy broke down into three parts: (1) the phased withdrawal of U.S. combat forces; (2) the reduction of draft calls (along with preparations to end the draft), coupled with continued air, naval, material, and advisory support for enlarged South Vietnamese fighting forces; and (3) the identification of the antiwar movement as the main impediment before the administration's "timetable" of withdrawal and eventual settlement. Nixon's November announcement worked two immediate effects. It snatched the issue of withdrawal from the reviving antiwar movement. And it forced the movement to the tactical defensive. Once more, antiwar activists were accused of being the main source of the continuing war.

With Vice-President Spiro Agnew leading the way, administration leaders attacked antiwar militants as a hypocritical corps of violence-prone malcontents. Pacifist leaders like Dellinger tried to point out the absurd disproportionality of administration charges. "We antiwar people may occasionally throw rocks," he allowed, "but the government drops six-ton bombs on Vietnam. It drops napalm. It drops fragmentation bombs. It doesn't break windows. It

wipes out whole towns and cities."[32] But the administration attack
did touch sensitive nerves within the movement. Radical bomb-
ings of banks and corporate headquarters increased in 1969, as the
New Left disintegrated into hopelessly competing factions. Indiscriminate street violence, or "trashing," also spread until the October 1969 "Days of Rage," when a few hundred members of the SDS
Weatherman faction were dispersed as they tried to "bring the war
home" to Chicago. Peace liberals showed deep distress over the
violence, while radical and liberal pacifists quarreled heatedly over
the propriety of destroying property. Internally divided and shoved
to the defensive, the antiwar movement lost momentum early in
1970. The Vietnam Moratorium Committee disbanded in April
after organizing some quiet taxpayer protests. The New Mobilization Committee tried to spread antiwar opposition within the military, but its leadership was divided and its followers distracted.

And then Nixon gave the movement new life. On April 30 the
President abruptly invaded Cambodia and renewed the bombing of
North Vietnam. In the process, he set off a roar of antiwar demonstrations on campuses across the country. On May 4 Ohio national
guardsmen shot down thirteen students—killing four—on the
Kent State University campus. On the next day, Mississippi police
killed two more students when they fired into a dormitory at
Jackson State University. Almost viscerally, students reacted to the
naked show of state power by lashing out in the greatest single
campus uprising in American history. Nearly 470 colleges and universities struck or closed, as the war came closer to home. Organized antiwar demonstrations were reported on nearly 60 percent of
the country's campuses, despite the thinly-veiled hostility of state
and local authorities. At state universities in New Mexico and
Kentucky, where antiwar activism was previously minimal, armed
troops patrolled the grounds in a show of force unknown in the
history of American higher education.

Inexplicably, however, neither antiwar leaders nor organizations
proved able to convert the high level of student unrest into a working agency of policy change. The New Mobilization Committee
tried to draw momentum from the May uprisings by holding a
major demonstration in Washington on May 9, but it failed to sustain its organizational energy. A number of recharged student liberals formed a variety of Washington pressure groups (including the
Movement for a New Congress and the National Coalition for a

Responsible Congress), but they worked only modest results on Capitol Hill. As much as anything, these accumulating failures underscored the fact that the May rebellions had been set off more by Nixon than by antiwar activists—a firm sign that full initiative over the determination of America's Indochina policy had returned to the White House. For the first time since 1967, warmaking Washington felt confident in its ability to contain the antiwar opposition. Yet the patent illegality of Nixon's invasion of Cambodia and his related attempts to overcome dissent through covert, anti-constitutional operations (most notably the 1970 Huston plan for mail opening, surveillance, and burglary) fixed him in a pattern of executive criminality that ultimately produced his own downfall and the collapse of his whole Indochina policy. Nixon had won out over the antiwar movement by the summer of 1970. But then Nixon never knew what to do when he had won.

There was much talk late in 1970 that the antiwar movement had reached a critical crossroads between electoral politics or radical street action. But the alternatives were never really that stark. Moved by the Cambodian invasion and consequent domestic uproar, peace liberals helped the Congress to pass the Cooper-Church amendment prohibiting the funding of further American ground action in Cambodia and Laos. The Senate also began for the first time to consider legislation designed to set a date for total U.S. withdrawal from Vietnam. More than forty national peace lobbies, ranging from the well-recognized SANE to the ad hoc Project Pursestrings, organized to press the politicians in their enlarging peace-mindedness.

Meanwhile, the radical wing of the antiwar movement cracked. In June politically minded elements seceded from the New Mobilization Committee and formed the National Peace Action Coalition (NPAC). Led mainly by the electoralist Socialist Workers Party, NPAC aimed to mobilize sympathetic trade unionists and local peace action centers around the single tactic of mass demonstrations and in pursuit of the single goal of immediate U.S. withdrawal from Vietnam. Other social radicals turned at the same time to create a multi-issue coalition that would work through any nonviolent means to effect domestic change. Reaching out to civil rights and poverty groups, pacifist leaders like Dellinger and McReynolds slowly gathered the Peoples Coalition for Peace and Justice (PCPJ) by January 1971, as another step in their continuing attempt to connect the country's parties of change upon a radical pacifist base.

Programmatically, the PCPJ demanded an immediate U.S. withdrawal from Vietnam, a $6,500 annual income for every American family, freedom for jailed dissidents, and national campaigns against racism and sexism. Operationally, it encountered some large problems. The very strategy of coalition-building on the autonomy of member groups enhanced the power of centrifugal forces within the antiwar movement. The impulses toward gay rights and women's liberation, welfare rights and Puerto Rican independence—all of which had grown in the climate created in the sixties by the collective struggles for civil rights and peace—moved at the turn of the seventies to stress the primacy of their individual needs. According to one observer, there emerged "a kind of Ptolemaic theory of the political universe: everything is in orbit around *my* movement, around *my* politics, around *my* collective."[33] Understandably, leaders of the PCPJ were hard pressed to maintain a functioning antiwar coalition in the face of the reformers' growing tendency to look inward.

Antiwar militancy received a much-needed boost in September 1970, when the three-year-old Vietnam Veterans Against the War (VVAW) organization launched Operation RAW (Rapid American Withdrawal) and its own rise toward national visibility. Moving in a three-day sweep through New Jersey to Valley Forge, Pennsylvania, VVAW troops armed with toy guns and outfitted in battle fatigues re-enacted their battlefield experiences in an exercise that was termed "a mixture of peace march, mobile speak-out, and guerrilla theatre."[34] Four months later VVAW leaders conducted in Detroit a three-day "Winter Soldier Investigation" of U.S. war crimes in Indochina. Featuring the testimony of U.S. war veterans and given legitimacy by the Mylai revelations, the Winter Soldier inquiry claimed more serious attention than did the earlier Russell War Crimes Tribunal. But most of the country preferred not to listen. As analysts depicted popular reaction to the Mylai atrocity, the general attitude toward allegations of U.S. war crimes was two-tiered: (1) American boys did not do such things; and (2), if they did, their victims deserved it.[35]

In retrospect, it is difficult to determine whether contemporaries were more disturbed by the VVAW's actions or by its very existence. Never before had American soldiers returned from a war to work against it. But then never before had they returned so ridden with drugs, so contemptuous of their superiors, and so convinced of the purposelessness of their sacrifice. The VVAW contributed greatly to the antiwar movement in that it forced middle-class America to face the possibility that the war was turning clean-cut young men into a rabble much more menacing than campus protestors. But it was even more important in that it dramatized the erosion of morale and effectiveness within the armed forces. The VVAW was only the best publicized of several groups, including the American Servicemen's Union and the Concerned Officers Movement, that worked for peace within a military at war. And these were only the organized forms of disaffection. There is no way of measuring the acts of individual and small group opposition—the deserters' search for sanctuary in churches, the sit-down protests in military prisons, the attacks on unpopular officers—that cut to the heart of the military command structure. Cumulatively, however, they revealed a system in crisis.[36]

Encouraged by GI dissidence, antiwar activists tried to retake the initiative over war policy from the Nixon administration early in 1971, following the failure of the U.S.-sponsored ARVN invasion of Laos. Working closely, a wide range of peace and social justice groups organized a five-phase spring offensive that aimed to force Congress to end the war and move toward domestic reform. In its most dramatic phase, the offensive featured a rag-tag collection of VVAW members—enraged by government rejection of their plans to hold a memorial service for their fallen comrades in Arlington National Cemetery—marching, limping, and rolling in wheelchairs toward the Capitol, where they threw their war medals over a jerry-built fence in a display of angry contempt over Congress' failure to halt the war. In its largest phase, the offensive mobilized over 300,000 people in Washington and 150,000 in San Francisco on April 24 behind the demand for immediate withdrawal. In its most militant phase, activists tried to shut down Washington.

Beginning on May 3, 1971, the May Day Collective of nonviolent radical actionists tried to seal off the city by blockading bridges and major thoroughfares with stalled cars, available debris, and their bodies. Invoking a virtual state of martial law, Nixon's Department of Justice ordered a massive police sweep that resulted in the indiscriminate arrest of over 12,000 people and the largest mass jailing in American history. The administration broke the blockade, but at a financial and constitutional cost. In January 1975 a Washington federal court ordered the government to compensate 1,200 victims of the police sweep $10,000 apiece in damages for the violation of their civil rights. It was the most expensive civil rights judgment in American courtroom history, and the first which held the government financially liable for attacking the constitutional rights of citizens.

Although it demanded careful preparation, the national spring offensive did not weaken the antiwar movement's unceasing local and educational efforts. In March 1971 a battery of Madison Avenue advertising talent opened the "Help Unsell the War Campaign," in an attempt to convert public opinion against the war through the subtle techniques that sold toothpaste and automobiles. At the same time, reports of the poisonous effects of U.S. chemical warfare upon Vietnam's fields and streams proved upsetting to that large number of domestic critics who were voicing growing concern over environmental matters and ecological balance. And Daniel Ellsberg released *The Pentagon Papers*. Dribbling out of a succession of major newspapers in May, the Pentagon's secret history of U.S. decision-making and Vietnam gave official imprint to what antiwar leaders had long maintained: that Vietnam was the well-calculated outcome of aggressive U.S. policy in Southeast Asia, and that American leaders had consistently misled the American people into believing otherwise.

Public awareness of official duplicity grew even larger in the spring of 1971, after files stolen from the FBI office in Media, Pennsylvania, were leaked to the press, inaugurating an investigative process that gradually revealed the unprecedented size of secret government attempts to destroy organized domestic dissidence. Naturally, the antiwar movement stood high among the government's targets. Expanding upon a counterintelligence program (abbreviated to COINTELPRO) initiated in 1956, the FBI strove covertly throughout the sixties to "expose, disrupt, and otherwise neutralize" antiwar critics through defamatory letters, warrantless wiretaps, the pressuring of employers, and the planting of disruptive stooges. In 1967 military intelligence officers joined the federal effort, organizing informants, infiltrators, and lines of collaboration with local police in an enterprise that a Senate investigating committee later called "the worst intrusion that military intelligence has ever made into the civilian community."[37] In the same year, the CIA launched Operation CHAOS, employing informants, burglars, and a computerized list of 300,000 individuals and groups in an attempt to help the FBI define the subversive nature of the antiwar movement.

Tellingly, the failure of the national-security agencies to establish the subversive bases of dissent only led them to expand their efforts. By June 1970 the FBI was submitting 1,000 reports on the peace movement every month to the CIA. A few months later (and shortly after the redundant Huston plan was dropped), the FBI "greatly intensified" its infiltration of the antiwar movement, while CIA burglaries, mail openings, and harassment at demonstrations grew in frequency.[38] More flagrantly, the security agencies felt freer after 1970 to unleash *agents provocateurs.* Starting with the trial of the draft card burning Camden 28 in 1971, police plants were central to political show trials that ranged from the Harrisburg 7 (mostly Catholic radicals charged with conspiring to bomb government buildings in Washington and kidnap presidential advisor Henry Kissinger) to the Gainesville 8 (VVAW leaders charged with conspiring to disrupt the 1972 Republican national convention). None of the trials set up by police *provocateurs* resulted in the conviction of antiwar dissidents. But they did divert precious economic, organizational, and emotional resources within the movement. And they moved antiwar activists into a fuller contempt for governing authority. "I think most of us assume that there are government agents at almost every meeting that we hold," wrote Stewart Meacham of the American Friends Service Committee, "and we simply don't worry about it." Peace workers had to be "a little bit careful" in dealing with proponents of questionable tactics. "But even after we have done all of that we have to operate under the assumption that big brother is listening."[39]

Undeterred by governmental actions, leaders of the Peoples Coalition for Peace and Justice opened a campaign in June 1971 for popular ratification of the People's Peace Treaty. Concluded a year earlier between student groups from the two Vietnams and America, the Treaty provided for U.S. withdrawal on terms essentially set down by the NLF. Other antiwar elements disliked the document's one-sided nature and chose alternative actions. Representatives from 24 religious denominations and liberals from the newly-formed public interest lobby, Common Cause, coalesced in a group called Set the Date Now in an attempt to press the Congress to fix December 31, 1971, as the end-point for total U.S. military withdrawal from Vietnam, while thirteen congressmen brought federal suit in Washington in another effort at testing the war's constitutionality. Liberal pacifists in the FOR and WILPF initiated in the fall the Daily Death Toll Project, which gathered 300–400 volunteers every day to lie near the White House as living reminders of the continuing carnage in Indochina. The AFSC sponsored Project Air War, an investigative enterprise geared to inform Americans of Washington's shift from ground to air warfare throughout Indochina. Citing government figures on the growth of the South Vietnamese military forces and the increase of U.S. bombing, antiwar leaders impressively analyzed and explained the changing nature of the war. Yet they could not control it. With the whole movement, they were still obliged to react to the war's rhythms and shifting Great Power politics.

In February 1972 Nixon visited the People's Republic of China, formally ending a generation of Sino-American hatred. The administration was planning a similar visit to the Soviet Union when North Vietnamese forces launched a major April offensive. Nixon reacted by ordering renewed bombing of North Vietnam and, on May 8, the mining of the ports of Hanoi and Haiphong. Almost instinctually, antiwar demonstrations erupted across the country in opposition to an escalatory act that threatened to provoke a nuclear confrontation. But the Russians ignored Nixon's affront and instead welcomed him to Moscow in June for the conclusion of the first phase of a strategic arms limitation agreement. After a ten-year absence, a spirit of détente returned to Great Power relations, lessening the danger of a nuclear standoff and reducing the last incentive to mass antiwar rallies.

During the summer of 1972 Nixon gained a free hand in the world and at home to deal with Vietnam. Some radical pacifists joined the AFSC in its People's Blockade Operation, placing their bodies in the way of military supplies bound for Vietnam. Anti-imperialists and former student radicals like Tom Hayden organized the Indochina Peace Campaign (IPC) as a means of reaching—especially through the actress Jane Fonda—general audiences unaware of the complexity of Indochinese politics and the prerequisites of peace. But most antiwar elements moved to advance the presidential candidacy of the long-time peace advocate, Sen. George McGovern (Dem.-South Dakota). Even radical anti-imperialists agreed with SANE that the contest between McGovern and Nixon provided "the clearest choice in this century" between the politics of peace and war.[40]

The war meanwhile moved according to its own rhythm, as the various belligerents decided in the course of 1972 to bring at least a temporary end to the violence. In late October, while the McGovern campaign sputtered toward disaster, Washington and the three Vietnamese parties devised a settlement formula. When Nixon demanded modifications in the formula, Hanoi refused; and the President ordered the most ferocious bombing raids in human history against the North Vietnamese during the Christmas holiday season in order to force them to his will, reassure the client Thieu government in Saigon of postwar protection, and forewarn the Communists of his capacity to take any action in pursuit of his post-armistice policies in Indochina. Antiwar activists again spilled into the streets in protest, capping their display of contempt with a counterinaugural rally of 100,000 people in Washington on January 20, 1973. It was the last march. Seven days later, the United States and the Vietnamese parties concluded in Paris the long-sought peace agreement.

Antiwar activists greeted the Paris peace accords with wary satisfaction. All welcomed the military ceasefire and Washington's recognition of "the independence, sovereignty, unity and territorial integrity" of Vietnam as established in the 1954 Geneva agreements. But all warned that the struggle was far from over. Insistently, antiwar spokesmen held that the fundamental question of who ruled in Saigon had only been raised from the military to a more complex political level on which the United States remained deeply involved. Some spoke of the Paris agreements as the opening segment—after the failed French and American military interventions—of the "Third Indochina War." All agreed that the uninterrupted U.S. bombing in Cambodia in behalf of the Lon Nol regime, the fate of antigovernment political prisoners in South Vietnam, and continued U.S. financing of the Thieu regime together pointed to an open-ended U.S. presence in Indochina. Unanimously, peace seekers agreed that, while armed conflict was in a state of suspension, peace in Vietnam had not yet broken out.

The anti-Vietnam War movement was unique in the history of American antiwar activism in the way that it persisted beyond the war's apparent end. Organizationally, NPAC expired with the Paris accords; and the PCPJ slipped into a slow descent. Yet social radicals in the IPC, peace liberals in SANE, and pacifists of all persuasions never let up in their defense of the peace settlement. Undeterred by flagging public interest, they pressed Washington to respect the Paris accords, worked to end U.S. bombing of antigovernment guerrillas in Cambodia and Laos, and sought to cut off all U.S. support of the Lon Nol and Thieu regimes. Domestically, they struggled for reconciliation, and for full and complete amnesty for anyone who had run afoul of draft or military law.

Antiwar leaders faced waning popular interest in the war issue following the conclusion of the Paris agreement. Yet their cause gained unusual power in Washington as the weakening Nixon administration began to crack during 1973 under the mounting Watergate crisis and related revelations of official criminality. In June 1973, as a Senate select committee under the chairmanship of Sam Ervin (Dem.-North Carolina) began to peel away the layers of executive crimes, Congress began to legislate the ending, in August, of U.S. bombing of Cambodia. Four months later a United Campaign of several antiwar factions organized to pressure Congress into cutting off all support of the Thieu and Lon Nol governments. Early in 1974 the centrist Coalition to Stop Funding the War joined the United Campaign in combined lobbying action. Their efforts—abetted by a deepening economic recession and the growing movement to impeach Nixon—paid off. In May 1974 Congress rejected an administration request for supplemental aid to Thieu and Lon Nol. It was the first time that Congress had rejected funds for the executive's war in Southeast Asia since the war's inception.

For the next six months Washington shuddered through the crisis provoked by the collapse of the Nixon regime and Gerald Ford's succession to power. In Indochina the war raged on. Over 4 million Vietnamese and Cambodians were killed, wounded, or forced to flee as refugees in 1974, as the Paris accords became daily more irrelevant. In December the Ford administration requested a half-billion dollar supplemental appropriation to shore up Washington's two Indochina clients. The White House action sparked antiwar leaders into convening in Washington in January 1975 the Assembly to Save the Peace Agreements, as a rallying point against the request and against future aid to the two governments. But battlefield developments again outraced the capacity of anyone in Washington to control Indochina's future. In March a large-scale Communist offensive precipitated the incredible disintegration of the South Vietnamese military and with it the Thieu regime. While Ford pressed the Congress for more aid, Thieu quit his government on April 21 and immediately set off for Taiwan and then London. Nine days later, U.S. Ambassador Graham Martin fled Saigon aboard a helicopter. In an act heavy with symbolism, he carried away the embassy flag in a plastic bag reminiscent of the kind that had borne home the remains of the war's 56,555 American dead.

Few antiwar leaders felt unmixed pleasure over the collapse of the South Vietnamese government. All were grateful for the end of Vietnam's anguish, but few had any illusions that the Communist victory would bring peace with freedom to a country that had long known neither. "In our defeat communism is inevitable and cleansing," wrote the poet Robert Lowell, "though tyrannical forever."[41] Most hoped that the U.S. defeat would force a reversal in Washington's preference for violent counter revolutionary action in the Third World. And all spoke of the work yet to be done: ending the war in Cambodia; initiating U.S. reconstruction aid to Vietnam; and issuing an amnesty for all military deserters, draft evaders, and resisters. "We have lost not only a war," argued Hayden, "we have lost the entire foreign policy of the last 30 years. Now we must find another policy and in that ordeal find ourselves."[42]

More positively, the end of the Vietnam War allowed antiwar activists to reconvert their energies behind an active new peace movement. "The war is over," declared one leading pacifist journal, *"The problem of war remains intact."*[43] Since 1965 the first concern of peace-minded Americans had been to reverse U.S. war policy in Asia. In the process, the burgeoning peace movement of the early sixties shifted its focus from international concerns to the domestic sources of U.S. foreign policy. Ideologically, it became less internationalist and more antimilitarist and anti-imperialist. Practically, it became less able to meet the mounting global problems presented by the spiraling arms race, nuclear proliferation, resource depletion, and the widening gap between rich and poor.

The critic W. Warren Wagar complained throughout the sixties that the very idea of a national peace movement was anachronistic in an era that demanded a revolutionary planetary consciousness which would carry mankind beyond the contentious nation-state system into a genuine Cosmopolis. Even a top antiwar activist like

Tom Cornell worried that a "symbiotic relationship" developed after 1965 between American peace seekers and the "misery in Indochina."[44] But their criticisms were irrelevant even if valid. Peace seekers could not begin after 1965 to address their highest concerns without struggling first against twentieth-century America's least necessary and most corrosive war. Grudgingly, they accepted the deferral of their first concerns, and resolved to learn from the memories of Vietnam how they could "better become a peacemaking community" within a violence-prone society.[45] It was the same challenge that faced seventeenth-century Quakers, only made more momentous through two centuries of struggle and sacrifice.

Afterthoughts

The largest challenge before the contemporary American peace movement is to build sizable antibodies within the U.S. body politic against the various war pathologies that afflict America and the world. It is a challenge rich in promise, frustration, and—for Americans—paradox. Hurrying toward the twenty-first century, the United States helps lead the world in levels of domestic violence, the production of thermonuclear warheads, arms sales at home and abroad—and in the tenacity of its citizen peace activism. There are many different reasons for and inferences to be drawn from the fact of U.S. leadership in each of these categories. But the curious consistency by which the United States excels both in its capacity for violence and in its ability to sustain an active peace movement points to the existence of a basic tension between culture and power, a tension that accounts for the strength as well as the weakness of the American peace tradition.[1]

In American history, volunteer peace activism has constituted a subculture that lives in the application of certain symbols esteemed by the larger culture. More specifically (if paradoxically), the peace subculture has developed in that it represents one expression of the same mystique of self-governance that fuels the country's high incidence of private violence. Americans more than any other people find meaning for their collective being in their identity as an independent and self-governing people. They govern themselves; and they are accountable to themselves. At the same time, many Americans have consistently resolved to govern themselves in ways accountable either to reform Christian sensibilities or to some humanitarian consciousness. Implicitly, they assume that, with self-governance and self-accountability, they are obliged to act in pursuit of some higher good. Over time, large numbers have perceived this good as world peace; and they have voluntarily struggled to make it real.

From the start, the peacemakers' guiding faith in self-governance and right conduct forged in them a determination to seek social and policy change through highly-charged but nonviolent methods. Predictably, this preoccupation with peaceable means has placed peace workers at the center of the nation's reform tradition. No large-scale reform campaign has advanced in American history on calls for mass violence.[2] On the contrary, every reform crusade— from prohibitionism through the civil rights movement—has progressed through an emphatic renunciation of violence and on explicit appeals for nonviolent activism. In part, the reformers' acceptance of the peacemakers' idiom of nonviolent change reflects an ideological deference to the values of Christianity, humanitarianism, and that rational preference for enlightened social progress traditionally favored by American progressives. In part, too, the reformers' nonviolence represents a tactical adaptation to the fact that defenders of the status quo have consistently managed to mass superior violence in defense of the old ways.[3] For the most part, however, the reformers' peaceability represents a functional adjustment to the need for order among a highly dynamic, self-governing people. In general, reformers have respected the vague but real rules governing the relationship of change and continuity in American life. They seek to win their way out of fidelity to—and not over the wreckage of—the mystique of self-governance.

The idiom of nonviolent change has defined a plot of common ground shared by organized peace seekers and other reformers from the time of the Napoleonic wars. For over 150 years, abolitionists, feminists, socialists, and other major reform forces have repeatedly involved themselves in the organized peace reform with an enthusiasm that led Roland Marchand to characterize volunteer peace seeking as the "protean reform."[4] Ironically, however, the very enthusiasm that associated reformers have felt at different times for the peace reform has compromised organized peace seeking in its search for independent solidity and fuller growth. Despite intermittent outbursts of popular antiwar sentiment, the organized peace reform has never approached the level of a genuinely mass movement in America.

The American peace movement has rather remained modest in

size and limited in effectiveness. Socially, it has exerted greatest appeal among those middle-class women, clergymen, educators, and businessmen who possessed a combination of advanced education, leisure time, and a reform Christian conscience. Intellectually, it has attracted greatest interest among religious liberals, political leftists, and cultural dissidents. Geographically, it has centered in the metropolitan northeast, although Chicago, the San Francisco bay area, and parts of the Midwest gradually developed respectable constituencies. Practically, however, organized peace seeking has never succeeded as a movement in penetrating the dense layers of American society. In the 1930s Merle Curti felt that the movement figured as little more than "chips and foam" atop the American mainstream.[5] More recent observers estimate the movement's core constituency at about 2 million people, less than 1 percent of the U.S. population.

Several factors account for the failure of organized peace seeking to mobilize a mass movement comparable even to the prohibitionist or suffragist campaigns. Partly, the very pool of potential recruits—people of good hope and great perseverance whose patriotism transcends the idea of the nation-state—is quite restricted. Partly, the very magnitude and complexity of the movement's goals have discouraged both potential recruits and active participants. Partly, the protean workings of the peace reform have periodically diverted those potential and real activists into other causes. Most of all, however, the peace movement stands as a minority reform in America because it constitutes a subculture opposed to the country's dominant power culture and power realities.

The peace subculture speaks of forebearance within a culture that has flowered in conquest. It speaks of reconciliation within a society that works better at distributing weapons than wealth. It speaks of supranational authority among a highly nationalistic people who dislike all authority. It speaks of a just global order to governing officials anxious for pre-eminence and profit. Accepting their distance from the country's dominant power values and realities, members of the peace subculture have consequently resolved to serve as the most vocal critics of power as traditionally pursued and applied. Rather than preparing to master the levers of national and international power, American peace seekers have progressively concluded that they would serve neither as "victims nor executioners" for those policy makers who ultimately perceive power in terms of violence.[6] Rejecting that perception of power, peacemakers instead work to uncover other means of moving men and women to seek justice and secure order. They really operate more as pathfinders than power seekers. They essentially guide forward a subculture of dissent that survives in the certainty that there are working alternatives to the dominant modern power drive toward national self-aggrandizement.

The real limitations of their subculture have not prevented peace seekers from effecting real achievements. Before all, they have plotted out the routes toward preferable world orders. They have devised and implemented creatively nonviolent ways of realizing fuller social justice. They have led the way in assailing Great Power attacks on the right of smaller peoples to self-governance. They have educated and organized the largest bodies of world-minded volunteer activists. They have fashioned and advanced some of the most acutely realistic criticisms of U.S. international policies and global developments. And they have struggled as the most resolute proponents of hope in a world grown sick with despair. In 1946, the French philosopher Albert Camus prophesied that a titanic struggle was beginning "between violence and friendly persuasion, a struggle in which, granted, the former has a thousand times the chances of success than that of the latter." "But I have always held," he added,

> that, if he who bases his hopes on human nature is a fool, he who gives up in the face of circumstances is a coward. And henceforth, the only honorable course will be to stake everything on a formidable gamble: that words are more powerful than munitions.[7]

Peace seekers in America are neither fools nor cowards. They are people of honor who have unhesitatingly gambled that their words and actions will yet yield a power that will heal and not hurt, harmonize and not atomize. And it is our lives that will turn in large part upon their fearlessness and fortunes.

BIBLIOGRAPHICAL ESSAY

This brief essay is intended only to highlight those works that have most directly shaped our understanding of the American peace tradition. References to other highly important—but less peace-oriented—studies can be found in the chapter notes.

The best surveys of peace activism in the early period of American history remain in the opening pages of Merle Curti's pioneering *Peace Or War: The American Struggle, 1636–1936* (New York: W. W. Norton & Co., 1936) and Peter Brock's authoritative *Pacifism in the United States: From the Colonial Era to the First World War* (Princeton: Princeton University Press, 1968). Both books furthermore provide great help in comprehending the evolution of citizen peace seeking through the Civil War. In addition, Curti's *The American Peace Crusade, 1815–1860* (Durham, N.C.: Duke University Press, 1929) and David C. Lawson's "Swords Into Plowshares, Spears Into Pruninghooks: The Intellectual Foundations of the First American Peace Movement, 1815–1865" (Ph.D. diss., University of New Mexico, 1975) are two essential introductions to the nineteenth-century peace movement. Arthur Ekirch's *The Civilian and the Military* (New York: Oxford University Press, 1956) explores the antimilitarist impulses that affected American peace activism from the Revolutionary period through the twentieth century.

No single monograph surveys popular peace seeking in the period 1865–1887, although the earlier chapters of Warren F. Kuehl's *Seeking World Order: The United States and International Organization to 1920* (Nashville, Tenn.: Vanderbilt University Press, 1969) are helpful. Kuehl's study is even more useful for the period after 1890, when the peace reform developed into an effective national movement that several scholars have since analyzed. Sondra R. Herman's *Eleven Against War: Studies in American Internationalist Thought, 1898–1921* (Stanford, Cal.: Hoover Institution Press, 1969) establishes a thoughtful framework for interpreting the governing assumptions of various peace leaders at the turn of the twentieth century. Quite valuable in different ways are C. Roland Marchand's *The American Peace Movement and Social Reform, 1898–1918* (Princeton: Princeton University Press, 1972); David S. Patterson's *Toward a Warless World: The Travail of the American Peace Movement, 1887–1914* (Bloomington: Indiana University Press, 1976); and Michael A. Lutzker's

"The 'Practical' Peace Advocates: An Interpretation of the American Peace Movement, 1898–1917" (Ph.D. diss., Rutgers University, 1969).

After 1914 American peace seeking became less nationalistic and more sharply critical, from a leftist perspective, of existing political and social structures at home and abroad. The changing assumptions and direction of private peace activism are examined in the latter chapters of Marchand's study; Charles Chatfield's *For Peace and Justice: Pacifism in America, 1914–1941* (Knoxville: University of Tennessee Press, 1971); and Blanche W. Cook's "Woodrow Wilson and the Antimilitarists, 1914–1917" (Ph.D. diss., The Johns Hopkins University, 1970). Peter Brock's *Twentieth-Century Pacifism* (New York: Van Nostrand Reinhold Co., 1970) intelligently compares the experiences of conscientious objectors in Britian, America, and India during and after World War I.

Citizen peacemaking in the interwar period is surveyed in Chatfield's work and in Charles DeBenedetti's *Origins of the Modern American Peace Movement, 1915–1929* (Millwood, N.Y.: KTO Press, 1978). Beginning with the 1930s, Robert Divine's *Second Chance: The Triumph of Internationalism in America During World War II* (New York: Atheneum, 1967) and Lawrence S. Wittner's *Rebels Against War: The American Peace Movement, 1941–1960* (New York: Columbia University Press, 1969) sympathetically reconstruct the major advances (and reverses) in organized peace activism. For the more recent period, Milton S. Katz's "Peace, Politics, and Protest: SANE and the American Peace Movement, 1957–1972" (Ph.D. diss., St. Louis University, 1973) and Neil H. Katz's "Radical Pacifism and the Contemporary American Peace Movement: The Committee for Nonviolent Action, 1957–1967" (Ph.D. diss., University of Maryland, 1974) remind us of the organizational and experiential underpinnings of opponents of the Vietnam War.

Two collections of essays—*Peace Movements in America*, edited by Charles Chatfield (New York: Schocken Books, 1973); and *Doves and Diplomats: Foreign Offices and Peace Movements in Europe and America in the Twentieth Century*, edited by Solomon Wank (Westport, Conn.: Greenwood Press, 1978)—merit attention for the originality and variety of their contributions. *The Encyclopedia of American Foreign Policy: Studies of the Principal Movements and Ideas*, edited by Alexander DeConde (3 vols.; New York: Charles Scribner's Sons, 1978), contains a number of useful essay-articles on such topics as peace movements, antiwar dissent, and arbitration, mediation and conciliation. Most valuable are the pieces by Charles Chatfield on "Pacifism" and Warren F. Kuehl on "Internationalism." Finally and most importantly, The Garland Library of War and Peace, edited by Charles Chatfield, Blanche W. Cook, and Sandi E. Cooper, and issued by the Garland Publishing Company of New York, represents an invaluable collection of over 300 reprinted peace classics (each prefaced by a historical introduction) and original anthologies of the major writings of the world's leading modern peace seekers. For serious students, it offers an essential apparatus for any larger understanding of the global peace tradition.

NOTES

1. The Sectarian Reform

1. Robert S. Smith, *Warfare and Diplomacy in Pre-Colonial West Africa* (London: Methuen & Co., Ltd., 1976), pp. 5, 51, 188.

2. Ruth Underhill, *Red Man's Religion: Beliefs and Practices of the Indians North of Mexico* (Chicago: University of Chicago Press, 1965), pp. 169–70, 194–97.

3. Sir George Clark, *War and Society in the Seventeenth Century* (Cambridge: Cambridge University Press, 1958), p. 10.

4. For the Puritan preference for the just war position, see Jon A. T. Alexander, "Colonial New England Preaching on War As Illustrated in Massachusetts Artillery Election Sermons," *Journal of Church and State* 17, no. 3 (Autumn 1975): 423–42. For the usefulness of the just war theory to the centralizing state, see James Turner Johnson, *Ideology, Reason and the Limitation of War: Religious and Secular Concepts, 1200–1740* (Princeton: Princeton University Press, 1975), pp. 8–25, 260.

5. Larzer Ziff, *Puritanism in America: New Culture in a New World* (New York: Viking Compass edition, 1973), p. 90. Also, Arthur Buffinton, "The Puritan View of War," *Transactions of the Colonial Society of Massachusetts*, December 1930–April 1931 (Boston, 1932): 67–86.

6. Increase Mather, quoted in Peter Carroll, *Puritanism and the Wilderness: The Intellectual Significance of the New England Frontier, 1629–1700* (New York: Columbia University Press, 1969), p. 211.

7. Richard Slotkin, *Regeneration Through Violence: The Mythology of the American Frontier, 1600–1860* (Middletown, Conn.: Wesleyan University Press, 1973), p. 5.

8. William Penn, "The Rise and Progress of the People Called Quakers," in Frederick Tolles and E. Gordon Alderfer, eds., *The Witness of William Penn* (New York: Macmillan, 1957), p. 29; and George Fox, quoted in Melvin Endy, Jr., *William Penn and Early Quakerism* (Princeton: Princeton University Press, 1973), p. 54.

For a splendid, brief survey of the main strands of Christian pacifism, see Geoffrey Nuttall, *Christian Pacifism in History* (London: Basil Blackwell & Mott, Ltd., 1958).

9. George Fox to Oliver Cromwell, 1654, excerpted in Peter Mayer, ed., *The Pacifist Conscience* (London: Penguin Books, 1966), p. 90. For the ambiguity of the early Quaker peace position, see Howard H. Brinton, *The Peace Testimony of the Society of Friends* (Philadelphia: American Friends Service Committee, 1958), pp. 5–6; and Hermann Wellenreuther, "The

Political Dilemma of the Quakers in Pennsylvania, 1681–1748," *The Pennsylvania Magazine of History and Biography* XCIV, no. 2 (April 1970): 141–44.

10. Margaret Hirst, *The Quakers in Peace and War* (New York: The George H. Doran Co., 1923), p. 115.

11. Frederick Tolles, "Nonviolent Contact: The Quakers and the Indians," *Proceedings of the American Philosophical Society* 107, no. 2 (April 1963), 94.

12. William Penn, "Essay Towards the Present and Future Peace of Europe," in Blanche W. Cook, ed., *Peace Projects of the Seventeenth Century* (New York: Garland Publishing, Inc., 1972), p. 4.

13. Peter Brock, *Pacifism in the United States: From the Colonial Era to the First World War* (Princeton: Princeton University Press, 1968), p. 5. Menno quoted in Arthur and Lila Weinberg, eds., *Instead of Violence: Writings by the Great Advocates of Peace and Nonviolence Throughout History* (New York: Grossman Publishing Co., 1963), p. 439.

For an excellent analysis of the Anabaptist peace vision, see James Stayer, *Anabaptists and the Sword* (Lawrence, Kan.: Coronado Press, revised edition, 1976).

14. Franklin Littell, *The Origins of Sectarian Protestantism* (New York: Macmillan, 1964), p. 106. For the ambiguous pacifism of another radical pietist sect, the Moravians (heirs to the Unity of the Czech Brethren or *Unitas Fratrum*), see Brock, ch. 7 et passim.

15. Penn, quoted in Gary Nash, *Quakers and Politics: Pennsylvania, 1682–1726* (Princeton: Princeton University Press, 1968), p. 49.

16. Penn, "Essay Towards the Present and Future Peace of Europe," pp. 5, 10.

17. For the significance of the Philadelphia merchants, see Frederick Tolles, *Meetinghouse and Countinghouse: The Quaker Merchants of Colonial Philadelphia, 1682–1763* (New York: Norton edition, 1963).

18. Alan Tully, *William Penn's Legacy: Politics and Social Structure in Provincial Pennsylvania, 1726–1755* (Baltimore: John Hopkins University Press, 1977), p. 143.

19. Sydney V. James, *A People Among People: Quaker Benevolence in 18th Century America* (Cambridge: Harvard University Press, 1963), pp. 2, 141–92, 317–20; Arthur J. Worrall, "New England Quakerism, 1656–1830" (Ph.D. diss., Indiana University, 1969), p. 95. Cf. David R. Korbin, "The Saving Remnant: Intellectual Sources of Change and Decline in Colonial Quakerism, 1690–1810" (Ph.D. diss., University of Pennsylvania, 1968), pp. 228, 269–70.

20. Tolles, *Meetinghouse and Countinghouse*, p. 24.

21. Tully, pp. 154–60; Jack Marietta, "Conscience, the Quaker Community, and the French and Indian War," *The Pennsylvania Magazine of History and Biography* CXV, no. 1 (January 1971): 5; and Wellenreuther, 140–44.

22. Quoted in Brinton, p. 8.

23. Quoted in Marietta, p. 14.

24. As Frederick Tolles put it, Quakers succeeded in creating in the wilderness "a commonwealth in which civil and religious liberty, social and political equality, domestic and external peace had reigned to a degree and for a length of time unexampled in the history of the Western world." Tolles, *Quakers and the Atlantic Culture* (New York: Macmillan, 1960), p. 39.

25. *The Journal of John Woolman and a Plea for the Poor*, introduction by Frederick Tolles (Secaucus, N.J.: The Citadel Press, 1972 edition), p. v.
26. Ibid., p. xi.
27. Woolman, quoted in Lillian Schlissel, ed., *Conscience in America: A Documentary History of Conscientious Objection in America, 1757–1967* (New York: E. P. Dutton & Co., Inc.; paperback edition, 1968), p. 37.
28. Richard Hofstadter, *America At 1750: A Social Portrait* (New York: Knopf, 1971), p. 194.

2. The Revolutionary Reform

1. Thomas Paine, *The American Crisis*, in William Van der Weyde, ed., *The Life and Works of Thomas Paine*, 10 vols. (New Rochelle, N.Y.: Thomas Paine National Historical Association, 1925), II, p. 326.
2. Thomas Paine, "Epistle to Quakers," in Philip S. Foner, ed., *The Complete Writings of Thomas Paine*, 2 vols. (New York: The Citadel Press, 1945), II, p. 59. Paine's emphasis.
3. Sydney Ahlstrom, "Religion, Revolution and the Rise of Modern Nationalism: Reflections on the American Experience," *Church History* 44, no. 4 (December 1975): 501. Also, Sidney Mead, *The Nation With the Soul of a Church* (New York: Harper, 1975), p. 73.
4. "I indulge a fond, perhaps an enthusiastic idea," George Washington wrote in a typical expression of rationalist peace hopes, "that as the world is evidently much less barbarous than it has been, its melioration must still be progressive; that nations are becoming more humanized in their policy, that the subjects of ambition and the causes for hostility are daily diminishing, and, in fine, that the period is not very remote, when the benefits of a liberal and free commerce will, pretty generally, succeed to the devastations and horrors of war." Washington to Marquis de Lafayette, August 15, 1786, in John C. Fitzpatrick, ed., *The Writings of George Washington from the Original Manuscript Scources, 1745–1799*, 39 vols. (Washington: Government Printing Office, 1938), 28, pp. 520–21.
In another sign of the rationalists' developing faith in peace, Jeremy Bentham coined the word *international* in 1770. Warren F. Kuehl, *Seeking World Order: The United States and International Organization to 1920* (Nashville, Tenn.: Vanderbilt University Press, 1969), p. 29; also, Michael Howard, *War and the Liberal Conscience: The George Macaulay Trevelyan Lectures in the University of Cambridge, 1977* (London: Temple Smith, 1978), pp. 28–31.
5. Rev. Abraham Ketaltas, quoted in Christopher Beam, "Millennialism and American Nationalism, 1740–1800," *Journal of Presbyterian History* 54, no. 1 (Spring 1976): 186; and Paine, *Common Sense*, in Van der Weyde, II, p. 179.
6. Ernest Lee Tuveson, *Redeemer Nation: The Idea of America's Millennial Role* (Chicago: University of Chicago Press, 1968), p. 24.
7. Richard H. Kohn, "The Murder of the Militia System in the Aftermath of the American Revolution," in James Kirby Martin, ed., *The Human Dimensions of Nation Making: Essays in Colonial and Revolutionary America* (Madison: The State Historical Society of Wisconsin, 1976), pp. 306–307.
For a detailed study of the roots of colonial antimilitarism, see Lois G. Schwoerer, *"No Standing Armies!": The Anti-Army Ideology in*

Seventeenth-Century England (Baltimore: Johns Hopkins University Press, 1974).

8. Rather impressively, Stephen Saunders Webb has argued that the life of colonial America was dominated by a "military and provincial system" much more fully than previously understood, suggesting that antimilitarism was a lived experience—and no mere abstraction—for American revolutionaries. See Webb, "Army and Empire: English Garrison Government in Britain and America, 1569 to 1763," *William and Mary Quarterly* XXXIV, no. 1 (January 1977): 1–31.

9. Kohn, pp. 306–308; Arthur E. Ekirch, *The Civilian and the Military* (New York: Oxford University Press, 1956), pp. 7–13; Jefferson, "The Declaration of Independence," in Henry Steele Commager, ed., *Documents of American History*, 2 vols. (New York: Meredith Publishing Co., 1963), I, p. 100.

10. E. Kidd Lockard, "Some Problems of the Draft in Revolutionary Virginia," *West Virginia History* 37, no. 3 (April 1976): 204–207.

11. For the severity of the war, by some estimates the second bloodiest (to the Civil War) in American history, see Howard Peckham, ed., *The Toll of Independence: Engagements and Battle Casualties of the American Revolution* (Chicago: University of Chicago Press, 1974), pp. 132–33; and John Shy, "The Legacy of the American Revolutionary War," in Larry Gerlach, ed., *Legacies of the American Revolution* (Logan, Utah: Utah State University Press, 1978), pp. 45–48.

12. Quoted in Lillian Schlissel, ed., *Conscience in America: A Documentary History of Conscientious Objection in America, 1757–1967* (New York: E. P. Dutton & Co., Inc.; paperback edition, 1968), p. 30.

13. Arthur Mekeel, "The Relation of Quakers to the American Revolution," *Quaker History* 65, no. 1 (Spring 1976): 3–18; and Sydney James, *A People Among People: Quaker Benevolence in 18th Century America* (Cambridge: Harvard University Press, 1963), pp. 240–58, 271–87.

14. Anthony Benezet, *Thoughts on the Nature of War* (Philadelphia, 1776), pp. 1, 5; and Nancy S. Hornick, "Anthony Benezet: Eighteenth-Century Social Critic, Educator, and Abolitionist" (Ph.D. diss., University of Maryland-College Park, 1974), p. 295. Benezet's emphasis.

15. Benezet to Henry Laurens, December 1776, in George S. Brookes, *Friend Anthony Benezet* (Philadelphia: University of Pennsylvania Press, 1937), p. 325.

16. Benezet to George Dillwyn, July 1781, ibid., p. 356.

17. John Ruth, *'Twas Seeding Time: A Mennonite View of the American Revolution* (Scottdale, Pa.: Herald Press, 1976), p. 22; and Mark A. Noll, *Christians in the American Revolution* (Washington: Christian University Press, 1977), pp. 123–47.

18. Richard K. MacMaster, "Neither Whig Nor Tory: The Peace Churches in the American Revolution," *Fides et Historia* 9, no. 2 (Spring 1977): 10; and Richard W. Renner, "Conscientious Objection and the Federal Government, 1787–1792," *Military Affairs* 38, no. 4 (December 1974): 142.

19. Thomas Jefferson, *Notes on the State of Virginia*, William Peden, ed. (Chapel Hill: University of North Carolina Press, 1955), p. 175. For Jefferson's private ambivalence toward the peace question, see Reginald C. Stuart, *The Half-way Pacifist: Thomas Jefferson's View of War* (Toronto: University of Toronto Press, 1978), pp. 3–4, 59–65.

20. Richard H. Kohn, *Eagle and Sword: The Federalists and the Creation of the Military Establishment in America, 1783–1811* (New York: The Free Press, 1975), p. xiii.

21. Quoted from Knox's plan, in John O'Sullivan and Alan M. Meckler, eds., *The Draft and Its Enemies: A Documentary History* (Urbana: University of Illinois Press, 1974), p. 30.

22. *The Federalist: A Commentary on the Constitution of the United States* (New York: The Modern Library, 1938[?]), pp. 43–45.

23. Cecelia Kenyon, ed., *The Antifederalists* (Indianapolis: The Bobbs-Merrill Co., Inc., 1966), pp. xlix, 58–59, 243; and Kohn, *Eagle and Sword*, pp. 81–83.

24. Rush, "A Plan for a Peace-Office, for the United States," in Benjamin Banneker, *Almanack and Ephemeries for the Year of Our Lord 1793 ...* (Philadelphia, 1794). Also, W. Freeman Galpin, *Pioneering for Peace: A Study of American Peace Efforts to 1846* (Syracuse, N.Y., 1933), pp. 4–5; and Dennis D'Elia, "Benjamin Rush: Philosopher of the American Revolution," *Transactions of the American Philosophical Society* 64, part 5 (Philadelphia, 1974): 97–98.

25. Renner, p. 143; Jefferson to John Wayles Eppes, November 6, 1813, in Paul Leicester Ford, ed., *The Writings of Thomas Jefferson*, 10 vols. (New York: G. P. Putnam's Sons, 1893–99), IX, p. 416; Jefferson to Eppes, September 11, 1813, ibid., p. 395.

26. Kohn, *Eagle and Sword*, pp. 88, 137–38.

27. Henry Steele Commager, *Jefferson, Nationalism and the Enlightenment* (New York: George Braziller, 1975), p. 22.

28. Rev. Nathaniel Ames, quoted in John A. Andrew III, *Rebuilding the Christian Commonwealth: New England Congregationalists and Foreign Missions, 1800–1830* (Lexington: University of Kentucky Press, 1976), p. 2.

29. Samuel Eliot Morison, "Dissent in the War of 1812," in Samuel Eliot Morison et al., *Dissent in Three American Wars* (Cambridge: Harvard University Press, 1970), p. 3.

30. Quoted, ibid., p. 5.

31. Peter Brock, *Pacifism in the United States: From the Colonial Era to the First World War* (Princeton: Princeton University Press, 1968), p. 356.

For the elaboration of Shaker pacifism during the War of 1812, see James M. Upton, "The Shakers As Pacifists in the Period Between 1812 and the Civil War," *The Filson Club History Quarterly* 47, no. 3 (July 1973): 267–73.

32. William Gribben, *The Churches Militant: The War of 1812 and American Religion* (New Haven: Yale University Press, 1973), p. 103; Richard Archer, "Dissent and Peace Negotiations at Ghent," *American Studies* 18, no. 2 (Fall 1977): 15.

33. Morison, p. 4.

34. John F. Berens, "The Sanctification of American Nationalism, 1789–1812: Prelude to Civil Religion in America," *Canadian Review of Studies in Nationalism* 3, no. 2 (Spring 1976): 183.

35. Nathan O. Hatch, *The Sacred Cause of Liberty: Republican Thought and the Millennium in Revolutionary New England* (New Haven: Yale University Press, 1977), p. 139.

3. The Humanitarian Reform

1. William Ellery Channing, *Discourses on War* (Boston: Ginn and Co., 1903), p. 3; Christina Phelps, *The Anglo-American Peace Movement in the*

Mid-Nineteenth Century (New York: Columbia University Press, 1930), pp. 12–13.

2. *Memorial of Mr. David L. Dodge, Consisting of an Autobiography Prepared at the Request and for the Use of His Children, with a Few Selections from His Writings* (Boston: published only for the family by S. K. Whipple & Co., 1854), p. 90.

3. William Gribben, *The Churches Militant: The War of 1812 and American Religion* (New Haven: Yale University Press, 1973), p. 138.

4. Donald Mathews, "The Second Great Awakening As an Organizing Process, 1780–1830," *American Quarterly* XXI, no. 1 (Spring 1969): 40–41; also, Don H. Doyle, "The Social Functions of Voluntary Associations in a Nineteenth-Century American Town," *Social Science History* 1, no. 3 (Spring 1977): 333–55.

5. Unfortunately, Quakers failed to contribute directly to the new societies because they were absorbed in internal religious schisms and "a narrowly conceived separatism." Peter Brock, *Pacifism in the United States: From the Colonial Era to the First World War* (Princeton: Princeton University Press, 1968), p. 377.

6. *Memorial of Mr. David L. Dodge . . .* , p. 23.

7. Ibid., pp. 80–81.

8. Noah Worcester, *A Solemn Review of the Custom of War; Showing That War Is the Effect of Popular Delusion, and Proposing a Remedy* (Hartford, Conn.: n.p., 1815), reprinted in Peter Brock, ed., *The First American Peace Movement* (New York: Garland Publishing Co., Inc., 1972), p. 4.

For the most comprehensive analysis of the pre-Civil War peace movement, see David C. Lawson, "Swords Into Plowshares, Spears Into Pruninghooks: The Intellectual Foundations of the First American Peace Movement, 1815–1865" (Ph.D. diss., University of New Mexico, 1975).

9. Worcester, in Brock, ed., pp. 17–18.

10. David L. Dodge, *War Inconsistent with the Religion of Jesus Christ*, also reprinted in Brock, ed., pp. 57–58, 140, 76.

11. *Memorial of Mr. David L. Dodge . . .* , p. 101.

12. William Ladd, *The Essays of Philanthropos on Peace and War* (Exeter, N.H.: n.p., 1827; New York: Garland edition, 1971), pp. 83, 10, 8–9. Emphasis in the original.

13. William Ladd, *The Harbinger of Peace*, I, p. 10, quoted by James Brown Scott in his introduction to Ladd, *An Essay on a Congress of Nations for the Adjustment of International Disputes Without Resort to Arms* (New York: Oxford University Press edition, 1916), p. 10. Emphasis in the original.

14. *Memoir of William Ellery Channing, With Extracts from His Correspondence and Manuscripts*, 3 vols. (Boston: American Unitarian Association, 1868), II, p. 112.

15. James Brewer Stewart, *Holy Warriors: The Abolitionists and American Slavery* (New York: Hill & Wang, 1976), p. 44.

16. *Memorial of Mr. David L. Dodge . . .* , p. 101.

17. Brock, *Pacifism in the United States*, p. 492.

18. Garrison to the President of the Anti-Slavery Convention . . . , January 30, 1836, in Louis Ruchames and Walter Merrill, eds., *The Letters of William Lloyd Garrison*, 4 vols. (Cambridge: Belknap Press of Harvard University, 1971), II, pp. 30, 32.

19. Garrison to the *New England Spectator*, July 30, 1836, ibid., p. 147. Emphasis in the original.

20. Lewis Perry, *Radical Abolitionism: Anarchy and the Government of God in Antislavery Thought* (Ithaca, N.Y.: Cornell University Press, 1973), pp. x–xii et passim.

21. John Demos, "The Antislavery Movement and the Problem of Violent Means," *New England Quarterly* XXXVII, no. 4 (December 1964): 502. For the story of one of the most fervent believers in the "religion of reform," see Jayme A. Sokolow, "Henry Clarke Wright: Antebellum Crusader," *Essex Institute Historical Collections* III, no. 2 (April 1975): 122–37.

22. Quoted in Merle Curti, *The American Peace Crusade, 1815–1860* (Durham, N.C.: Duke University Press, 1929; New York: Octagon edition, 1965), p. 76.

23. Garrison to Orson S. Murray, August 11, 1837, in Ruchames and Merrill, II, p. 279. Statement by May et al., ca. July 1838, in Gilbert H. Barnes and Dwight L. Drummond, eds., *Letters of Theodore Dwight Weld and Angelina Grimke Weld and Sarah Grimke, 1822–1844*, 2 vols. (Washington: American Historical Association, 1934; Gloucester, Mass.: Peter Smith edition, 1965), II, pp. 686–87.

24. "Non-resistance Society: Declaration of Principles, 1838," in Peter Mayer, ed., *The Pacifist Conscience* (Chicago: Henry Regnery Co., Gateway edition, 1967), pp. 124–27. Emphasis in the original.

25. Garrison to Maria W. Chapman and Edmund Quincy, March 1, 1839, in Ruchames and Merrill, II, p. 436; Garrison to Helen E. Garrison, September 21, 1838, ibid., p. 391. Chapman, quoted in Perry, p. 247. Emphasis in the original.

26. Garrison to Orson S. Murray, August 11, 1837, in Ruchames and Merrill, II, p. 280.

27. Ralph Waldo Emerson, "War," in Emerson, *Miscellanies* (Boston: Houghton, Mifflin and Co., 1888), pp. 187, 189. Emphasis in the original.

28. Ibid., pp. 196–98; and George M. Fredrickson, *The Inner Civil War: Northern Intellectuals and the Crisis of the Union* (New York: Harper & Row, Inc., 1965), p. 39.

29. Ladd to William Lloyd Garrison, November 7, 1838, in John Hemmenway, *The Apostle of Peace: Memoir of William Ladd* (Boston: American Peace Society, 1872; Jerome S. Ozer, Publisher, edition, 1972), p. 77.

30. Garrison to *The Emancipator*, May 21, 1839, in Ruchames and Merrill, II, p. 484.

31. "Philanthropos" (William Ladd), *On the Duty of Females to Promote Peace* (Boston: American Peace Society, 1836; New York: Garland edition, 1971), pp. 5, 8; Harris's introduction, ibid., p. 10. Also, Nancy F. Cott, *The Bonds of Womanhood: "Woman's Sphere" in New England, 1780–1835* (New Haven: Yale University Press, 1977), pp. 126–59.

32. Ladd, *An Essay on a Congress of Nations . . .* , pp. xlix, 1, 6, 101. More generously, David Lawson believes that Ladd's plan "was the antebellum peace movement's single most important proposal for the abolition of war, its most innovative and substantive contribution to the Anglo-American peace effort of the first half of the nineteenth century, and its greatest bequest to the post-Civil War campaign to put an end to war." Lawson, p. 377. Also, Phelps, pp. 103–128.

33. Douglas Maynard, "Reform and the Origin of the International Organization Movement," *Proceedings of the American Philosophical Society* 107, no. 3 (June 1963): 220–31.

34. Robert Trendel, "William Jay and the International Peace Move-

ment," *Peace and Change* II, no. 3 (Fall 1974): 17–23; Phelps, pp. 127–28, 150–64.

35. Curti, p. 188.

36. Quoted in Peter Tolis, *Elihu Burritt: Crusader for Brotherhood* (Archon, Conn.: Shoestring Press, 1968), p. 128.

37. Quoted in Peter Brock, *Radical Pacifists in Antebellum America* (Princeton: Princeton University Press paperback edition, 1968), p. 200. Emphasis in the original.

38. Curti, p. 92; quoted in Tolis, p. 122. George C. Beckwith, *The Peace Manual, Or War and Its Remedies* (Boston: American Peace Society, 1847; New York: Garland edition, 1971), p. 4. Emphasis in the original.

39. Beckwith, p. 9.

40. Ibid., pp. 223, 210–11.

41. Charles Sumner, "The True Grandeur of Nations," *Orations and Speeches*, 2 vols. (Boston: Ticknor, Reed, and Fields, 1850), II, pp. 66, 69–70, 127. Emphasis in the original.

42. Theodore Parker, "A Sermon on War," June 7, 1846, in Parker, *Sermons on War* (New York: Garland edition, 1973), pp. 23–24. For the larger story of antiwar dissent, see John H. Schroeder, *Mr. Polk's War: American Opposition and Dissent, 1846–1848* (Madison: University of Wisconsin Press, 1973).

43. Garrison to Elizabeth Pease, April 1, 1847, in Ruchames and Merrill, III, p. 476.

44. Parker, *Sermons on War*, p. 4.

45. Quoted in Curti, p. 145; quoted in Tolis, p. 169.

46. Quoted in Curti, p. 145; quoted in Tolis, p. 144.

47. In Merle E. Curti, ed., *The Learned Blacksmith: The Letters and Journals of Elihu Burritt* (New York: Wilson-Erickson, Inc., 1937; New York: Garland edition, 1971), pp. 10–11; Curti, *American Peace Crusade*, p. 150.

48. Charles Sumner, "The War System of the Commonwealth of Nations: An Address before the American Peace Society, at Its Anniversary in Boston, May 28, 1849," *Orations and Speeches*, II, pp. 6, 85, 97, 99.

49. Staughton Lynd, ed., *Nonviolence in America: A Documentary History* (Indianapolis: Bobbs-Merrill, Inc., 1965), p. xxv.

50. Quoted in Curti, *American Peace Crusade*, p. 223.

51. Quoted in Demos, p. 522; quoted in Perry, pp. 240–41.

52. Quoted in Perry, p. 258; quoted in Brock, *Radical Pacifists in Antebellum America*, p. 237.

53. Perry, pp. 239–67.

54. Burritt to Henry Richard, May 26, 1861, in Curti, ed., *The Learned Blacksmith*, p. 139. Emphasis in the original.

55. Quoted in Gerda Lerner, *The Grimké Sisters from South Carolina: Rebels Against Slavery* (Boston: Houghton Mifflin Co., 1967), p. 389.

56. Brock, *Pacifism in the United States*, p. 769.

57. Ibid., p. 866; also, Richard L. Zuber, "Conscientious Objectors in the Confederacy: The Quakers of North Carolina," *Quaker History* 67, no. 1 (Spring 1978): 1–19.

58. Edward Needles Wright, *Conscientious Objectors in the Civil War* (Philadelphia: University of Pennsylvania Press, 1931; New York: A. S. Barnes and Co., Inc., 1961), p. 180. Also, Samuel Horst, *Mennonites in the Confederacy: A Study in Civil War Pacifism* (Scottdale, Pa.: Herald Press, 1967).

In addition, Robert E. Sterling, "Civil War Draft Resistance in the Middle West" (Ph.D. diss., Northern Illinois University, 1974), provides an extremely useful study of this topic, including several tables which detail antidraft opposition on a state-by-state and county-by-county basis.

59. Michael Howard, *War and the Liberal Conscience: The George Macaulay Trevelyan Lectures in the University of Cambridge, 1977* (London: Temple Smith, 1978), p. 47; Ladd, *An Essay on a Congress of Nations* . . . , p. 7.

4. The Cosmopolitan Reform

1. Benjamin Trueblood, in *First Annual Report of the Lake Mohonk Conference on International Arbitration 1895* (n.p.; published by the Lake Mohonk Arbitration Conference, 1895), p. 8; Hannah Bailey, ibid., p. 69.

2. Edson L. Whitney, *The American Peace Society: A Centennial History* (Washington, D.C.: The American Peace Society, 1928), p. 118.

3. Ibid., p. 123.

4. Peter Brock, *Pacifism in the United States: From the Colonial Era to the First World War* (Princeton: Princeton University Press, 1968), p. 925; Robert Doherty, "Alfred H. Love and the Universal Peace Union" (Ph.D. diss., University of Pennsylvania, 1962), p. 57.

5. Ibid., p. 37.

6. Laura Richards and Maud Howe Elliott, *Julia Ward Howe, 1819–1910* (Boston and New York: Houghton Mifflin and Co., 1925), p. 160; and Julia Ward Howe, *Reminiscences, 1819–1899* (Boston and New York: Houghton Mifflin and Co., 1899), pp. 330, 336.

7. David S. Patterson, *Toward a Warless World: The Travail of the American Peace Movement, 1887–1914* (Bloomington: Indiana University Press, 1976), p. 7.

8. Morton Keller, *Affairs of State: Public Life in Late Nineteenth Century America* (Cambridge: Harvard University Press, 1977), pp. 5, 122.

9. James P. Piscatori, "Law, Peace and War in American International Legal Thought," in Ken Booth and Moorhead Wright, eds., *American Thinking About Peace and War* (New York: Barnes & Noble, 1978), p. 136.

10. Arthur Nussbaum, *A Concise History of the Law of Nations* (New York: The Macmillan Co., 1947), p. 219; and F.S.L. Lyons, *Internationalism in Europe, 1815–1914* (Leyden: A.W. Sythoff, 1963), pp. 295–307.

11. Charles S. Campbell, *The Transformation of American Foreign Relations, 1865–1900* (New York: Harper Colophon edition, 1976), p. 45.

12. Lyons, p. 14; Louis Sohn, "The Growth of the Science of International Organizations," in Karl Deutsch and Stanley Hoffman, eds., *The Relevance of International Law* (New York: Doubleday Anchor edition, 1971), p. 329.

13. "We must be no longer hedged about by the artificial boundaries of states and nations"; Willard declared during her conversion, "we must utter, as women, what good and great men long ago declared as their watchword: 'The whole world is my parish and to do good my religion.'" Quoted in Anna A. Gordon, *Frances Willard: A Memorial Volume* (Chicago: Women's Christian Temperance Union, 1898), pp. 147–48; also, Mary Earhart, *Frances Willard: From Prayers to Politics* (Chicago: University of Chicago Press, 1944), pp. 261–70.

14. Warren F. Kuehl, *Seeking World Order: The United States and In-*

ternational Organization to 1920 (Nashville, Tenn.: Vanderbilt University Press, 1969), pp. 38–48; and Patterson, pp. 101, 114–15.

15. Kuehl, p. 50.

16. Trueblood, in *First Annual Report of the Lake Mohonk Conference on International Arbitration 1895*, p. 25.

17. John Bassett Moore, in Henry S. Clubb, ed., *Full Proceedings of the Conference in Favor of International Arbitration, February 22, 1896* (Philadelphia: Universal Peace Union, 1896), p. 26.

18. Josiah Strong, in *Fourth Annual Report of the Lake Mohonk Conference on International Arbitration 1898* (n.p.; published by the Lake Mohonk Arbitration Conference, 1898), p. 74.

19. "Annual Meeting of the American Peace Society," *The Advocate of Peace* LVI, no. 6 (June 1894): 129.

20. Patterson, p. 18.

21. Merle E. Curti, *The Roots of American Loyalty* (New York: Columbia University Press, 1946; Atheneum edition, 1968), pp. 190–91.

22. Richard Hofstadter, *Social Darwinism in American Thought* (Boston: Beacon Press paperback edition, 1955), pp. 172–84; and Bradford Perkins, *The Great Rapprochement: England and the United States, 1895–1914* (New York: Atheneum, 1968), p. 82 et passim.

23. Edwin D. Mead, in *Third Annual Report of the Lake Mohonk Conference on International Arbitration 1897* (n.p.; published by the Lake Mohonk Arbitration Conference, 1897), p. 25.

24. Patterson, pp. 36–44.

25. For Tolstoy's diverse influence, see Peter Frederick, *Knights of the Golden Rule: The Intellectual As Christian Social Reformer in the 1890s* (Lexington: University of Kentucky Press, 1976).

26. Until 1898, Mormons reserved the right to reject service in the wars of the state. D. Michael Quinn, "The Mormon Church and the Spanish-American War: An End to Selective Pacifism," *Pacific Historical Review* XLIII, no. 3 (August 1974): 342–66; and Gerald F. Linderman, *The Mirror of War: American Society and the Spanish-American War* (Ann Arbor: University of Michigan Press, 1975), p. 64.

27. "A Fearful Responsibility," *The Advocate of Peace* LX, no. 5 (May 1898): 101–102.

28. From the platform of the Anti-Imperialist League, in James R. Cobbledick, "Anti-Imperialism in the United States, 1893–1902" (Ph.D. diss., Tufts University, 1966), p. 132. For a valuable anthology of anti-imperialist writings, see Gerald E. Markowitz, ed., *American Anti-Imperialism, 1895–1901* (New York: Garland Publishing Co., Inc., 1976).

29. Robert L. Beisner, *Twelve Against Empire: The Anti-Imperialists, 1898–1900* (New York: McGraw-Hill, Inc., 1968); E. Berkeley Tompkins, *Anti-Imperialism in the United States: The Great Debate, 1898–1920* (Philadelphia: University of Pennsylvania Press, 1970); and James A. Zimmerman, "Who Were the Anti-Imperialists and Expansionists of 1893 and 1898?: A Chicago Perspective," *Pacific Historical Review* LXVI, no. 4 (November 1977): 589–601.

30. Fred H. Harrington, "The Anti-Imperialist Movement in the United States, 1898–1900," *The Mississippi Valley Historical Review* XXII, no. 2 (September 1935): 224; or Frank Friedel, "Dissent in the Spanish-American War and the Philippine Insurrection," in Samuel Eliot Morison, et al., *Dissent in Three American Wars* (Cambridge: Harvard University Press, 1970), pp. 83–86.

31. Quoted in Daniel B. Schirmer, *Republic Or Empire: American Resistance to the Philippine War* (Cambridge, Mass.: Schenkman Publishing Co., 1972), p. 151.

32. Willard B. Gatewood, Jr., *Black Americans and the White Man's Burden, 1898–1903* (Urbana: University of Illinois Press, 1975), p. 184.

33. Schirmer, pp. 219–20; John M. Gates, "Philippine Guerrillas, American Anti-Imperialists, and the Election of 1900," *Pacific Historical Review* XLVI, no. 1 (February 1977): 51–64.

34. Quoted in Richard E. Welch, Jr., "American Atrocities in the Philippines: The Indictment and the Response," *Pacific Historical Review* XLIII, no. 1 (May 1974): 241.

35. Richard E. Welch, Jr., "Organized Religion and the Philippine-American War, 1899–1902," *Mid-America* 55, no. 3 (July 1973): 204–205.

36. For the origins and evolution of Jordan's peace activism, see Edward McNall Burns, *David Starr Jordan: Prophet of Freedom* (Stanford, Cal.: Stanford University Press, 1953), pp. 78–127; and James L. Abrahamson, "David Starr Jordan and American Antimilitarism," *Pacific Northwest Quarterly* 67, no. 2 (April 1976): 76–87.

37. "A Conflict of Two Civilizations," *The Advocate of Peace* LXI, no. 3 (March 1899): 54; Trueblood, "Greatness and Permanence of the Arbitration Cause," in *Fourth Annual Report of the Lake Mohonk Conference on International Arbitration 1898*, p. 7.

38. Calvin D. Davis, *The United States and the First Hague Conference of 1899* (Ithaca, N.Y.: Cornell University Press, 1962), pp. 54–61, 190–97.

39. Robert Treat Paine, in *Report of the Fifth Annual Meeting of the Lake Mohonk Conference on International Arbitration, 1899* (n.p.; published by the Lake Mohonk Arbitration Conference, 1899), p. 23; and *Report of the Sixth Annual Meeting . . . 1900* (n.p.; published by the Lake Mohonk Arbitration Conference, 1900), p. 105.

40. Trueblood, "The Present Position of the International Peace Movement," in *The American Friends' Peace Conference, December 12–14, 1901* (Philadelphia: published by the Conference, 1902), pp. 157, 153.

41. C. Roland Marchand, *The American Peace Movement and Social Reform, 1898–1918* (Princeton: Princeton University Press, 1972), p. 24.

5. The Practical Reform

1. Michael A. Lutzker, "The 'Practical' Peace Advocates: An Interpretation of the American Peace Movement, 1898–1917" (Ph.D. diss., Rutgers University, 1969), p. 169 et passim.

2. Charles Chatfield, "More Than Dovish: Movements and Ideals of Peace in the United States," in Ken Booth and Moorhead Wright, eds., *American Thinking About Peace and War* (New York: Barnes & Noble, 1978), p. 116.

3. Barbara Kraft, "Peacemaking in the Progressive Era: A Prestigious and Proper Calling," *Maryland Historian* I, no. 2 (Fall 1970): 121.

4. David S. Patterson, "An Interpretation of the American Peace Movement, 1898–1914," in Charles Chatfield, ed., *Peace Movements in America* (New York: Schocken, 1973), p. 36.

5. Hamilton Holt, quoted in Warren F. Kuehl, *Hamilton Holt: Journalist, Internationalist, Educator* (Gainesville: University of Florida Press, 1960), p. 66.

6. Michael A. Lutzker introduction, in reprint of Hayne Davis, ed., *Among the World's Peacemakers* (New York: Garland Publishing Co., Inc., edition, 1972), pp. 8–9.

7. Calvin DeArmond Davis, *The United States and the Second Hague Peace Conference: American Diplomacy and International Organization, 1899–1914* (Durham, N.C.: Duke University Press, 1976), p. 97; also, David S. Patterson, "Andrew Carnegie's Quest for World Peace," *Proceedings of the American Philosophical Society* CXIV, no. 5 (October 20, 1970): 371–83.

8. Sondra R. Herman, *Eleven Against War: Studies in American Internationalist Thought, 1898–1921* (Stanford, Cal.: Hoover Institution Press, 1969), p. 24. More generally, Judith Shklar argues that legalism is "the ethical attitude that holds moral conduct to be a matter of rule following, and moral relationships to consist of duties and rights determined by rules." Judith N. Shklar, *Legalism* (Cambridge: Harvard University Press, 1964), p. 1.

9. For the growth of legalism, see C. Roland Marchand, *The American Peace Movement and Social Reform, 1898–1918* (Princeton: Princeton University Press, 1972), pp. 39–73; for the legalists' devotion to the court idea, see David S. Patterson, "The United States and the Origins of the World Court," *Political Science Quarterly* 91, no. 2 (Summer 1976): 279–95.

10. Lutzker, pp. 252–53; and Lutzker, "The Pacifist As Militarist: A Critique of the American Peace Movement, 1898–1914," *Societas* V, no. 2 (Spring 1975): 87, 97.

11. Quoted in Davis, pp. 163–64.

12. David S. Patterson, *Toward A Warless World: The Travail of the American Peace Movement, 1887–1914* (Bloomington: Indiana University Press, 1976), p. 136.

13. Marchand, p. 99; and Michael A. Lutzker, "The Formation of the Carnegie Endowment for International Peace: A Study of the Establishment-Centered Peace Movement, 1910–1914," in Jerry Israel, ed., *Building the Organizational Society: Essays on Associational Activities in Modern America* (New York: The Free Press, 1972), pp. 143–62.

14. Marchand, p. 106; and Peter Filene, "The World Peace Foundation and Progressivism, 1910–1918," *New England Quarterly* XXXVI, no. 4 (December 1963): 484–501.

15. *Yearbook* for 1912 of the Carnegie Endowment for International Peace (Washington: for the CEIP, 1913), pp. 1, 3.

16. Quoted in Charles DeBenedetti, "The American Peace Movement and the State Department in the Era of Locarno," in Solomon Wank, ed., *Doves and Diplomats: Foreign Offices and Peace Movements in Europe and America in the Twentieth Century* (Westport, Conn.: Greenwood Press, 1978), p. 209.

17. Harold E. Fey, ed., *Kirby Page, Social Evangelist: The Autobiography of a 20th Century Prophet for Peace* (Nyack, N.Y.: Fellowship Press, 1975), p. 70.

18. William James, "The Moral Equivalent of War," in Bruce Wilshire, ed., *William James: The Essential Writings* (New York: Harper & Row, Inc., 1971), p. 356.

19. Ibid., pp. 358–59.

20. Herman, pp. 7, 10.

21. Ibid., pp. 115, 128; and Allen F. Davis, *American Heroine: The Life and Legend of Jane Addams* (New York: Oxford University Press, 1973), pp. 140–49.

22. Quoted in E. James Hindman, "The General Arbitration Treaties of William Howard Taft," *The Historian* XXXVI, no. 1 (November 1973): 52.

23. Ibid.: 56.

24. Michael A. Lutzker, "Can the Peace Movement Prevent War?: The U.S.-Mexican Crisis of April, 1914," in Wank, pp. 141–42, 146–47.

25. Marchand, p. 208.

26. Quoted in Lutzker, "The 'Practical' Peace Advocates," p. 315.

27. Ruhl J. Bartlett, *The League to Enforce Peace* (Chapel Hill: University of North Carolina Press, 1944), pp. 38–39; and Warren F. Kuehl, *Seeking World Order: The United States and International Organization to 1920* (Nashville, Tenn.: Vanderbilt University Press, 1969), p. 213.

28. Blanche Wiesen Cook, "Woodrow Wilson and the AntiMilitarists, 1914–1917" (Ph.D. diss., Johns Hopkins University, 1970), p. 10; also John C. Farrell, *Beloved Lady: A History of Jane Addams' Ideas on Reform and Peace* (Baltimore: The Johns Hopkins Press, 1967), pp. 17–20, 140–216.

29. Marie L. Degen, *The History of the Woman's Peace Party* (New York: Garland Publishing Co., Inc., 1971), pp. 38–63. For Catt's peace activism, see David Katz, "Carrie Chapman Catt and the Struggle for Peace" (Ph.D. diss., Syracuse University, 1973).

30. Quoted in Barbara S. Kraft, *The Peace Ship: Henry Ford's Pacifist Adventure in the First World War* (New York: Macmillan, 1978), p. 20.

31. Herman, p. 138. Also, Gertrude Bussey and Margaret Tims, *Women's International League for Peace and Freedom, 1915–1965: A Record of Fifty Years' Work* (London: George Allen & Unwin, 1965); and Barbara Steinson, "Female Activism in World War I: The American Women's Peace, Suffrage, Preparedness, and Relief Movements, 1914–1919" (Ph.D. dis., University of Michigan, 1977).

For some powerful essays by a leading antiwar feminist, see Blanche Wiesen Cook, ed., *Crystal Eastman on Women and Revolution* (New York: Oxford University Press, 1978), pp. 235–68.

32. Kraft, *The Peace Ship*, p. 297.

33. Quoted in James C. Duram, "In Defense of Conscience: Norman Thomas As an Exponent of Christian Pacifism During World War I," *Journal of Presbyterian History* 52, no. 1 (Spring 1974): 24.

34. David S. Patterson, "Woodrow Wilson and the Mediation Movement, 1914–1917," *The Historian* XXXIII, no. 4 (August 1971): 535–56.

35. Quoted in Merle Eugene Curti, *Bryan and World Peace* (New York: Octagon edition, 1969), p. 236.

36. John Milton Cooper, Jr., *The Vanity of Power: American Isolationism and the First World War, 1914–1917* (Westport, Conn.: Greenwood Press, 1969), pp. 90–98; and John Patrick Finnegan, *Against the Specter of the Dragon: The Campaign for American Military Preparedness, 1914–1917* (Westport, Conn.: Greenwood Press, 1974), pp. 141–57.

37. Arthur S. Link, *Woodrow Wilson and the Progressive Era, 1910–1917* (New York: Harper Torchbook edition, 1963), p. 241; and Cook, pp. 66–67, 140–71.

38. Wilson, "Conditions of Peace," in Albert Bushnell Hart, ed., *Selected Addresses and Public Papers of Woodrow Wilson* (New York: Boni and Liveright, 1918), pp. 175, 172.

39. Quoted in Edson L. Whitney, *The American Peace Society: A Centennial History* (Washington: American Peace Society, 1928), p. 285.

40. Blanche Wiesen Cook, "Democracy in Wartime: Antimilitarism in England and the United States, 1914–1918," in Chatfield, ed., pp. 44–48; and

Donald Johnson, *The Challenge to American Freedoms: World War I and the Rise of the American Civil Liberties Union* (Lexington: University of Kentucky Press, 1963), pp. 10–25.

41. Quoted in Charles DeBenedetti, *Origins of the Modern American Peace Movement, 1915–1929* (Millwood, N.Y.: KTO Press, 1978), p. 36.

42. DeBenedetti, *Origins of the Modern American Peace Movement, 1915–1929*, pp. 4–18; and Charles F. Howlett, *Troubled Philosopher: John Dewey and the Struggle for World Peace* (Port Washington, N.Y.: Kennikat Press, 1977), pp. 27–33.

43. John P. Diggins, *The American Left in the Twentieth Century* (New York: Harcourt Brace Jovanovich, Inc., 1973), p. 73; and Randolph S. Bourne, "Twilight of Idols," in Carl Resek, ed., *War and the Intellectuals: Essays by Randolph S. Bourne, 1915–1919* (New York: Harper Torchbook edition, 1964), p. 57.

44. John Whiteclay Chambers II, ed., *The Eagle and the Dove: The American Peace Movement and United States Foreign Policy, 1900–1922* (New York: Garland Publishing Co., Inc., 1976), p. 48.

45. Quoted in H. C. Peterson and Gilbert C. Fite, *Opponents of War, 1917–1918* (Madison: The University of Wisconsin Press, 1957), p. 17.

46. Norman Thomas, "The Christian Patriot," reprinted in Bernard K. Johnpoll, ed., *Norman Thomas on War: An Anthology* (New York: Garland Publishing, Inc., 1974), p. 91.

In addition to the COs, approximately 171,000 men evaded the draft, while another 450 "unconditionalists" (who demanded unconditional exemption from military service and refused to work in military camps) were court-martialed and imprisoned. Peter Brock, *Twentieth-Century Pacifism* (New York: Van Nostrand Reinhold, Co., 1970), pp. 56–59; and Charles Chatfield, *For Peace and Justice: Pacifism in America, 1914–1941* (Knoxville: University of Tennessee Press, 1971), pp. 10, 70–86.

47. Quoted in Chatfield, *For Peace and Justice*, p. 51; emphasis in the original.

48. Quoted in Ray Ginger, *Eugene V. Debs: A Biography* (New York: Collier paperback edition, 1962), p. 327; also, Frederick C. Griffin, *Six Who Protested: Radical Opposition to the First World War* (Port Washington, N.Y.: Kennikat Press, 1977), pp. 34–48.

49. Peterson and Fite, p. 194.

6. The Necessary Reform

1. Fosdick to Manley O. Hudson, July 14, 1919, Box 35, Manley O. Hudson Papers, Harvard Law School Library.

2. Charles F. Howlett, "John Dewey and the Crusade to Outlaw War," *World Affairs* 138, no. 4 (Spring 1976): 336–55. For the full scope of the Outlawry of War crusade, see John E. Stoner, *S. O. Levinson and the Pact of Paris: A Study in the Techniques of Influence* (Chicago: University of Chicago Press, 1943).

3. Libby to Carrie Chapman Catt, September 7, 1923, and Libby to John Barrett, November 15, 1921, Records of the National Council for Prevention of War, Swarthmore College Peace Collection. Also, George P. Marabell, "Frederick Libby and the American Peace Movement, 1921–1941" (Ph.D. diss., Michigan State University, 1975).

4. Charles Chatfield, ed., *International War Resistance Through World War II* (New York: Garland Publishing Co., Inc., 1975), pp. 22, 29.

5. Charles DeBenedetti, "The $100,000 American Peace Award of 1924," *The Pennsylvania Magazine of History and Biography* 98, no. 2 (April 1974): 224–49.

6. Robert M. Miller, *How Shall They Hear Without A Preacher?: The Life of Ernest Fremont Tittle* (Chapel Hill: University of North Carolina Press, 1971), p. 403.

7. For the full story of the first Court battle, see Robert Accinelli, "The United States and the World Court, 1920–1927" (Ph.D. diss., University of California-Berkeley, 1968).

8. Paul H. Douglas, "The American Occupation of Haiti, II," *Political Science Quarterly* XLII, no. 3 (September 1927): 396.

9. "America—World's Banker," *Foreign Policy Association News Bulletin* 4, no. 36 (July 17, 1925): 2.

10. Paul L. Murphy, *The Meaning of Freedom of Speech: First Amendment Freedoms from Wilson to FDR* (Westport, Conn.: Greenwood Press, 1972), p. 26.

11. Charles Chatfield, *For Peace and Justice: Pacifism in America, 1914–1941* (Knoxville: University of Tennessee Press, 1971), p. 157. For reproductions of the "spider web" chart, see Frederick J. Libby, *To End War: The Story of the National Council for Prevention of War* (Nyack, N.Y.: Fellowship Publications, 1969), pp. 46–47; and Allen F. Davis, *American Heroine: The Life and Legend of Jane Addams* (New York: Oxford University Press, 1973), p. 265.

12. Chatfield, p. 157; Davis, pp. 262–71.

13. Daniel W. Barthell, "The Committee on Militarism in Education, 1925–1940" (Ph.D. diss., University of Illinois-Urbana, 1972), provides the most comprehensive examination of this fascinating organization.

14. Charles DeBenedetti, "Alternative Strategies in the American Peace Movement in the 1920's," in Charles Chatfield, ed., *Peace Movements in America* (New York: Schocken Books, 1973), pp. 57–67.

15. Detzer to Emily Greene Balch, June 23, 1928, Box 5, Records of the WILPF, Swarthmore College Peace Collection. For the evolution of the Paris Pact, see Robert H. Ferrell, *Peace In Their Time: The Origins of the Kellogg-Briand Pact* (New Haven: Yale University Press, 1952); and Charles DeBenedetti, *Origins of the Modern American Peace Movement, 1915–1929* (Millwood, N.Y.: KTO Press, 1978), pp. 185–236.

16. Chatfield, *For Peace and Justice*, p. 162.

17. Charles DeBenedetti, "The Origins of Neutrality Revision: The American Plan of 1924," *The Historian* XXXV, no. 1 (November 1972): 75–89; and John F. Greco, "A Foundation for Internationalism: The Carnegie Endowment for International Peace, 1931–1941" (Ph.D. diss., Syracuse University, 1971), pp. 38–61.

18. Devere Allen's words, quoted in Charles Chatfield, ed., *Devere Allen: Life and Writings* (New York: Garland Publishing, Inc., 1976), p. 33; Charles Chatfield, ed., *The Americanization of Gandhi: Images of the Mahatma* (New York: Garland Publishing, Inc., 1976), p. 58.

19. For the divisive effect that these questions had within the FOR, see Peter Brock, *Twentieth-Century Pacifism* (New York: Van Nostrand Reinhold Co., 1970), pp. 142–50.

20. Earl Browder, "The American Communist Party in the Thirties," in Rita James Simon, ed., *As We Saw the Thirties: Essays on Social and Political Movements of a Decade* (Urbana: University of Illinois Press, 1967), p. 223.

21. A. J. Muste, "My Experience in the Labor and Radical Struggles of the Thirties," ibid., p. 139; and Jo Ann Robinson, "A. J. Muste and the Ways to Peace," in Chatfield, ed., *Peace Movements in America*, pp. 81–85.

For two detailed studies of Muste's evolving pacifism, see Jo Ann Robinson, "The Traveler from Zierkzee: The Religious, Intellectual, and Political Development of A. J. Muste from 1885 to 1940" (Ph.D. diss., Johns Hopkins University, 1972); and William G. Batz, "Revolution and Peace: The Christian Pacifism of A. J. Muste" (Ph.D. diss., University of Minnesota, 1974).

22. Chatfield, *For Peace and Justice*, p. 210; and Chatfield, ed., *The Americanization of Gandhi*, pp. 59–61.

23. William E. Leuchtenburg, "The New Deal and the Analogue of War," in John Braeman, ed., *Change and Continuity in Twentieth-Century America* (New York: Harper Colophon edition, 1966), pp. 81–143.

24. Justus Doenecke, "The Debate Over Coercion: The Dilemma of America's Pacifists and the Manchurian Crisis," *Peace and Change* II, no. 1 (Spring 1974): 47–52.

25. Dennis Mihelish, "Student Antiwar Activism During the Nineteen Thirties," *Peace and Change* II, no. 3 (Fall 1974): 29–40; and Eileen M. Eagan, "'War Is Not Holy'—The American Student Peace Movement in the 1930s," ibid., 41–47.

26. Chatfield, *For Peace and Justice*, p. 211.

27. Patricia F. McNeal, "Origins of the Catholic Peace Movement," *The Review of Politics* 35, no. 3 (July 1973): 346–72.

28. Patricia F. McNeal, "The American Catholic Peace Movement, 1928–1972" (Ph.D. diss., Temple University, 1974), p. 46.

29. Ibid., pp. 36–47; John L. LeBrun, "The Role of the Catholic Worker Movement in American Pacifism, 1933–1972" (Ph.D. diss., Case Western Reserve University, 1973), pp. 27–81; and William D. Miller, *A Harsh and Dreadful Love: Dorothy Day and the Catholic Worker Movement* (New York: Liveright, 1973), pp. 159–70.

30. Quoted in Chatfield, *For Peace and Justice*, p. 265. Emphasis in the original.

31. Although the term "collective security" did not become current until 1934, the idea of independent states cooperating automatically in the impartial enforcement of peace first seriously attracted internationalists during World War I. In the 1930s the term was used to characterize several internationalist strategies, including some that excluded the notion of enforcement. Recent historians have therefore suggested that the phrases "collective concern" or "collective responsibility" would more accurately convey the many-sided internationalist attempt to move the United States after 1928 into some collaborative defense of the Versailles order. Richard N. Current, "The United States and 'Collective Security': Notes on the History of an Idea," in Alexander DeConde, ed., *Isolation and Security: Ideas and Interests in Twentieth-Century American Foreign Policy* (Durham, N.C.: Duke University Press, 1957), pp. 33, 44–48; Roland N. Stromberg, *Collective Security and American Foreign Policy: From the League of Nations to NATO* (New York: Praeger, 1963), pp. 4, 65, 85, 111; and Warren F. Kuehl, "The Principle of Responsibility for Peace and National Security, 1920–1973," *Peace and Change* III, nos. 2–3 (Summer/Fall 1975): 85.

32. Greco, pp. 195–216; and Harold Josephson, *James T. Shotwell and*

the Rise of Internationalism in America (Rutherford, N.J.: Fairleigh Dickinson University Press, 1975), pp. 221–23.

33. Robert E. Bowers, "The American Peace Movement, 1933–1941" (Ph.D. diss., University of Wisconsin-Madison, 1950), p. 20.

34. Chatfield, *For Peace and Justice,* pp. 271–72.

35. Quoted, ibid., p. 285. For the larger story of the war-referendum idea, see Ernest Bolt, *Ballots Before Bullets: The War Referendum Approach to Peace in America, 1914–1941* (Charlottesville: University of Virginia Press, 1977), pp. 152–85.

36. Bernard Johnpoll, *Pacifist's Progress: Norman Thomas and the Decline of American Socialism* (Chicago: Quadrangle, 1970), p. 206; and Justus D. Doenecke, "Non-intervention of the Left: 'The Keep America Out of the War Congress,' 1938–41," *Journal of Contemporary History* 12, no. 2 (April 1977): 221–36.

37. Glen Zeitzer, "The Fellowship of Reconciliation on the Eve of the Second World War: A Peace Organization Prepares," *Peace and Change* III, nos. 2–3 (Summer/Fall 1975): 46–51.

38. Quoted in Lillian Schlissel, ed., *Conscience in America: A Documentary History of Conscientious Objection in America, 1757–1967* (New York: E. P. Dutton & Co., Inc., 1968), p. 214.

39. Quoted in Greco, p. 281. Also, see Clark M. Eichelberger, *Organizing for Peace: A Personal History of the Founding of the United Nations* (New York: Harper and Row, 1977), p. 104.

40. Mark Lincoln Chadwin, *The Warhawks: American Interventionists Before Pearl Harbor* (Chapel Hill: University of North Carolina Press, 1968; New York: Norton edition, 1970), pp. 173–76, 189, 236.

41. Robert A. Divine, *Second Chance: The Triumph of Internationalism in America During World War II* (New York: Atheneum, 1967), pp. 38–39.

7. The Subversive Reform

1. "Findings and Recommendation of the Personnel Security Board," *In the Matter of J. Robert Oppenheimer: Texts of Principal Documents and Letters of Personnel Security Board* (Washington: Government Printing Office, 1954), p. 13.

2. Gordon C. Zahn, "Peace Witness in World War II," *Worldview* 18, no. 2 (February 1975): 53.

3. Mulford Sibley and Philip Jacobs, *Conscription and Conscience: The American State and the Conscientious Objector, 1940–1947* (Ithaca, N.Y.: Cornell University Press, 1952), p. 192.

4. Gordon C. Zahn, *Another Part of the War: The Camp Simon Story* (Amherst: University of Massachusetts Press, 1979), p. x; emphasis in the original. For other aspects of conscientious objection in World War II, see Patricia McNeal, "Catholic Conscientious Objection During World War II," *Catholic Historical Review* LXI, no. 2 (April 1975): 222–42; W. Edward Roser, "World War II and the Pacifist Controversy in the Major Protestant Churches," *American Studies* XIV, no. 2 (Fall 1973): 5–24; Theodore R. Wachs, "Conscription, Conscientious Objection, and the Context of American Pacifism, 1940–1945" (Ph.D. diss., University of Illinois-Urbana, 1976); and Michael Young, "Facing the Test of Faith: Jewish Pacifists During the Second World War," *Peace and Change* III, nos. 2–3 (Summer/Fall 1975): 34–39.

5. *War, Transition and Peace* (neither author, place, nor date of publication indicated; endorsed by the WILPF, FOR, AFSC, and WRL), p. 32.

6. Lawrence S. Wittner, *Rebels Against War: The American Peace Movement, 1941–1960* (New York: Columbia University Press paperback edition, 1970), p. 58.

7. E. Raymond Wilson, *Uphill for Peace: Quaker Impact on Congress* (Richmond, Ind.: Friends United Press, 1975), p. 13.

8. For a comprehensive analysis of the origins and evolution of the connection between black protest and Gandhian pacifism, see August Meier and Elliott Rudwick, "The Origins of Nonviolent Direct Action in Afro-American Protest: A Note on Historical Discontinuities," in Meier and Rudwick, *Along the Color Line: Explorations in the Black Experience* (Urbana: University of Illinois Press, 1976), pp. 344–89.

9. Clark M. Eichelberger, *Organizing for Peace: A Personal History of the Founding of the United Nations* (New York: Harper and Row, 1977), pp. 209–17; and Harold Josephson, *James T. Shotwell and the Rise of Internationalism in America* (Rutherford, N.J.: Fairleigh Dickinson University, 1975), p. 256.

10. Robert A. Divine, *Second Chance: The Triumph of Internationalism in America During World War II* (New York: Atheneum, 1967), p. 104.

11. Thomas M. Campbell, *Masquerade Peace: America's UN Policy, 1944–1945* (Gainesville: The University Presses of Florida, 1973), pp. 58–59, 86–89, 115, 145–47, 198–204; and Martin J. Sherwin, *A World Destroyed: The Atomic Bomb and the Grand Alliance* (New York: Alfred A. Knopf, 1975), pp. 3–9 et passim.

12. Excerpt from The Franck Report, in Alice Kimball Smith, *A Peril and a Hope: The Scientists' Movement in America, 1945–1947* (Chicago: University of Chicago Press, 1965), p. 45.

13. Clyde Eagleton, "World Government Discussion in the United States," *London Quarterly of World Affairs* XII, no. 3 (October 1946): 251.

14. Michael Yavenditti, "The American People and the Use of Atomic Bombs on Japan: The 1940's," *The Historian* XXXVI, no. 2 (February 1974): 240–41.

15. Charles DeBenedetti, "The American Peace Movement and the National-Security State, 1941–1971," *World Affairs*, 141, no. 2 (Fall 1978): 118–29.

16. Max Lowenthal, *The Federal Bureau of Investigation* (New York: William Morrow, Inc., 1950; Greenwood reprint, 1971), pp. 422, 439; and Sanford J. Ungar, *FBI* (Boston: Little, Brown and Co., 1975), pp. 104–108, 123–33.

17. Michael S. Sherry, *Preparing for the Next War: American Plans for Postwar Defense, 1941–1945* (New Haven: Yale University Press, 1977), p. 234.

18. *Historical Statistics of the United States: Colonial Times to 1970*, Part 2 (Washington: U.S. Bureau of the Census, 1975), p. 1102.

19. Sherry, p. 235.

20. Smith, p. v.

21. Federation of American Scientists, "Survival Is At Stake," in Dexter Masters and Catherine Way, eds., *One World Or None: A Report to the Public on the Full Meaning of the Atomic Bomb* (New York: McGraw-Hill Co., Inc., 1946), p. 78. Emphasis in the original.

22. Walter Lippmann, ibid., p. 70.

23. Morton Grodzins and Eugene Rabinowitch, eds., *The Atomic Age: Scientists in National and World Affairs* (New York: Basic Books, Inc., 1963), p. 352.

24. Wittner, pp. 170–74; and Jon A. Yoder, "The United World Federalists: Liberals for Law and Order," in Charles Chatfield, ed., *Peace Movements in America* (New York: Schocken Books, 1973), pp. 100–101. Also, Harrison Brown, "The World Government Movement in the United States," *The Bulletin of the Atomic Scientists* III, no. 6 (June 1947): 156–57, 167; and Alan Cranston, "Memoir of a Man," in Norman Cousins and J. Garry Clifford, eds., *Memoirs of a Man: Grenville Clark* (New York: W. W. Norton & Co., Inc., 1975), pp. 252–64.

25. Cord Meyer, Jr., *Peace Or Anarchy* (Boston: Little, Brown and Co., Inc., 1947), p. 65. For Washington's diminishing interest in even the existing UN, see George T. Mazuzan, "America's UN Commitment, 1945–1953," *The Historian* XL, no. 2 (February 1978): 309–30.

26. Milton S. Katz, "Peace, Politics, and Protest: SANE and the American Peace Movement, 1957–1972" (Ph.D. diss., St. Louis University, 1973), pp. 7, 51–57.

27. Quoted in Charles Chatfield, ed., *International War Resistance Through World War II* (New York: Garland Publishing, Inc., 1975), p. 37.

28. Dwight Macdonald, "The Bomb," *Politics Past: Essays in Political Criticism* (New York: The Viking Press paperback edition, 1970), p. 179.

29. Muste, "Sketches for an Autobiography," in Nat Hentoff, ed., *The Essays of A. J. Muste* (New York: Simon and Schuster Clarion edition, 1970), p. 12. The leading internationalist Raymond Fosdick was equally troubled. "It seems to me that America has taken her place among the conquerors of history who have won by utter ruthlessness," he wrote shortly after Nagasaki. "Nothing that Attila or Genghis Khan ever dreamed of can match our wholesale slaughter of civilians in Hiroshima and Nagasaki." Fosdick to Warren Weaver, August 29, 1945, Box 28, Raymond B. Fosdick Papers, Seeley G. Mudd Library, Princeton University.

30. Jo Ann Robinson, "A. J. Muste and Ways to Peace," in Chatfield, ed., *Peace Movements in America*, p. 88; her emphasis; and Hentoff, ed., p. 138.

31. August Meier and Elliott Rudwick, *CORE: A Study in the Civil Rights Movement, 1942–1968* (New York: Oxford University Press, 1973), p. 39.

32. Martin E. Marty, *Righteous Empire: The Protestant Experience in America* (New York: Dial Press, 1970), pp. 256–57.

33. Christopher Lasch, "The Cultural Cold War: A Short History of the Congress for Cultural Freedom," in Barton J. Bernstein, ed., *Towards a New Past: Dissenting Essays in American History* (New York: Random House; Vintage edition, 1969), p. 323.

34. *Final Report of the Select Committee to Study Governmental Operations With Respect to Intelligence Activities* (Church Committee), U.S. Senate, 94th Cong., 2d sess. (Washington: Government Printing Office, 1976), pp. 4, 40; also, DeBenedetti: 118–29.

35. Zelle Larson nonetheless believes that the practice of conscientious objection made "substantial progress" during the War, encouraging more men "to say 'No' to conscription." Zelle A. Larson, "An Unbroken Witness: Conscientious Objection to War, 1948–1953," (Ph.D. diss., University of Hawaii, 1975), pp. ix, 324.

36. For the rise of the peace research movement, see Wittner, pp. 250–51; Kenneth E. Boulding, "The Peace Research Movement in the U.S.," in Ted Dunn, ed., *Alternatives to War and Violence* (London: James Clarke and Co., Ltd., 1963), pp. 4–51; and Cynthia Earl Kerman, *Creative Tension: The Life and Thought of Kenneth Boulding* (Ann Arbor: University of Michigan Press, 1974), pp. 47–48, 68–71.

37. Peter Brock, *Twentieth-Century Pacifism* (New York: Van Nostrand Reinhold Co., 1970), p. 230; and David L. Lewis, *King: A Critical Biography* (New York: Praeger, 1970), p. 88.

38. Lewis, p. 86.

39. Robert Gilpin, *American Scientists and Nuclear Weapons Policy* (Princeton: Princeton University Press, 1962), p. 136.

For a superb retelling of the testing controversy, see Robert A. Divine, *Blowing on the Wind: The Nuclear Test Ban Debate, 1954–1960* (New York: Oxford University Press, 1978).

40. Wittner, pp. 235–37; and Otto Nathan and Heinz Norden, eds., *Einstein on Peace* (New York: Simon and Schuster, 1960), pp. 633–35.

41. Neil H. Katz, "Radical Pacifism and the Contemporary American Peace Movement: The Committee for Nonviolent Action, 1957–1967" (Ph.D. diss., University of Maryland-College Park, 1974), pp. 35, 90.

42. Donald F. Keys, quoted in Milton Katz, p. 137.

43. Ibid., p. 89.

44. Ibid., p. 127.

45. Muste, quoted, ibid., p. 146; also, Milton S. Katz and Neil H. Katz, "Pragmatists and Visionaries in the Post-World War II American Peace Movement: SANE and CNVA," in Solomon Wank, ed., *Doves and Diplomats: Foreign Offices and Peace Movements in Europe and America in the Twentieth Century* (Westport, Conn.: Greenwood Press, 1978), pp. 268–71.

46. Cousins, quoted in Katz, "Peace, Politics, and Protest," p. 118.

8. The Deferred Reform

1. Daniel Berrigan to Gordon Zahn, November 4, 1966, The Berrigan Papers, Department of Rare Books, Olin Library, Cornell University; Daniel Berrigan, "David Darst Memorial," *The Catholic Radical* II, no. 2 (December 1969): 7.

2. Constitution of the Student Peace Union, Box 25a, Social Protest Project, Bancroft Library, University of California-Berkeley; also, George R. Vickers, *The Formation of the New Left: The Early Years* (Lexington, Mass.: D.C. Heath and Company, Lexington Books, 1975), pp. 51–61.

3. Pamphlet, *The Committee of Correspondence: A Statement*, The Committee of Correspondence Folder, Social Protest Project, Bancroft Library.

4. Brochure on the Institute for International Order, Carton 7, Records of the World Without War Council (WWWC), Bancroft Library.

5. Kenneth Boulding, "After Civilization, What?" *Bulletin of the Atomic Scientists* XVIII, no. 8 (October 1962): 4.

6. "The American Peace Movement: What Is It; What Has It Accomplished?" *Vital Issues* XIII, no. 6 (February 1964): 3.

7. "The Cuban Crises and the Peace Movement," *Common Sense* 4, no. 2 (December 1, 1962): 2.

8. On the origins and significance of the New Left, see Vickers; Irwin

Unger, *The Movement: A History of the American New Left, 1959–1972* (New York: Dodd, Mead and Co., 1974); Massimo Teodori, ed., *The New Left: A Documentary History* (Indianapolis: Bobbs-Merrill Co., Inc., 1969); Edward J. Bacciocco, Jr., *The New Left in America: Reform to Revolution, 1950 to 1970* (Stanford, Cal.: Hoover Institution Press, 1974); and James Weinstein, *Ambiguous Legacy: The Left in American Politics* (New York: New Viewpoints, 1975), pp. 115–59.

9. *Kirkpatrick Sale, SDS* (New York: Random House, Inc.; Vintage edition, 1973), passim.

10. *PREP Newsletter*, no. 12 (January 1964), 3, Box 32, Records of the Students for a Democratic Society, The State Historical Society of Wisconsin; Richard Flacks, "New Crisis in Vietnam," PREP Memo, February 29, 1964, Box 8, ibid.

11. Steve Max, form letter, September 30, 1963, Box 8, ibid. Also, *Vietnam: A Documentation of Disaster*, issued by the Student Peace Union (author unknown), October 1963, Box 25a, Social Protest Project, Bancroft Library.

12. "WILPF Speaks Up On Vietnam," *Four Lights* XXIV, no. 5 (May 1964): 1–2; "Students Act for Protest on Vietnam," *The National Guardian*, March 21, 1964, p. 3; Teodori, ed., p. 297; and *Peace Activity: General Statement*, in DuBois Clubs Folder, Social Protest Project, Bancroft Library.

13. Brochure, *Silent Vigil for Ending the War in Vietnam*, p. 1, Records of Women Strike for Peace, The State Historical Society of Wisconsin; "Protest Vietnam War Dec. 19th," *The Catholic Worker* XXI, no. 5 (December 1964): 1; and David McReynolds, form letter, December 5, 1964, Records of the War Resisters League, Swarthmore College Peace Collection, Swarthmore, Pennsylvania.

14. For a superb survey of radical pacifists and Vietnam (plus valuable biographical profiles), see Robert Cooney and Helen Michalowski, eds., *The Power of the People: Active Nonviolence in the United States* (Culver City, Cal.: People Press, Inc., 1977), pp. 182–209.

15. I. F. Stone categorized the antiwar movement another way: (1) the "democratic forces" that sought to win U.S. public opinion against the war; (2) the "religious forces" that preferred to testify against the war's immorality, through nonviolent civil disobedience; and (3) the "revolutionary forces" that tried to obstruct the U.S. war effort and assist Vietnamese revolutionaries. "What Should the Peace Movement Do?" reprinted in Stone, *In A Time of Torment* (New York: Random House, Inc.; Vintage edition, 1968), pp. 78–79.

For a valuable insider's account of intramovement politics, see Fred Halstead, *Out Now!: A Participant's Account of the American Movement Against the Vietnam War* (New York: Monad Press, 1978).

16. Sally Honan, "On the Peace Front," *War/Peace Report* 5, no. 3 (March 1965): 15–16; and Rev. Daniel Berrigan, S.J., "In Peaceable Conflict," *The Catholic Worker* XXXI, no. 8 (March 1965): 1. Also, Louis Menashe and Ronald Radosh, eds., *Teach-Ins: U.S.A.; Reports, Opinions, Documents* (New York: Frederick A. Praeger, 1967 paperback edition).

17. "Youth Has Its Day," *The Economist* 233, no. 6587 (November 22, 1969): 47; and Noam Chomsky, *American Power and the New Mandarins: Historical and Political Essays* (New York: Random House, Inc.; Vintage edition, 1969), p. 379.

The numerical estimates are drawn from James O'Brien, "The Anti-War Movement and the War," *Radical America* 8, no. 3 (May-June 1974): 58; and "Mailing List of Organizations Opposing the War in Vietnam, September, 1967," prepared by the Central Committee of Correspondence, in Citizens Committee of Correspondence Folder, Social Protest Project, Bancroft Library.

18. Spock to Gen. Hugh Hester, February 26, 1968, Box 13, Benjamin Spock Papers, George Arents Memorial Library, Syracuse University.

19. Warren Hinckle, "The Social History of the Hippies," *Ramparts* 5, no. 9 (March 1967): 9–12, 17–20, 24–26; Edgar Z. Friedenberg, ed., *The Anti-American Generation* (New Brunswick, N.J.: Transaction Books, Inc., 1971); and William L. O'Neill, *Coming Apart: An Informal History of America in the 1960's* (New York: Quadrangle/The New York Times Book Co., 1971 paperback edition), pp. 233–71.

20. Martin Luther King, Jr., "Declaration of Independence from the War in Vietnam," reprinted in Lillian Schlissel, ed., *Conscience in America: A Documentary History of Conscientious Objection in America, 1757–1967* (New York: E. P. Dutton paperback edition, 1968), pp. 426, 433; and Thomas Powers, *The War At Home, Vietnam and the American People, 1964–1968* (New York: Grossman Publishers, 1973), pp. 139–63.

For the fuller range of black antiwar opposition, see Clyde Taylor, ed., *Vietnam and Black America: An Anthology of Protest and Resistance* (Garden City, N.Y.: Anchor Press edition, 1973).

21. "The Dilemma of Dissent," *Time* 89, no. 16 (April 21, 1967): 20.

22. Louis Harris, *The Anguish of Change* (New York: W. W. Norton, 1973), pp. 66–68.

23. Philip S. Foner, *American Labor and the Indochina War: The Growth of Union Opposition* (New York: International Publishers, 1971 paperback edition), pp. 48–59.

24. Lawrence M. Baskir and William A. Strauss, *Chance and Circumstance: The Draft, the War, and the Vietnam Generation* (New York: Alfred A. Knopf, 1978), pp. 5, 30; and Lawrence M. Wittner, *Rebels Against War: The American Peace Movement, 1941–1960* (New York: Columbia University Press, 1969 paperback edition), p. 41.

For more on the resistance and exile, see Alice Lynd, ed., *We Won't Go: Personal Accounts of War Objectors* (Boston: Beacon Press, 1968); Michael Ferber and Staughton Lynd, *The Resistance* (Boston: Beacon Press, 1971); Michael Useem, *Conscription, Protest, and Social Conflict: The Life and Death of a Draft Resistance Movement* (New York: John Wiley & Sons, Inc., 1973); David M. Mantell, *True Americanism: Green Berets and War Resisters* (New York: Teachers College Press, Columbia University, 1974); Renée G. Kasinsky, *Refugees from Militarism: Draft-Age Americans in Canada* (New Brunswick, N.J.: Transaction Books, Inc., 1976); Willard Gaylin, *In the Service of Their Country: War Resisters in Prison* (New York: The Viking Press, 1970); and Jack Colhoun, "The Exiles' Role in War Resistance," *Monthly Review* 30, no. 10 (March 1979): 27–42.

25. Peter R. Lieurance, "Negotiation Now!: The National Committee for a Political Settlement in Vietnam," in David S. Smith, ed., *From War to Peace: Essays in Peacemaking and War Termination* (New York: Columbia University; The International Fellows Public Policy Series, 1974), pp. 171–201; and Kenneth Keniston, *Young Radicals: Notes on Committed Youth* (New York: Harcourt, Brace & World, Inc., 1968).

26. Robert McAfee Brown, "'In Conscience, I Must Break the Law,'" *Look* 31, no. 22 (October 31, 1967): 48. For a useful list of the major (involving 1,000 people or more) antiwar demonstrations of this period, see Irving Louis Horowitz, *The Struggle Is the Message: The Organization and Ideology of the Anti-War Movement* (Berkeley, Cal.: The Glendessary Press, 1970), pp. 148–67; and Jerome H. Skolnick, *The Politics of Protest* (New York: Ballantine Books, 1969), pp. 25–78.

27. For an overview of the significance of the Spock and other antiwar trials, see John F. and Rosemary Bannan, *Law, Morality and Vietnam: The Peace Militants and the Courts* (Bloomington: Indiana University Press, 1974).

28. Oral history interview of Arleen Hynes, p. 1, Eugene R. McCarthy Oral History Project, Georgetown University.

29. McReynolds to Roy Finch, August 1, 1968, Box 1, WRL Records; emphasis in the original.

30. Paul Hoffman, *Moratorium: An American Protest* (New York: Tower Publications, Inc., 1970); Sam Brown, "The Politics of Peace," *The Washington Monthly* 2, no. 6 (August 1970): 24–46; and Ken Hurwitz, *Marching Nowhere* (New York: W.W. Norton & Co., Inc., 1971).

31. Barbara Trimmer to author, January 9, 1977.

32. "Dellinger's Washington Speech," *Liberation* 14, no. 9 (January 1970): 4.

33. Andrew Kopkind, "The Greening of America: Beyond the Valley of the Heads," *Ramparts* 9, no. 8 (March 1971): 52. Emphasis in the original.

34. VVAW History, Box 6, Records of the Vietnam Veterans Against the War, The State Historical Society of Wisconsin.

35. Edward M. Opton, Jr., and Robert Duckles, "Mental Gymnastics on Mylai," *The New Republic* 162, no. 8 (February 21, 1970): 14–16.

36. Matthew Rinaldi, "The Olive-Drab Rebels: Military Organizing During the Vietnam Era," *Radical America* 8, no. 3 (May-June 1974): 17–51; and David Cortright, *Soldiers in Revolt: The American Military Today* (Garden City, N.Y.: Doubleday, Anchor Press edition, 1975), pp. 3–27.

37. U.S. Senate, 94th Cong., 21 sess., "Intelligence Activities and the Rights of Americans," Book II, *Final Report of the Select Committee to Study Governmental Operations with Respect to Intelligence Activities* (Washington: U.S. Government Printing Office, 1976), p. 88; Book III, p. 792.

38. Ibid., Book II, p. 116.

39. Meacham to Lorena Jeanne Tinker, March 5, 1971, File: PE-VN-Peoples Coalition, Records of the American Friends Service Committee, AFSC Headquarters, Philadelphia, Pennsylvania.

40. *SANE Action,* August 2, 1972, Box 74, SANE Records, SCPC.

41. Lowell, in symposium, "The Meaning of Vietnam," *The New York Review of Books* XXII, no. 10 (June 12, 1975): 27; also Hendrik Hertzberg, "The Collapse of America's Indochina Empire," *WIN* 11, no. 15 (May 1, 1975): 7.

42. Tom Hayden, "Peace," *Rolling Stone,* no. 187 (May 22, 1975): 31.

43. "At Last, At Last . . . ," *Fellowship* 41, no. 6 (June 1975): 3. Emphasis in the original.

44. W. Warren Wagar, *Building the City of Man: Outlines of a World Civilization* (San Francisco: W. H. Freeman & Co., 1971), pp. 30–36; and Tom Cornell, "The Mobe: A Look Toward The Future," *Fellowship* 44, no. 9 (September 1978): 18.

45. "At Last, At Last . . .": 3.

Afterthoughts

1. For some suggestive insights on the relationship of power and culture in the making of American foreign policy, see Akira Iriye, "Culture and Power: International Relations as Intercultural Relations," *Diplomatic History* 3, no. 2 (Spring 1979): 115–28.

2. Richard Hofstadter and Michael Wallace, eds., *American Violence: A Documentary History* (New York: Random House; Vintage edition, 1971), p. 38; and Rhodri Jeffreys-Jones, *Violence and Reform in American History* (New York: New Viewpoints, 1978), p. 39 et passim.

3. See, for instance, Richard Maxwell Brown, "Historical Patterns of Violence in America," in Hugh Davis Graham and Ted Robert Gurr, eds., *The History of Violence in America: Historical and Comparative Perspectives* (New York: Praeger, 1969), pp. 67–76, 805; and Leonard L. Richards, *"Gentlemen of Property and Standing": Anti-Abolition Mobs in Jacksonian America* (New York: Oxford University Press, 1970), pp. 131–50, 165–70.

4. C. Roland Marchand, *The American Peace Movement and Social Reform, 1898–1918* (Princeton: Princeton University Press, 1972), p. 387.

5. Merle Eugene Curti, *Peace Or War: The American Struggle, 1636–1936* (New York: W. W. Norton & Co., Inc., 1936; Garland edition, 1972), p. 262.

6. Albert Camus, *Neither Victims Nor Executioners*, trans. by Dwight Macdonald (Chicago: World Without War Publications, 1972), was a statement that worked profound effect upon post-WW II American peace workers.

7. Ibid., p. 55.

INDEX

Abernathy, Ralph, 159

abolitionism, 15, 21, 56, 60, 198; humanitarian peace reform and, 39–45; nonresistant (Garrisonian) pacifism and, 41–42, 44

"activist-repressionists," 118

Addams, Jane, 70, 72, 77, 80, 87–88, 97, 119; and World War I, 93–94, 99; and Women's International League for Peace and Freedom, 111, 114

Aguinaldo, Emilio, 73, 75–76

Alcott, Bronson, 44

Ali, Muhammad, 179

Allen, Devere, 121

Allen, Florence E., 114

America First Committee, 133

American Alliance for Labor and Democracy, 101

American Anti-Imperialist League (1899), 74

American Association for International Conciliation (1906), 81

American Bible Society: peace movement and, 34

American Board of Commissioners for Foreign Missions (ABCFM): peace movement and, 34

American Civil Liberties Bureau, 99

American Defense Society, 101

American Federation of Labor, 99, 154

American Friends Service Committee (AFSC; 1917), 157, 159; liberal pacifism and, 103; post-World War I era and, 121; anti-Vietnam War movement and, 191–92

American League Against War and Fascism, 123

American League for Peace and Democracy, 123

American League to Limit Armaments (1915): antipreparedness campaign and, 96

American Legion: attacks peace movement in 1920s, 118–19

American Peace Award (1923–1924), 116

American Peace Society (APS; 1828): origins and early activities, 32, 38–39; promotes congress of nations, 38–39, 45–46, 50, 60, 91; promotes international arbitration, 39, 47, 64, 89; nonresistant (Garrisonian) pacifism and, 42–43; Transcendentalists and, 44; humanitarian peace reform and, 47–51, 54, 56; cosmopolitan peace reform and, 59–60, 64–65, 67, 69, 71, 80–81; activities in early 20th century, 84–85, 89, 91, 98

American School Peace League (1908), 83

American Servicemen's Union, 189

Americans for Democratic Action (ADA): formation of, 155; anti-Vietnam War movement and, 171, 174, 181

American Society for the Judicial Settlement of International Disputes (ASJSID; 1910): formation of, 82–83; relations with Carnegie Endowment for International Peace, 85; supports Taft's arbitration treaties, 89

American Society of International Law (ASIL; 1906), 82, 85, 98

American Student Union, 131

American Union Against Militarism (AUAM; 1916): leads antipreparedness campaign, 96; calms Mexican-American tensions, 96; internal divisions, 99

Andrews, Fannie Fern, 83

anti-Communism: American liberals and, 151, 154–55; peace reformers and, 168

anti-expanionists: late 19th century base of anti-imperialism, 71

Antifederalists, 25

227

peace movement and, 34–36; and
Civil War, 58; tribal attractions of,
86–87; necessitates peace reform, 129;
and Cold War radical pacifists, 152,
161; as threat to survival, 164; and
anti-Vietnam War movement, 175
—as a crime: Outlawry of War program,
111; and War Resisters League, 115
—crimes of: U.S. and, 179, 188
—war economy, 162
—relief during, 21, 58, 139–40
—taxes: resistance to, 14–15, 20–22, 27,
51, 57, 115, 152–53, 161
—rules of, 77
—veterans of: and Cold War federalism,
149
War Resisters League (WRL; 1924): origins
of, 109, 115; and World War II, 139–40;
protests Korean War, 155; attacks nu-
clear testing, 160; and 1960s peace
movement, 166, 171
—War Resisters International, 115n
Washington, Booker T., 72
Washington, George, 20–21, 24, 26
Washington Conference (1921–22), 108,
112, 125
Watson, Tom, 101
Weld, Angelina Grimké, 55–56
Weld, Theodore, 40
Whig Party, 50–51
White, William Allen, 136
White Fright, 102–105
Wickersham, George, 113
Willard, Frances, 65
W(illiam).E.B. DuBois Clubs, 171
Willkie, Wendell, 142
Willoughby, George, 161
Wilson, Dagmar, 166, 173
Wilson, E(dward). Raymond, 119, 140
Wilson, Woodrow: intervenes in
Mexico, 89–90; and European war, 91;
and League to Enforce Peace, 93; and
neutral mediation, 93; supports mili-
tary preparedness, 95–96; and pro-
gressive peace movement, 96–97; at-
tacks wartime domestic violence, 105;
and Paris Peace Conference, 109–10;
loses League fight, 112; inter-
nationalists and, 120; World War II in-
ternationalists and, 142–43
"Winter Soldier Investigation" (1971), 188
Witherspoon, Frances, 115
Wofford, Harris, Jr., 149
Woman's Peace Party (1915), 93–94,
98–99
Woman's Pro-League Council (Non-

Partisan). See The Woman's Pro-
League Council (Non-Partisan)
women: and humanitarian peace re-
form, 40, 43, 45–46; and Universal
Peace Union, 61; and post-Civil War
peace work, 61–62; and 1896 National
Arbitration Conference, 67; and Anti-
Imperialist League, 72; and post-World
War I peace movement, 114–16; and
World War II peace movement, 145;
and Cold War peace activism, 154; and
peace movement of 1960s, 166; and
U.S. peace movements, 199
—women's liberation: and anti-
Vietnam War movement, 188
—women's rights: and Universal Peace
Union, 61
Women's Christian Temperance Union
(WCTU), 65
Women's International League for Peace
and Freedom (WILPF; 1919): origins of,
94, 109, 111, 114; actions in 1920s, 118;
work in 1930s, 121–22, 125–26, 132; and
World War II, 138–40; and Cold War,
152; and Korean War, 155; protests
nuclear testing, 160; and peace move-
ment of 1960s, 165–66; and Cuban
missile crisis, 168; and anti-Vietnam
War movement, 171, 173, 192
Women's Peace Society (WPS; 1921),
114–15
Women's Peace Union of the Western
Hemisphere, 115
Women Strike for Peace (WSP; 1960),
166–68, 171, 173
Woodrow Wilson Foundation (1923), 143
Woolman, John 13–15
Worcester, Noah, 34–37
workmen's compensation, 97
World Alliance for International Friendship Through the Churches (WAIFTC;
1914), 86, 98, 110
World Association of Parliamentarians
for World Government, 160
world congress: favored by practical
peace reformers, 80
world court: supported in pre-World War
period, 65, 67, 81, 91, 111. See also Permanent Court of International Justice
world federalism, 146, 149
world federation, 78, 80–81, 141–42
world government: and world
federalism, 149–51, 155, 160, 162
World Law Fund (1961), 166
Worldover Press (No-Frontier News
Service), 121